TO THE SEA IN SHIPS

Captain J. C. Robinson
of the
Union-Castle Line

– and his brother Damnation Joe
(Captain J. T. Robinson)

edited by Felicity Potter

RP

Published by Royd House
The Book Case
29 Market Street
Hebden Bridge
West Yorks.
HX7 6EU
www.bookcase.co.uk

Cover design: D&P Design and Print

Cover pictures:
Captain J. C. Robinson – thanks to the Union-Castle Staff Register.
La Hogue and *Duncan Dunbar*, reproduced with permission of
the State Library of NSW; Mitchell Library.
Armadale Castle – 1910 postcard.

ISBN: 978-1-907197-10-9

PREFACE

I was actually hoping for family information when I started searching for the memoirs of my great-great-uncle Captain J. C. Robinson. I'd been working on the Robinsons for years: a series of solid Westmorland farmers and millers whose line came to an abrupt halt in the 1850s when nearly a whole generation died within a few years of each other, leaving their penniless orphans in England to reinvent themselves as best they could. We had vague family stories of a missionary in Jamaica and clearer ones of a Union-Castle[1] Captain, my great-grandfather Joseph Trutch Robinson, known as "Damnation Joe". We had his silver pocket watch, his family photograph, and tales of his temper and of his clever grey parrot Polly.

All we knew about his elder brother "JC" was that he was a commodore and "very religious".

Looking for information on the Union-Castle Line, I found a second-hand copy of Marischal Murray's *Union-Castle Chronicle* (1953) and there in the Acknowledgements was a reference to the Memoirs of Captain J. C. Robinson published in the journal *South Africa*. I started visiting the National Newspaper Library in Colindale – but the volumes of *South Africa* are massive. The paper was weekly, unindexed, the print small, and trawling through 1900 to 1912, I found only occasional references and a nice photo of JC (p. 224). A helpful member of staff at the NLSA in Cape Town also checked the volumes they had there but with no success.

Then an online reference to JC's report on Rhodes's plan for a Cape Town university, dated 1920, sent me back to Colindale: JC died in 1925, and I hadn't expected him to be writing his memoirs so long after his retirement. And there they were, in 36 instalments, from 26 July 1919 to 27 March 1920.

Having transcribed them all, although he says very little about his family, he has much to say on topical matters and a very engaging style. There are storms at sea, passenger dramas, mechanical problems, fauna and flora on board and off, a hair-raising ghost story, pen portraits of Rhodes, Sir Donald Currie, Gladstone, African kings; Rider Haggard smoking in his bunk in a flooded cabin; the casual severing of the Java-Sumatra submarine communications cable; unemployed Scottish fishermen recruited to work on South African docks; the benign episode of the hymn-singing Boer POWs; and a distressing story of a spoiled top

---

[1] The Union-Castle Line ran mail, passenger and cargo steamships regularly between England and Africa from 1900 to 1977. It was formed from the previously separate Castle and Union companies.

hat (which clearly still rankled decades later). JC was devoutly conservative and paternalistic, but he was also thoughtful and humane (except to snakes, porcupines and the Salvation Army who he considered unseemly), opposed racism in the context of those days, delighted in problem solving, and had a nice sense of humour. I liked him and his enthusiasm and his pride in his competence.

Characteristically, JC took his title from the Bible: "They that go down to the sea in ships, that do business in great waters; These see the works of the Lord, and his wonders in the deep." - *Psalm 107*, 23-4. He waits till the final instalment to let rip with his evangelical message (in the form of a West Indian *Dies irae*) but his religious beliefs are bubbling away throughout.

JC's memoirs form the bulk of this book. Also included is an exciting account by the passengers of the shipwreck of the *Duncan Dunbar* in 1865, when JC was 2nd officer (from when it's said his fervent Christianity dated), along with more of his yarns and a factual summary of his life and voyages, reconstructed from genealogical and maritime records, newspaper references and other sources.

Sadly JC's younger brother and fellow Union-Castle Captain Joseph Robinson left no memoirs, but JTR's youngest son preserved his 1862 indenture and voyage discharge certificates, and from these and other sources the outlines of his life could also be reconstructed. A list of both brothers' voyages is at the back.

I hope you enjoy these stories and JC's "yarning"!

Felicity Potter

iv

CONTENTS

ILLUSTRATIONS

Acknowledgements and sources

Thanks to the hardworking staff of the British Newspaper Library at Colindale, where J. C. Robinson's memoirs are at the time of publication (the building is scheduled for closure in 2013).

Amongst "Robinsons," thanks to Geoffrey K. Robinson for his material on the life of his grandfather Joseph Trutch Robinson, to Bunty Robinson, and to Nicole Ansell, Bryan Clark, Angie Gibson, Reid Robinson and Andy Shepherd for their help and information. I am very much indebted to the late Frances Burt for passing on her family records and memories.

The online British Newspaper Archive has been a most useful source of information, as has the online Australian Newspaper Archive, Trove. The online Union-Castle Staff Register is a splendid resource for those interested in the history of the shipping company and its men: address changing from unioncastlestaffregister.co.uk to bandcstaffregister.co.uk

Acknowledgements: illustrations

Page 1: Logo from JC's memoirs © The British Libraries Board – *South Africa*.
Thanks to Tony Haslett for permission to reproduce the photos of Union Castle ships on pp. 16, 42, 47, 63, 68, 81, 161, 209, 250-1 & 254-6
Page 94: The *La Hogue* outside Sydney Heads, reproduced with permission of the State Library of NSW; Mitchell Library.
Page 112: Concert on deck. Thanks to Barry Eagles.
Page 188: Morning Prayers © The British Libraries Board – *South Africa*.
Page 210: JC on deck: thanks to the Union-Castle Staff Register
Page 222: Wreck of the Duncan Dunbar, reproduced with permission of the State Library of NSW; Mitchell Library.
Page 224: *South Africa* portrait © The British Libraries Board – *South Africa*.
Page 230: *La Hogue*. John Oxley Library, State Library of Queensland via Wikimedia Commons.
Page 238: "High Seas: tea-clipper *Leander*" by Derek G. M. Gardner. Thanks to Mrs Mary Gardner for her kind permission to reproduce this.

The photographs on page 236, 245-6 and 259-60 are in the possession of the Robinson family. The illustrations from the *Strand* and *Illustrated London News* are from originals held by the editor, as are uncredited illustrations. The family trees were produced with Family Tree Maker, version 10.

TO THE SEA IN SHIPS

CAPT. J. C. ROBINSON'S REMINISCENCES.

Captain J. C. Robinson

No. 1.

AS a young man, serving in sailing ships, it was my good fortune to "Home" always in the Port of London, and generally in the East India Docks, Blackwall, which in those days afforded convenient room and rest between their voyages for all, or nearly all, the grand old argosies that went to build up British history abroad.

It was one of the sights of London in those early days to walk along the North Quay under the outrigged bowsprits of those mysterious bulwarks of Great Britain and examine the wonderful and artistic figureheads that reached out towards you along the way, indicating the name and often the destination of the Greens, and Wigrams, and Dunbars, and Soames, and Marshalls, and Lidgetts, all spick and resplendent in outward-bound uniform of paint and gold leaf; the familiar black and white ports of most of the hulls, with their towering spars and rope rigging, and their white covered sails bunted professionally along the great yardarms, providing a fascinating and enthralling picture against sea and sky that filled the timid imagination of the uninitiated with wonder and apprehension. There were lots of nice properties about Poplar in those days, and many owners lived in the neighbourhood of their ships, and loved them – and truly they were lovable!

On a Sunday afternoon in fine weather the North Quay became Lovers' Walk. I am not sure it was not called so; but I am quite sure that from a British educational point of view it had no competitor.

Compared with the restless whirl and worry of our steamers up to date, these ships went about their business in a dignified and orderly manner; not very fast perhaps, but with a good deal of style and success, the fruits of sound seamanship and commercial excellence. Seamen were sailors then, and none but sailors could manage their ships. The superiority also of British manufactures in those days admitted of no successful competition, so that around all coasts the Red Ensign floated fearlessly, and made us by universal consent mistress of the seas. My personal experiences extend over a period of 55 years – 1858 to 1913; and I may fairly claim for that interval all the extraordinary developments that have marked the evolution of things maritime from the old to the new, so quickly have science and invention revolutionised our conditions at sea.

In the year 1873 I was first mate of one of Soames' crack East Indiamen,[1] and had the promise of the next vacancy for command. When at home I used to lodge with an old one-eyed rigger and his wife,

---

[1] The *Star of India*.

who lived in a small house in Harrap Street, Poplar. For 13 years I used these rooms. On the occasion I am about to refer to, having safely moored our beautiful ship in her allotted berth, I went as usual to my old quarters – and found them occupied. My old friend Mrs. Parker sent me to inquire for rooms in Bisterne Place, and being vacant I took them on at once. I remained there about two or three weeks, when my landlady on bringing in my tea after the day's work informed me in a sad tone of voice that she had been obliged to refuse an old captain and his wife, regular clients of hers, because I was in possession of their rooms. I told her to wire acceptance at once, and I would vacate after tea. Finding, on inquiry, that my own old rooms were again vacant, I went round to them bag and baggage after paying my score, and thought no more of the matter. I made another East Indian voyage in the same vessel, and again moored her securely as before. Before leaving the ship I went along the quay from one end to another to inspect everything, and correct any points that were contrary to smart seamanship and the credit of the finest frigate in the Fleet; after which, I was standing at the bows admiring the *tout ensemble,* and feeling very proud of my work, when I was nearly knocked into the dock by a sound thump on the back, and wheeling round resentfully faced a old sailor with a grey beard and a loud smile offering me his hand. So absorbed had I been in my duty that I was unaware of his presence. For a moment his appearance reminded me strongly of a turtle. Declining the proffered civility, I more or less politely enquired upon what grounds he presumed upon such impertinent familiarity. He laughed aloud and, advising me not to expose my linen, said his name was Tom Smith. "Neither the first nor last of that name," I replied, with fine originality. Still laughing, he told me that he knew me, though I did not apparently know him; and then he said:

"Look here, young man, you turned out of your diggings to accommodate me twelve months ago, and I am going to turn out of my ship now to do you a good turn. There she is opposite. Isn't she a beauty?"

It was the *Carnarvon Castle* of the Donald Currie line – more like a great yacht than a merchantman. Somewhat mollified, I suggested that he was perhaps exceeding his commission or his powers; but he insisted that I should come with him there and then and be introduced to their Superintendant, Captain Gibson, who was on board at the time, and he, having evidently been primed beforehand, invited me to meet him and Mr. Currie the following morning at Fenchurch Street.

Somewhat dazed by the hasty and unexpected march of events, I kept the appointment, and was ushered into the great man's presence, who, after the usual civilities, looking me through and through, asked Captain Gibson whether he considered me a proper person to have charge of that ship. He replied that he did. Beetling his brows and drawing his whiskers meditatively into his lips, Mr. Currie said:

"I don't like putting an entire stranger over the heads of my own men." I rose at once and said:

"Excuse me, sir; I am not seeking to deprive any man of his birthright. I am in no need of a ship, but I understood that you were in need of a commander."

"That is so," he replied; "and at the moment our senior men are not available. Go and discharge your ship and do the right thing by your owners. I will write a note to Soames myself. In the meantime Captain Smith will take the ship round to Cardiff, and you can join her there, and pick up a cargo of coal for my steamers in Cape Town. Then you will go on to Calcutta, and thence to New York and Home. See me again when you are quite free."

The whole interview lasted perhaps some fifteen minutes, and no papers or references were asked for, no questions asked. Where they got all their information from regarding me and my antecedents I never heard, but I can only surmise that Mr Soames was in the know beforehand, and that the plan had been arranged to accommodate Mr. Currie previous to our arrival in England. Anyhow, the ship sailed a week afterwards round to Cardiff, where she remained about a fortnight awaiting her turn at the tips, whilst I did the handsome thing by the "old love" in preparation for embracing the "new".

On reaching Cardiff along with my friend C.W.W. and taking over the ship from Captain Smith, I indulged in a little extravagance by entertaining the old man and his wife at a champagne supper and taking them to the theatre afterwards – such a quaint little provincial place, with wooden forms in the dress circle and floors carpeted with sawdust. But if merriment may be taken as an indication of enjoyment, we certainly had a good time. The play was *Pygmalion and Galatea,* and Mrs Chrysos had an altogether extraordinary lisp; all her "s's" had an "h" after them. "So" became "sho" and "Chrysos" became "Chryshosh", and Tom Smith nearly had an attack of apoplexy. After the champagne supper Mrs. Chrysos was too much for him, and the audience was convulsed. I have never gone to the theatre since for fear of spoiling this royal memory!

The following day was devoted to business. I took over sundry properties necessary to navigation from my predecessor, amongst which were two old chronometers for which he accepted £20 and all his charts, which he valued at £10, but unfortunately he left me only an old bundle of "blues" which were no use to any one; a number of ancient well-thumbed books which had to be replaced at the end of the voyage by editions up to date, £5; and a few other more or less useful things that he found it difficult to cart away without exciting remark. He had a large chest made of teak by the ship's carpenter on the way round from

London, which along with other sundry and manifold parcels went ashore and passed through Customs as the personal effects of the late Captain and his wife. The chest, by the weight of it, must have contained the accumulation of voyages and the sailors pronounced it "bricks". I am afraid Captain Smith was a little careless about provisioning the ship that voyage, for there was an unaccountable shortage of small stores and medical comforts after his departure, which made the daily menu somewhat monotonous. Perhaps it was all the better for us.

And so we started on my first voyage in command, in the infancy of a firm which was destined to become one of the most important shipping concerns of the age – the "Castle," afterwards the "Union-Castle Royal Mail Line," embracing the whole of Africa, under whose colours I have, by the grace of God, served ever since.

How strange it seems that such far-reaching issues should spring from a circumstance so small and apparently insignificant! And yet is it not according to universal law, though it may not always be so easy to discover the source? The acorn becomes the oak. A simple act of spontaneous and forgotten courtesy towards an utter stranger and his wife has led to forty years' enjoyment of the highest honours that glorify life at sea – the command of steamers in the Mail, Transport and Passenger services that hold first place with the finest in the world – privileged intercourse and many lasting friendships amongst all ranks and professions of British and foreign society – Royalty and rebels, millionaires and mendicants, Jews and Gentiles; constant opportunity of kindly service to old and young, to rich and poor, invaluable to all. A handsome income during these 40 years that has aggregated over £20,000 without mentioning the frequent "recognitions over his signature" that Sir Donald Currie was so fond of lavishing upon his servants, and a "pensioned rest" at last for a poor old sailor of 70 – all parallel with happy home circle and surroundings; an astonishing harvest surely to spring from one poor grain of human kindness!

Though my 55 years of active service have flowed calmly compared with the experience of many nautical men in less favoured vessels and under less favourable conditions, still, they have not been altogether uneventful, and should reminiscences of this kaleidoscopic period of ocean history be judged readable matter, I propose to contribute them until the Editor shall cry "Hold, enough!"

No. 2.

MEN in every vocation of life have their occasional moments of exaltation and depression; due to temperament, or circumstances. They are not machines. Health no doubt has a lot to do with it; but success beats the big drum, and failure pulls down the blinds.

There is one calling, however, that has a barometer peculiar itself, the conditions of service being so totally different from all others. Brought up – I'm speaking of the so-called palmy days of "Auld lang syne" – brought up under rough and ready notions of discipline – arbitrary despotism very often, and arrogant brutality occasionally, our ancient mariners had a rough training as a rule: too often submitting to tyranny that would have wrecked any business commonwealth ashore, because the tyrant was, perhaps with truth, regarded as the undesired but necessary angel of safe conduct for the ship and all on board. Besides, mutiny had a disagreeable sound, and somewhat unpleasant consequences, on returning to the cold sympathy of wigs and gowns. Insubordination on the wet side of the world was quite a different thing from sporting rebellion on dry land.

Yes, it was rough at the best when canvas was the motive power of British supremacy, and nothing but an albatross or a stray whale broke the beautiful monotony of sea and sky for months together sometimes. "Salt junk" and "hard tack," briny pork and pea soup, "duff" and dirty water were poor substitutes for Christian food even when full allowance was available – which was not always the case. Watch and watch[2] continually, when the weather and the captain permitted it, did not conduce to inspiration for writing poetry during the intervals of duty; and in bad spells it was very bad – apart from all the danger and suffering connected with the handling of sails and rigging, and the periodical pump – all tended to promote a species of settled depression that took the form of spontaneous submission to constituted authority under all circumstances, and of a dogged disposition that defied all difficulties – along with a shyness and absence of ordinary self-assertion when ashore, that found favour amongst landsmen, and especially amongst the gentler sex. Strangely enough, these men have, perhaps, since the days of good Queen Bess unconsciously exercised more influence over the history of our Empire than any other section of society.

When homeward bound, and especially during fair winds and fine weather, the nautical barometer would commence to rise, and the habitual disposition would occasionally thaw out into actual levity. Now

---

[2] Alternately on and off watch.

and then, of an evening, some musical genius would dig out an ancient accordion from the bowels of his sea chest, and commence drawing out melancholy dirges at the "fore end," varied by an unpublished accompaniment to a love-song several yards in length, mostly referring to a beautiful virgin of prehistoric times, whose front name had apparently been Mary Ann – with chorus *ad lib.;* whilst not seldom a couple of swarthy seamen with pipes in their mouths would solemnly embrace one another in the orthodox manner, and perform a "pas de deux" to the rhythm of the tune by way of a practical contribution to the concert. But such frivolity vas indulged in only when the ship was homeward bound – probably, but quite unconsciously, by way of getting their hands and feet in against possible future occasions. Faces grew brighter as England, Home, and Beauty loomed nearer; but when "land ahead" was proclaimed from the "look out," the exaltation was complete. Nine months' pay due – and a glorious time ashore! Poor fellows. Many of them – too many of them, alas, drugged by crimps and robbed of every penny of their hard-earned wages the very first night after being "paid off"– and away down the docks the following day to find another ship, and to draw another month's pay in advance, to be lost in the same manner, and to sail away from a delusive dream of two or three days' misery to work off their "dead horse" for the first four weeks of a fresh voyage at sea – short of the necessary outfit, and provided only with a few bars of soap, some boxes of matches, half a dozen clay pipes, perhaps the same number of plugs of black Virginia tobacco! The only and invariable consolation was found in the old sea proverb – "There's a sweet little cherub that sits up aloft to look after the life of poor Jack." Poor Jack! It's precious little your ungrateful country has done for you in days gone by – even within the scope of one old seaman's experience. "It's only a damned sailor – what's the odds?" I am criticising history, but history, previous to the Board of Trade's activities between the years, say, 1870-80. Since then, many improvements in shipping and the protection of sailors have been developing.

If our men before the mast had a rough time of it in the "Blood Boats," so called when the captain was a brute, the officers were not much better off. They were quite a middle class "between the Devil and the deep sea." But who shall estimate the exaltation of soul, the suppressed joy of the young commander, when for the first time, the pilot, the last link with the shore, has left him "Lord of all he surveys." King, magistrate, and minister of a truly royal and unlimited monarchy upon the limitless ocean; father of his crew, though perhaps the youngest of them all, and henceforth to be known as the "Old Man" – the brains of the ship – and the arbiter of fate to all the lives and property on board. Courses to be set, and winds to be courted – nothing less than a heavy gale and grievous anxiety with no appeal will knock the stuffing out of him, and help him to realise the fact that eminent privilege carries equally heavy responsibility to level up the compensations – accountable to none but the powers unseen, often unknown, seldom acknowledged, no wonder if some of the less refined natures split upon the rocks of arrogance and egotism, and gravitate into the brutes and bullies of our noble profession.

Before passing away from the subject of Board of Trade regulations and our English legalised limitations to the industry of Messrs. Crimp[3] and Co., it may be interesting to contrast British improvements during the period referred to above with the manners and customs of ports in America for instance. The *Carnarvon Castle* sailed in July, 1874, on a voyage from London to Cardiff to pick a cargo of coal for the Castle Company's steamers in Cape Town and thence in ballast to Calcutta, to load Indian produce for New York and home again with "notions for the natives" and cake for cattle, &c. The whole voyage occupied about eleven months. Now on arrival at New York – say, nine months out from home – the chief mate awoke the captain[4] from dreams of peace and prosperity to inform him that during the night fourteen of the crew had disappeared, and that only five seamen and four apprentices remained on board, their loyalty being also under suspicion. Inquiries elicited blank information buttressed by bland smiles. The captain interviewed the agents of the ship upon the subject and was politely referred to the British Consul, as the matter was none of their business. The latter received him very graciously and suavely informed him that we were up against one of the customs of the port, and that it would, perhaps, be judicious to submit to the rule, unless he was firmly persuaded that his owners would agree to fight the hydra-headed sea serpent of Manhattan, in which case the matter would go before the Supreme Court in Washington, and in process of time would probably go in favour of the ship, which would then be officially attached for expenses. Further that such ruling would only affect the particular cause and ship at the time, and would in no case alter the custom of the port. Angry and dispirited, the captain, finding no friend in the hour of need, determined to beard the enemy in his den – a so-called shipping master named O'Flaherty, who, by specious arguments of greatly increased pay and improved conditions of service marched the men off the ship and kept them "perdu" until he could "Shanghai" them in a drunken state on to another vessel and draw a month's pay for each man as his own commission. Prodigious! The gentleman referred to was

---

[3] Press gang.
[4] In No. 36, JC explains he was trying to avoid saying "I" so much, so he tried writing about himself in the third person – which he then decided was even worse. Anyway "the captain" is JC.

9

good enough to tell the Captain that it was no use running his head against a stone fence – that before the ship could leave the port he would have to hand over the whole of the men's wages "due up to the date of his agreement to do so" (amounting in the aggregate to about £280), and that he would then supply him with a new crew at double the old crew's pay, and would draw a month's pay in advance for each man supplied. After which the captain might take his ship to sea with his, the shipping master's blessing, and with half the amount of the crew's wages to put in his (the captain's) own pocket. Whereupon the captain indignantly protested that such money should at all events go to pay the new crew for the run across the Atlantic; and the graceless scamp smiled sardonically, and said that if the captain was such a blanketty blanketty fool in his own interests, it was none of his business! All this meant, of course, that the new crew would receive no pay on arrival in England unless the ship made a very long voyage across. As a matter of fact, the captain fought the question out to the last day, vaguely intending to risk the voyage with the few men he had, when a United States Marshal was put on board the ship, and she was "legally detained" in port. Then there was no help for it, and the whole of the shipping master's programme was carried out in the most "honourable" manner, the Marshal's pay and expenses being deducted from the "captain's share" in the plunder. Wonderful! No doubt the "custom of the port" has been altered since then; at least, I hope so!

On the following voyage, profiting by the above bitter experience, a couple of days before arriving in New York the captain called the whole crew aft, and told them the story from beginning to end, rubbing it well in; and it had the desired effect, only three men leaving the ship during her stay in port, and "our" shipping master, on that occasion a certain Mr. Lafferty (for they take regular turns), complimented the captain on the loyalty of his crew, saying that they were about the saintliest lot of sailors he had struck. They drew their nine months' pay in London in due course – but whether they profited by it or not, who shall say?

Peculiar virtues were not strictly confined to shipping masters on the Western side of the herring pond in those 1874 days, but such things have no doubt long disappeared. Under Mr. Wilson[5] they would be impossible. The captain had to cut his eye teeth in more ways than one before he laid in a sufficient stock of wisdom to meet the everyday emergencies of business. Two examples may be interesting.

The ship arrived and berthed in New York during the evening on the captain's first voyage, and, having had a trying time, he was the last at the breakfast table on the following morning, when an ungainly figure

---

[5] President Woodrow Wilson.

marched in and sat down in a friendly manner. Extinguishing the sugar basin with his high plug hat and arranging his leg gracefully over the arm of the settee, he desired the steward to bring him a cup of coffee, and then informed the captain that he was his Custom House Officer, and that his name was Major Crawford.

Having accorded him a sailor's welcome and conferred upon him the obviously superfluous freedom of the ship, a little newsy and local conversation followed.

The Major was good enough to say: "Waal, Cap., I like you; you're one o' my sort. I'm a great admirer of nature, too; I find quite a deal of pleasure looking at the river; so if you've any trifle of your own that you are anxious to land, just give me a cigar and I'll go down to the end of the jetty and get some new ideas from the craft navigating up and down stream. It's quite a pleasant study, and" – (in a far-away voice) – "my price is 25 dollars."

Hardly grasping the situation, and fully persuaded that he had not heard aright, or had misunderstood the gallant officer, the captain looked straight at him and said:

"I beg your pardon?"

"Oh, that's all right, Cap. Just say when you want any news about the traffic and send for your waggon. We're all in the same boat."

"But, Major," said the astonished Commander, "I have nothing of a contraband nature to land if that is what you mean, and surely you would not have me understand that you would sell your complaisancy as a Customs Officer for money if I were disposed to smuggle anything ashore?"

"Waal, Cap., I should smile; but I see you're white, so I'll give you a friendly warning. Never give hard names to soft customs – 'taint polite – nor safe. Of course I know you haven't any private property to land, and if you had you wouldn't be fool enough to say so; but when you put it ashore just give me a long cigar and I'll smoke it at the Pier end – and my price is 25 dollars."

"May I, without any offence, Major, ask you a simple question?"

"Why certainly, Cap. Cough it up."

"If I were to report this conversation when I go up to enter the ship at the Custom House, what would likely be the result?"

"Waal, I reckon you might – I don't say you would – but there's just a possibility that you might meet with an accident, and come back to the ship on a ladder. 'Fact is, Cap', we all come in and quit along with the President, and have to buy store clothes while we're there; and those that are out now ain't going to spoil their chances against a change of office, and might be as mad as anybody against a crank. Enough said!"

"That so, Major? I was seeking information."

"Jest so."

11

No. 3.

IN my last paper, treating of "shipping master" troubles and "Customs officers"' complacency in New York, I casually remarked that American peculiarities of that period were not limited to the two classes above mentioned. I should like to give an example of smartness and practical business capacity that was particularly vexatious at the time, but which I have long since forgiven, and have remembered as something remarkably funny, all things considered.

It refers to our second voyage in the *Carnarvon Castle* sailing ship. I may mention, by the way, that I am blessed – and it is undoubtedly a very great blessing – with a particularly keen appreciation of all the wonders of Creation, "alow and aloft." Amongst these things, I dearly love floral life, though I know nothing whatever about the science of botany. During my two years' travelling and visits to many ports I had collected quite a varied assortment of rare and curious plants and orchids, as a supplement to the eternal glories of sea and sky; and I had constructed a nice little greenhouse for them on the after deck.

These were a source of continual pleasure and occupation to me in my spare time.

On arrival in New York, a delightful acquaintance of mine, a resident of Haarlem, near Brooklyn, being interested in the collection, asked if he might bring a friend of his to see the show. The friend was, however, away at the time, and it was our last day in port before he returned to town.

The two gentlemen came on board to breakfast, during which a little good-natured chaff was indulged in by our visitor regarding McArthur's enthusiasm over my wallflowers and daisies. After we had put on cigars we went upstairs and opened up my treasures, and badinage ceased. Questions were asked, localities discussed, and careful examinations made; and our visitor expressed his astonishment at seeing so many healthy specimens quite unknown in the States flourishing on board a ship.

After dwelling very lovingly upon them for quite a time – in a tentative, far-away voice he "guessed" that he would like to take a cutting or two away with him if he had my permission. Of course that was granted at once – *Cela va sans dire* – knowing with whom I was dealing. He might take anything he liked – the sole proviso being that he must be careful not to injure any of the plants in the process.

Having a good deal to do at our agents and at the Custom House, &c., in preparation for sea, it was late in the afternoon when I returned to the ship and found the tugs and the pilot fuming to be off.

Once under way, the chief came to me and asked if I had authorised "that man" to help himself to those plants of mine, and I set his mind at rest.

Getting a ship under sail in a smart breeze on a moonlight evening, correcting the compass, and setting the course, &c., takes time, and it was getting late when I went down below for a little rest and refreshment. Then, for the first time, the potential inwardness of the chief officer's inquiry occurred to me; and I jumped up on deck, took the binnacle lamp, and looked into my greenhouse.

Dead Caesar! there was nothing else to look into! I was dazed! The thing was impossible! I fear I must confess that I said many things that should have been left unsaid that night – to my chief officer – and about a certain pirate!

Time has long since cast the charitable veil of absolution over the delinquent; but my virtuous indignation reached a climax that night on finding a note pinned to my cabin table cloth, written on my own paper, and presumably with my own pen and ink, thanking me in the name of the Horticultural Society of the U.S.A. for the interesting parcel of uncommon plants presented to them that day through – I will not give him away now – but it was about the year 1875 or 1876, and the signature was over the words, if I remember rightly, "Curator-General." He had taken my permission and proviso quite literally, and had sent for a cart to remove all but a few odds and ends of little value – without injuring them in the process! Hail Columbia: the world is made up of People.

I have never been to the States since. In spite of many troubles – mostly due to ignorance of the uninitiated – that used to ruffle the business surface of life in Port, I look back with profound appreciation on the great kindness and hospitality I received on all hands. I certainly had a royal time of it each voyage. Dined, fêted, driven around, entered as a member on the "distinguished visitors list" of the U.S. Club, all in the most friendly and natural way, simply because I was an Englishman and captain of a fine ship. It is all a matter of surprise to me now, thinking it over after 40 odd years.

The sequel to it was worth the story. One of my kind hosts was Mr. George A. Stevens, the designer and, I think, the builder also of the celebrated schooner yacht, *America*, which came over and carried off the highly-esteemed, much-coveted, and jealously guarded English Yacht Club Cup.

He greatly admired the shapely proportions of the *Carnarvon Castle,* and suggested making up a party to cross the Atlantic with us as passengers.

Our agents offering no objection, I consented with pleasure, and carefully prepared our limited accommodation, and supplemented our meagre outfit for the modest comfort of two ladies and four gentlemen of New York society – to the astonishment and chagrin of the mail steamer on turn. We had beautiful weather on passage, and all went well from first to last. Our friends thoroughly enjoyed their 27 days' trip and treated it as a huge joke.

On arrival in London, Sir Donald – then plain Mr. Currie – opened up the question of emoluments – and laughed heartily when I told him that the gross passenger receipts exactly balanced total expenditure, but that the resultant advertisement of the ship in New York was an asset of considerable and lasting value.

This was my last voyage in the stately *Carnarvon Castle*, and flatter myself that I handed over to my successor the smartest and best equipped sailing ship that ever flew the colours of the British Mercantile Marine. It was with anything but a light heart that I furled my canvas to boil the kettles of the Castle Mail.

I would fain linger longer on the loving memories of those sailor days, but the powers that be deride romance, and clamour for adventures up to date.

Lay in the lead. The sun has set upon Drake and Frobisher, and Admiral Noah is no doubt antique.

Beyond all question the poetry and fascination of a life on the ocean wave cannot germinate upon coal and smoke. The relative conditions between sail and steam are as the poles asunder. The latter is too mechanical, too matter of fact, and compassed about with over much red tape and regularity. It lacks the mystery, the majestic solitude, the continual expectation of the unexpected – backed by a sturdy resourcefulness, the result of manifold experiences – that can hardly be considered indigenous to funnels and bare poles. Sailors are not grown in steamers; they are an imported article, but essential to them nevertheless.

After leaving the *Carnarvon Castle*, and having six weeks' leave of absence, on pay, wherein to get married, I was sent by Mr. Currie, as a passenger, for a trip coastwise in a primitive kind of steamer called the *Iceland* to "learn steam," along with an old sea dog, named Thomas, in command.

We left Hull for Hamburg to pick up a cargo of crude sugar for Liverpool, and had a very heavy westerly gale in the Channel on the way round. The ship was loaded down to the scuppers, and by the time we reached Portland, in the middle of a black November night, the poor little vessel was making such heavy weather of it, waterlogged most of the time, enveloped in foam, and losing steerage way, that I got alongside the "old man" and shouted into his sou'-wester, "How long are we going to cut these capers, with Portland lights abeam?" His reply was to the man at the wheel: "Keep her away a couple of points"; and we gradually edged in towards the land and crept into Weymouth Harbour to relief and to rest.

When we had some hot coffee in front of us, and a couple of "German Smokes" under way, I asked old Thomas whether our recent diving bell performance was a frequent occurrence on these coasting voyages, and whether the old motto, "any port in a storm" was not a wise one at such times? He smiled and said if it was good enough for me it was good enough for him. Evidently a case of being between two stools – an old Captain and a young one each waiting for the other to give a hint that both were more than anxious to act upon, in a case that might easily have led to disaster, for lack of independent initiative. Anyhow it was none of my business to interfere – I was a passenger, of sorts.

I was relating this incident to dear old Captain Johnnie Winchester; and he told me that on one occasion he was in precisely similar circumstances as regards time, place, and weather, when he was in the *Betty Martin*. He had gone down to his cabin (which was under the bridge) to try and rest his weary bones for a few minutes after nearly 24 hours on deck leaving the chief officer in charge. He had just turned the lamp down dim, and propped himself upon the sofa facing the door, dressed as he was in sea boots, oilskins, and sou'-wester, and had closed his eyes, when the ship suddenly lifted herself forward at a an unusual angle and took a header over the crest into the lap of an awful sea, trembling all over and staggering like a drunken man under the overwhelming weight of a roaring deluge; and a moment after the upper panels of his door were completely smashed in and a cow's head, horns and all, forced inwards, with glaring eyes and a terrified and protracted moan! "Man J.C.," he, said, "I thought for a moment I was sent for." The poor beast was on freight, and was in a box lashed before the bridge, which was wrecked by the flood. It was a very difficult matter to release the innocent intruder from its unpleasant predicament, and get rid of the surplus water out of the captain's cabin.

On our arrival at Liverpool I took train for London and told Sir Donald that I had "learned steam" most thoroughly, and had no yearning desire to learn any more of the same kind.

He rather took me aback by telling me to go back to Liverpool and take command of the *Lapland*[6] for another voyage to Hamburg and back. I did not go, however. He changed his mind and sent me up to Glasgow instead to join the first *Balmoral Castle* (then building) as chief officer – Captain Howson being in command. This ship, some years afterwards, was sold to the Spaniards and burnt out in the Bay of Biscay.

---

[6] JC's younger brother Joseph worked on the *Lapland* to Cape Town as 3rd and 2nd officer, and then as 1st Mate, from 1879 to 1883.

From all accounts it was a dreadful tragedy. Amongst other horrors, the Spanish Captain went mad, and jumped down the main hatch into the roaring furnace below.

Strangely enough the shell of the ship remained afloat. She was picked up and towed into port, and practically rebuilt, the engine-room having escaped the general destruction.

Poor Captain Howson lost his wife before we sailed from the Clyde; and Alec Winchester came up to relieve him. He, Alec, was very seedy, and confined to his bed all the way round so the whole responsibility devolved upon the chief officer. The two brothers Winchester became very popular commanders in the Castle mail steamers. They were wonderful seamen and full of fun. I loved them both.

Carnarvon Castle - Tony Haslett Collection

No. 4.

THE bee will stick to its honey, and old memories crop up periodically and assert themselves to the temporary obliteration of every other interest. They are so deeply ingrained and so full of youthful vitality.

In the year 1866, I joined a sailing ship in London called the *Orient*, a strong, steel-built vessel of 11,000 tons, belonging to the Clints, of Liverpool. She was loading rails and railroad material in the East India Docks for Calcutta. I was to be second mate.

The captain was a French-Canadian named Wolfe, a clever, smart little man, an excellent navigator, but an awful bully, and the possessor of other little peculiarities that did not immediately appear until circumstances later on revealed him in his native tints.

The chief mate, when I joined the ship, was a canny Scot named Maur; a tall, easy-going, but masterful seaman who had a mind and notions of his own. He quarrelled with the captain before we sailed, for interfering with his plan for the stowage of the heavy cargo above mentioned. The difference of opinion became so acute, and relations so strained between them, that it led to his walking ashore, after telling the captain, "Weel, I'm no for being drooned mysel' just yet, so ye can gang yer ain gait, and gae to —" (well, it was some port that was not charted), "and be — to ye." The turning over of a case of cargo at the moment prevented me from catching the word.

I have no hesitation in saying now, after-events being considered, that Mr. Maur's plan would have saved us a very close shave upon the brink of eternity.

As we had not then "signed articles," that captain had no choice but just to hunt up another mate in a hurry; and he picked up a loud-voiced, burly bounder, who promised badly for the peace of the ship – and, by the way, fulfilled the promise. His name, if I remember right, was Jenkins, an East-end Cockney. Every soul on board when we sailed was new to the ship, from the captain downwards.

We started about a week after the Maur *fracas*. Plimsoll did not exist as a ship marker in those days, or we should have been detained for inquiries. We had a thousand tons of rails stowed in the lower hold, and the 'tween decks were partly laden with material of every kind required in railway construction; the upper half of the lower hold being practically empty.

As a model, our ship could not be classed amongst the clippers exactly. She was evidently not built for speed. Her lines forward were finer above than below the water-line, on account of the forecastle being drawn out to the figure-head; and the lower form at both ends had evidently been moulded with a view to carrying capacity rather than to quick voyages. And yet she was a smart-looking and well-found ship in every way, hull and rigging, inside and out. We carried a crew of 29 all told – very mixed ingredients, as usual.

All went well at first. We had fair winds and moderate weather; and as the ship was "as stiff as a church" we made the best of our way south, across the Equator and through the south-east trades, at quite a creditable speed, until we commenced to run down our easting – and then the trouble began.

Before we reached the longitude of the Cape we experienced a succession of bad samples of weather, with heavy seas, and the *Orient* began to display her abilities as a roller of no mean capacity. She had need to be staunch and strong, and well rigged. The captain seemed to lose his nerve, too, and would not keep the ship under canvas enough to steady her. To make matters worse, a strange and unaccountable noise commenced to accompany the rolling, gradually increasing, and proceeding apparently from the bowels of the ship. This got more and more pronounced, until from a rumble it became a sort of submarine thunder, with a distinct trembling sensation as of a distant earthquake. There is no disguising the fact that we were all more or less scared, not knowing what it meant. The weather, too, was getting worse and worse until we were "hove to" off St. Francis, under a close-reefed main topsail and fore-staysail, with a weather cloth in the mizzen rigging.

As I endeavour to describe that awful gale, accompanied by the terrible conditions I have referred to, it makes me shiver now to think of it, after 52 years. To add to the pandemonium, some of the upper tiers of rails in the lower hold worked loose, and began to slide across from side to side. If one of those bars should get a fair "end-on" smack at the ship's side we could only hope and pray that it would not pierce the plating. We managed pass some sails and awnings down through the lazarette and fore-scuttle into the 'tween decks, and dropped them down into the hold at each side of the rails, hoping they would "cushion the contacts" and save the sides. We could do nothing else. All the King's horses and all the King's men could not have gone below and lived – let alone do any good there. It was a desperate expedient, but it partly succeeded – at the cost of our canvas.

The gale commenced from the eastward, and we were "hove to" on the port tack with a dangerous sea, continually increasing in height, and the weather dark and threatening. The glass was low and falling fast. About 2 p.m. an enormous waterspout was observed to windward, apparently coming straight down upon us and lashing the seas into fury over a wide area. The clouds seemed almost to touch the waves. We could do nothing to help ourselves. Even the old tradition of gun-fire to create atmospheric shock was an experimental impossibility; our two six-pounder carronades were on the main deck, and almost continually under water; though, considering the terrible rolling to windward as well as to leeward, it seemed very remarkable that she did not take more and heavier water on board than she did.

I was on watch when the waterspout appeared through the driving spindrift and rain, and I shouted down the companion way for the captain, who climbed up the stairs, and put his head out the narrow opening at the top. After taking a hasty glance, he called to me that "this was an occasion which must be left to the skill and discretion of the man in charge, and that he was going below." He closed the slide again and disappeared. Providentially for us, that waterspout passed by us about half a mile away, and brought the wind round a couple of points more to the northward, so that we headed the sea a bit better for the time being, and were thankful.

During a hurricane squall that accompanied the sudden change of wind, the fore-staysail sheet was carried away, and for a few minutes the dreadful artillery of the released canvas added an energetic feature to the howling tempest. There was no need to make any attempt to haul down the sail; in a very few minutes there was nothing left of it except the head rope and a string of noisy ribbons, not worth risking men's lives to save. How the main-topsail held on was a mystery – but it was small and brand new – and we should have done badly without it indeed.

It was the winter season down south and no moon at the time, so that, as night came on, the dense cloud, and driving rain and spume made the blackness of darkness visible. The sea was increasing all the time, and hauling round more to the nor'ard like the wind, which was blowing a furious gale, and I shall never forget the watch I had to keep from eight to twelve. The "wheels" had been lashed, and the helm secured with relieving tackles early in the evening.

I kept the four helmsmen along with me behind the weather cloth ready for any emergency, but none the less also for human companionship during that dreadful night. Life-lines had been stretched along the decks fore and aft, for those to hang on to who had to risk moving – and it was indeed at no small risk that any attempt of the kind was made.

The experiences of that four hours' watch are graven upon my memory for life.

The mysterious pandemonium below, the sliding rails, the howling storm, and the roaring seas, added to the thrashing of the ship from side to side, and the angry swish of the deluge on deck, left nothing to be desired by the most adventure-loving enthusiast.

But there was an item of terror added that would require an abler pen than mine to do full justice to.

As I have said, the night was darkness visible – overhead: but the combing seas were brilliantly phosphorescent along their wicked crests, and like moving avalanches they raced one after another as if determined

19

to engulf the labouring ship. As she rolled from 20 to 30 degrees to windward over the fiery crown into the yawning trough of each succeeding sea, the relative angle of deck and masts made every approaching crest appear nearly vertical; and it quite impossible that she could recover herself in time to escape the awful wall of water that appeared actually to overhang us from a dreadful height above; but she flung herself over every time at an angle of some 40 degrees to leeward under the foaming crest, and back again as before, in the same terrifying manner continually, accompanied by the never ceasing thunder below, which even the roaring of the tempest could not drown.

It would be quite impossible to do justice to the fearful conditions that existed towards midnight on that never-to-be-forgotten occasion. None of us expected to come through it afloat, and if ever a ship in distress was preserved from destruction by universal and soul-agonised prayer, it was surely the *Orient* in that hurricane of the southern seas.

Nothing less than an Almighty Supervisor and special Providence could have pulled her through. Nothing less! How the hull and rigging stood the test no practical seaman's experience could comprehend, especially when we discovered the causes of the submarine thunder and the volume of rails that had been working loose below!

At midnight, a hurricane squall and mighty downpour of hail and rain, accompanied by blinding flashes of lightning (thunder could not be heard) struck the apparently doomed ship just at the change of the watches, and we all held on, lashed as we were to the rigging, awaiting the end. Why should we attempt to move? We were all no doubt too deeply occupied in pleading for help – and to our inexpressible surprise help came in what appeared to be a critical moment of time!

The ship was observed to be climbing up an inaccessible mountain of water, and through an altogether obliterating cloud of foam and spray she pitched through the crest and dived down into the lap of the next advancing wave end on, comparatively free from all rolling motion!

"Look at the compass," roared the mate, and at the risk of being washed overboard, as the stern of the ship sat down under water, I dragged myself over and shouted – "E.S.E.: the wind has hauled round six points." I caught no vocal expression in reply – but I am certain that our Guardian Angels heard every heart scream out "Thank God!" and that the salt water dripping from all faces as not entirely Agulhas current.

That squall was the climax and conclusion of our troubles – the christening of a great deliverance. The gale commenced to moderate; and though the swell was very heavy, the vice was knocked out of it, and the ship took the changed conditions very kindly.

The captain showed his head suddenly through the narrow

opening of the companion cover, asking for information; and having shouted to us that the barometer had risen a tenth, and that we were to call him if there should be "any change," he again disappeared – probably to attend to his navigation.

I left the mate in charge with very different feelings from those experienced on relieving him at 8 p.m.; and lay down as I was, in oilskins and sea boots, on a settee in the cuddy for a rest, ready for a call should anything unforeseen arise.

At 4 a.m. when I again relieved the deck, the stars were shining, the heavy sea had become a long swell, and a moderate gale was blowing. We decided to let things remain as they were until daylight, and then call all hands to make sail and get the ship on her course, as the wind had hauled still further round, and was settling down to a fresh breeze and fair weather.

We found that the ship had been making a good deal more water than usual, and we had a long spell at the pumps. This was easily accounted for later on when we went into the question of the submarine thunder.

The last voyage log book revealed the fact that in order to make room for a light homogeneous cargo and to stiffen the ship – she being rather tender – the floor spaces under the ceiling had been filled with rock ballast. This was "supposed to have been all removed in London"; but the work had evidently been imperfectly done, and the excessive rolling, and loose water in the bilges, had dislodged and started the remaining rocks going from side to side over the rivet heads, to our grave anxiety, and no small danger to the ship.

When we opened our hatches to examine the cargo, we were not surprised to find the entire surface of rails grievously disarranged. But all's well that ends well.

No. 5.

IN March, 1877, we started in the new steamer *Balmoral Castle*, Captain John Howson being in command and I chief officer. We made two voyages together in her. I am sorry to say that we did not agree very well. Good old J. H. had been brought up in Brocklebank's employ of Liverpool, and there was a marked difference in those days – whatever there may be now – between Liverpool and London ships in the matter of discipline. The explanation of this was not hard to find.

London had for many years enjoyed a monopoly of the grand old firms and splendid ships of the East Indian and Australian services: Green's, Wigram's, Dunbar's, Somes', Marshall's, &c., as previously mentioned. The education, discipline, and style were the same in all – based upon the system of the Royal Navy and the old East Indiamen. They were all passenger ships, and it was an axiom that work must be carried on in a quiet and orderly manner.

In Liverpool, the trade was almost entirely confined to cargo – excepting, of course, in the Transatlantic steam services. But, steam or sail, the so-called "Packet-rat"[7] order of crew was always a troublesome factor, requiring to be dealt with in a somewhat unceremonious manner. It was practically impossible to carry out orders systematically and work quietly. Emphasis in language and action seemed to be considered necessary. I do not for a moment say it was always so, but it certainly was too frequently the rule.

I had sailed out of London all my life, and my manners and customs did not please J. H. He told me bluntly one day that he liked "to hear the work go on." I had to submit to a good deal in that way, and at the termination of the voyage handed in my resignation. Whereupon he asked my reasons for taking such a step. I reminded him that he had only quite recently informed me that he would not take me with him again under any consideration. In reply, he said he did not remember ever having said or thought such a thing, and requested me to alter my decision and continue with him.

I suppose he had begun to realise that sound seamanship did not depend altogether upon "sound" of any other kind.

On our first voyage we were honoured by having Sir Bartle Frere[8] and his family on our passenger list. Poor man, he went out just in time to pilot that South African Ship of State through a sea of troubles. Wars and rumours of wars – fightings without and fears within. The whole of the native tribes seemed to be in the melting pot, until the White

---

[7] A tough seaman in the old Transatlantic sailing packets.

[8] High Commissioner for Southern Africa.

Colonists themselves were drawn in – with what disastrous results we know too well.

I was on the quay in Cape Town when Captain Joe Morton, of the Union Company's little *Natal*, came in with Cetewayo on board as a prisoner. There was a crowd to receive him on landing. As the grand old Zulu passed close to me I respectfully saluted him – much to the disgust of another of our captains, with whom I was standing at the time.

"Why do you raise your hat to that — Black n—?"

"The name and reputation of that 'Black n—'," I said, "will go down to history in the annals of our country as an honourable and patriotic foe, when ours will be forgotten even on our grave-stones. Out of pure patriotism he fought us heroically; and his remarkable dignity and self-possession now, as a prisoner of war, surrounded by crowds of inquisitive strangers and enemies, excite my admiration for him as a man."

On that first passage out to Cape Town Lady Frere was good enough to admire a sketch I had made for the benefit of the Missions to Seamen. It was sold on board, but I quite forget what it went for. In Cape Town I was surprised to receive an invitation to breakfast at Government House one morning. I went, of course, for such an invitation was tantamount to a command. During the meal her ladyship told me she was intending to inaugurate an Art Gallery in Cape Town, and asked me to contribute a picture! I was startled, and exclaimed, "My dear Lady Frere, I am not equal to such a commission." For once in her life she forgot her graceful courtesy, and with a smile replied, "Don't let that trouble you; there will, no doubt, be lots of other daubs there!" It could have been eased away more gently, however correctly it might apply to future contributions. At all events, my talents in that line were far below the zero of the Royal Academy, and I was constrained to decline the honour.

After our second voyage in the *Balmoral*, I was taken out of the ship and appointed to the command of the *Taymouth Castle*. Her commander, Fiery Fulton, had managed to get himself into hot water abroad, by altering the pitch of his propeller in Cape Town Dock, at considerable expense, without consulting anyone.

I joined the ship in London, but wisely carried on the work in chief officer's uniform, until such time as my name should appear on the ship's register. It was as well that I did so. A week before sailing, I saw Sir Donald and Captain Fulton walking along the quay towards the ship – and at once jumped to conclusions. The new ship *Conway Castle* was lying opposite to us, and Howson was going in command.

As Sir Donald came up the gangway he shook hands, and asked me what I was doing – I pointed over to the *Conway*, and said: "I believe I am to go there as chief officer." He smiled a broad smile, slapped me on the back, and said "Well done." I lost no time in carting my odds and ends over to the *Conway* whilst he and Captain Fulton had lunch together on "my ship." *Sic transit gloria mundi.*[9]

It was only for one voyage, however. Poor old Fulton got into trouble again by cutting corners too closely, and narrowly escaped putting his ship ashore in the process. It made very little difference to him, however. He had married money at the Cape – and was probably trying to make the voyage shorter in order to get back to his comfortable home the sooner.

It was then my turn – May, 1878; my first command of a steamer[10] – and a very bonny one she was. It was about time too, from the point of view of home finance. I had been drawing chief officer's pay for the last 18 months; and with the lease of a house on hand, and a brand-new bride, I found it little enough, without even a motor-car.

Those were the easy-going days of the Castle Line. We used remain 14 days in Cape Town and three weeks in Algoa Bay, which was, as a rule, the terminus of the ocean steamers.

James Murison, of the firm of Anderson Murison, was our agent in Cape Town – a grand old Scotsman of the first water. He was the figurehead of Table Mountain; always the same – bluff, blunt, and amiable – brimming over with human kindness, a prince among men. He seldom smiled, but when he did relax it was good to hear him!

On arrival in dock on my first voyage, I donned my silk "bell topper" and holiday togs in order to make my bow in correct form. Being directed to the office (now the Union-Castle Company's premises) – I had never been up town before – I saw a big, burly figure in snuff-and-butter colour with a hat to match, standing at the door like a huge letter X, thumbs in waistcoat, and solemn as a judge. I asked him politely to allow me to pass. He gruffly replied:

"What do you want?"

"To see Captain Murison."

"And what if I'm Captain Murison?"

"Well, sir, if you are, I'm Captain Robinson, of the *Taymouth*."

"What! you a sailor? I took you for some out o'-work doctor looking for a job. What have you been doing this long while? I could have walked out in half the time." Then he offered me his great paw and said, "Come in and crack a bottle of champagne." I succumbed.

Our agent in Port Elizabeth was Fred Blaine, afterwards Sir Frederick. Courteous, gentle, refined, and correct to his finger tips, full of droll humour and amiability, he was immensely popular. The Castle Line was agreeably represented in the Eastern and Western Provinces.

---

[9] Thus passes the glory of the world.

[10] *Taymouth Castle.*

24

At the time I am speaking of, the middle of 1878, the Kafir war[11] was just over, and Cetewayo (or Ketchwayo) with his Zulu impis was defying creation. We were sent up to East London to pick up a consignment of stores for Natal. But oh! the muddle, the somnolence, the official ignorance and incapacity! We were hanging about at East London for many weary days, doing nothing continually and fruitlessly signalling for instructions of some kind. The Union Company's *Saxon* was lying there when we arrived, with the men of Schermbrucker's Horse on board – about 80 of them. These were ordered to be transferred to us without any apparent cause; and during the process one boat load was nearly lost through a trooper grounding his musket rather too emphatically on a rotten plank in the bottom of the ship's boat.

Colonel Schermbrucker was one of the original German Legion, who, I believe, had been rather liberally treated in the way of concessions by the Cape Government. He was a most amusing and interesting companion. I was glad to make his acquaintance as such, but I did not like to trust him altogether. One of his anecdotes will suffice to give an idea of the man. He made no secret of his "hide and seek" manner of making a livelihood. He had been everything and everywhere in South Africa; in comparative affluence occasionally, but bankrupt most of the time – had served in the police, had dabbled in produce, had tried farming on nothing except another man's land, and for some time had edited a paper of sorts at East London. The latter was his undoing. His too candid way of showing up his neighbours to one another led him deeper and deeper into hot water, and at last brought down the fury of the local gods upon his head. Having heard rumours of a prepared ceremony in which he was destined to play the principal part to the accompaniment of tar and feathers, he said, in his delightful broken English, "I just told my Irish servant Mike to load up the Cape cart, and be ready for a start. Then I wrote a last, slashing article for the 'Rag' on the coming day, and leaving the plant to look after itself, we just trekked away for anywhere, with my two Basuto ponies in harness, and Mike's 'shackass' tied on behind. So we travelled and camped for days and completely lost our bearings. Nothing but endless Karoo and sand, and our water fast giving out. The poor ponies were the first to go. One after the other they failed and fainted for thirst, and died. Good cattle they were, too – genuine Basuto blood. There was nothing for it but to unload everything that we could do without, and harness the 'shackass' to the cart. The poor beast soon gave in, and we had to leave the cart and tramp along on foot, Mike leading the moke carrying our last keg of water, and I with my gun on the look out for anything that never turned

---

[11] Kafir here means Xhosa. In the 9th Kaffir War, 1877-8, the Xhosas attacked the Fingus who were in alliance with the Cape government.

up. It was broiling weather and blistering sand; and at last I sat down and left Mike and the 'shackass' to tramp along ahead. I said to myself 'Schermy, old man, your lease is out; you've played your last trick; but let Mike get out of hearing before you "touch her off."' So I just sat and watched them plodding wearily along, until it suddenly occurred to me that it was playing it pretty low down for a man to cave in while that patient beast was wagging his long ears backwards and forwards to the stride of his tired legs; so I struggled up on to my own, and decided that the 'shackass' should be the first man to give in. And that 'shackass' was the wisest of us three; for, led by Nature's unerring instinct, he was nosing for a native kraal that we reached before dark on that dreadful day, just a fortnight after we left East London."

The way he related this incident was too comically dramatic for anything, and cannot be reproduced in writing. Now, here he was again, in the region of his former exploits, in command of a regiment of horse, and bent on honourable warfare.

Some considerable, time after this I heard a strange story about my friend's narrowly escaping the award of a V.C. for an act of gallantry under fire. It was something to this effect:-

In a hot engagement with an impi of Zulus one of his men had his horse shot under him, and was in imminent peril of being slaughtered. Observing the man's helpless condition, the Colonel turned, and galloped through a storm of bullets and spears, caught up the poor chap, who was wounded, behind him, veered round, and tore back to his lines in triumph through a horde of howling savages, and saved his man. As Commanding Officer he reported the matter to headquarters in due course, switching on the limelight.

The investiture was, it appears, suspended *sine die*, owing to the incident becoming mixed up with a cock-and-bull story of an officer having had his own horse shot under him during a scrimmage, jumping on to a fallen trooper's mount, and galloping off for bare life.

Sic transit once again.

No. 6.

LISTENING to Schermbrucker's romances, however amusing they might be, was not bringing grist to our mill. The R.M.S. *Taymouth Castle*, Commander J. C. Robinson, was being shamefully neglected in spite of signalling, steam whistling, and indignant messages whenever an opportunity offered for their dispatch. The earth's balance in the solar system was being compromised, let alone the material welfare of South Africa, which depended so much upon our proper recognition and employment. I have always felt that way – and feel so still: "my ship and I!"

It must not be forgotten that East London, in 1878, was not the port it is to-day, with its breakwaters, its tugs and steam-launches, harbour lights, and civilised conveniences; far from it. The one and only means of ordinary communication with the shore was remarkably primitive. A "sea buoy" was anchored in 7 fathoms of water off the river entrance, to which a coir warp was attached, the other end being fast to another buoy anchored just inside the mouth of the river. Lighters -- very small things in those days – had to be towed out by a whale boat to the "river buoy," and thence hauled out by hand to the other one. The ship "on turn" outside steamed up as close to this buoy as circumstances and the captain's nerve would permit, and anchored; after which she ran a line from her own bow to the buoy, which enabled the lighter to warp along to the ship's side, ready for work; the return journey being in reversed order.

I fear that more accidents happened than were reported. Raw "boys,"[12] unaccustomed to the rough and tumble of the Bar, were frequently lost overboard, and – well – perhaps least said soonest mended – poor fellows! Under the most favourable circumstances it was dangerous work from beginning to end. The Bar was almost always in evidence. It is in a straight coast-line with no protection of any kind; and the Agulhas current runs from two to five miles an hour according to the prevailing wind and weather – and these are never to be relied upon at East London for more than an hour at a time. We had to keep a sharp look out therefore and to order the lighter away on the first premonitory symptoms of change; work was, therefore, a business of anxiety as well as of delay.

The authorities could not complain of any want of enterprise and preparedness on the *Taymouth*'s account. I made it a regular practice, weather permitting, to be anchored close to the sea buoy at break of day, with our line attached ready for action; and before dark we returned to

---

[12] He is probably referring to black workers here – see No. 25.

anchor in twelve fathoms for the night. When there were several ships waiting, there was keen competition for the buoy anchorage at dawn; but we were never forestalled. Captain Rigby, in the *Betty Martin*, was determined to get to windward of us, but I knew my man. One morning – it was pouring with rain, and as black as ink, no wind, and smooth water – we got in quietly about four o'clock by instinct and "the lead," and let go our anchor; and over the rattle of the chain I heard Rigby's howl of rage as he yelled out, "Full steam astern. There's that 'something or other' there again!" and as he diminuendoed into the darkness he shouted out, "All right, my love, I'll be even with you yet." Good old Harry Rigby.

A lighter at last was sent out to us with war stores. It was a beautiful sunny day for a change.

My chief officer came to me whilst I was at breakfast, and said he did not like the way they were sending the stuff off.

Following him on deck to inspect – to say that I received a shock would be to put it very mildly. A flour barrel, with the head out, about two-thirds full of loose gunpowder, was standing on deck before the bridge – and lo! three of Schermbrucker's troopers, smoking three large pipes, with Boer tobacco, stood round the barrel sifting the fascinating stuff through their fingers!

I said, very calmly, "Step back, please – further off – now clear out! Away aft everybody!"

Then we covered the barrel with sacking, and stuck it back into the lighter.

I trust that my remarks to the chief officer will be remembered. He might well take exception to the state of the shipment. Any lunatic might. He told me that all they had so far received on board was more or less leaky. As a matter of fact, the deck between the gangway and the hatch was literally strewn with the shiny black explosive. It was sent off in second-hand flour barrels and boxes, a disgrace to somebody.

J. J. Irvine was our agent there then, and I sent him a bit of my mind by the lighter. This brought him off the following day by another boat with "war stores."

Now I know that Mr. Irvine was an honourable, upright, and faithful agent; but I was exasperated by delays, neglect of signals, absence of instructions, and inexcusable carelessness on the part of someone in sending off such a shipment, and I refused to listen to any explanation. He said the blame lay on the other side of him altogether.

I threatened to report the whole thing to Sir Donald, and as a matter of fact I did; and it may have led to the appointment of our own Company's men as agents, for I brought out Georgeson for East London and McLean for Cape Town. Captain Ridge was sent to Algoa Bay and D. C. Andrew to Natal.

During our protracted stay at East London we had several interesting people with us on their way to Natal. Digby Willoughby, Captain Bettington, who afterwards raised a Company of Horse, and a fine old gentleman who claimed to be the oldest living Natal colonist. Mr. Wolhuter was, I think, his name.

He told us some capital stories about the earlier struggles between British, Dutch, and Zulus. One of these is perhaps worth repeating, allowing the particulars to be within low water mark of truth.

He was out with Sir Harry Smith's Commando to check the inroads of the Boer farmers. The British, who were on the south bank of the Tugela, possessed two small six-pounder field pieces, which were a source of annoyance to the Dutch on the opposite bank. They made a raid during the darkness of night and captured one of these; so that honours were equal in the matter of artillery, but not in the munitions of war. The Dutch had powder enough but no balls of their own; so a sharp look-out was kept for every shot fired at them, and searchers at once proceeded to unearth the missile when it could be found, and it was returned by means of their captured cannon.

In a short time, however, the supply of balls was getting scarce and the periodical "bang" on either side became less frequent, and finally ceased. Then some clever mechanic managed to form a ball of sorts, by amalgamating some small chain with molten lead (from bullets). This ball was by no means round and in transit, it loudly announced its evil purpose by a "worra, worra, worra" that warned its objectives to "embrace cover" until it had earthed; when it was immediately dug up, reloaded, and sent backwards and forwards until it fell short in the river and was lost.

This sociable kind of duel contrasted very innocently with what has been taking place during the last four years on the Continent and elsewhere. The old gentleman used his walking stick to illustrate his descriptions with dramatic action and expression that were quite delightful, and kept us in fits of laughter.

All things come to an end in process of time. We landed our moss troopers at East London, and took up our strange assortment of "war stores" to Natal; after which, we commenced loading wool for the homeward voyage at various coast ports, Natal, East London, Port Alfred, Algoa Bay, Mossel Bay, and Cape Town. But owing to the wars and droughts, cargo was very scarce, particularly at Algoa Bay.

I consulted with Fred Blaine. We invited merchants on board to a nice luncheon, and I made my maiden speech. It was not very long, but it was to the point. I asked them if they were going to let me, on my first voyage as captain, return with an empty ship to face the music – and so on? Afterwards, on deck, good old Harry Mosenthal asked me what room we had, and I told him about a thousand bales. "We'll arrange that," he said. Then Newsome asked the same question, and got the same reply; and several other well-known wool merchants did likewise.

The next morning our shipping clerk, Bob Jones (who afterwards became the Union Company's agent at Port Elizabeth), came off in a tantrum, and asked what I had been up to, ordering wool – that bills of lading had been issued already for 2000 more bales than the ship could take, and that there would be "the deuce to pay and no pitch hot." I pacified him by suggesting that he could leave the freight to stand in our ship's name, and transfer the surplus wool to the *Walmer Castle*, then loading in the Bay. So we booked good returns ourselves, and both ships had full cargoes.

(N.B.– Must make a note of this for further service, before the lure of "first command" becomes threadbare).

Lunching at the Club with Fred Blaine one day, I was introduced to another guest of his, a gentleman from "foreign," whose name I cannot recall, nor does it affect the subject. He referred to the competition existing between the Union and Castle Companies: and asked how it was that the latter engaged such a lot of rough sailors for commanders, as compared with the gentlemen of the former. I am afraid I took an unfair advantage of a stranger in a strange land, but I could not help it. I replied that, "Being one of the Castle ruffians, I am afraid the explanation is beyond me."

There was one man in Port Elizabeth, the memory of whose gentle personality and cardinal virtues, shyly veiled under a transparent veneer of brusque mannerism, will ever remain with me as a sunshine over the briny -- James Searle. The mere mention of his name is a pleasure to me. For thirty years he was my never-failing friend in the Bay – where a friend was often a friend indeed. He had been a seaman himself, and, in fact, as active manager of the Port Elizabeth Boating Company he was a seaman still, until he had to give it up to act as one of the representatives of Port Elizabeth in the Cape Parliament.

Port Elizabeth, like East London, was, in those early days, very crudely served as regards communication between ships and shore. There were no tugs or steam launches of any kind. Passengers and officials had to sail backwards and forwards in a funny little half-decked cutter that might take any time, more or less, according to wind or weather, in reaching its objective; and many a hearty curse lay upon it for thoroughly upsetting the dignity of passengers who had long since forgotten their liability to mal de mer.

When numbers had to be landed, ladies and gentlemen, as from arriving steamers, they had to be dumped over by means of the cargo basket into a lighter, bag and baggage, sailed ashore, backed stern first on to the beach through the surf and carried out beyond water mark pick-aback by naked Fingos, whose sole, and somewhat startling adornment was the totally unfamiliar native feathery "mucha."

It was, I think, in 1880 that the brothers Mesina embarked upon the perilously speculative enterprise of bringing out and starting a small but real steam launch, which was the blessed harbinger of great developments in the bay.

About the same time our Company built and sent out a launch for East London. It was designed for crossing the bar by our Marine Adviser, Captain Small, and on arrival was damned by expert opinion as an "impossible absurdity." Well, I am not going to condemn expert opinion because I was of the same way of thinking. The *Dolphin*, however, lived down her detractors, and did remarkably well, and was followed later on by a larger edition of the same plan.

The building of the latter had a strange history. Her designer acquired by purchase a second-hand engine and boiler out of a disused tug on the Thames, and installed it in the new launch. There had been a slight error made in the calculations however and when the vessel was floated, with empty boiler and bunkers, it was found that she had on board already more than she could carry. In this case second-hand economy was an expensive luxury.

We made a double mistake the same year for the Natal Bar service. A really beautiful little vessel, but too fine-lined and powerful for the work, was sent out. Fortunately the Government wanted her services higher up the coast, and she was sold. I think she was called the *Carnarvon*. Improving on her, we went to the opposite extreme, and built a great lumbering twin-screw, double-decked affair called the *Lion*. Very appropriately named! She required a great deal of persuasion to come alongside a ship quietly. I daresay my good friend, Captain Tyzack, will disagree with me; but he always elevates a wheel-barrow into a motor-car, and would never allow a yellow cur to be called a bad dog!

No. 7.

IN July, 1879, after Lord Chelmsford's defeat of Cetewayo on the field of Ulundi, there was some competition between the Cape Town agencies of the "Union" and "Castle" Companies as to whether Lord Gifford, with peace despatches, should sail for England in the *Mexican*[13] or the *Taymouth Castle*, both steamers being billed to leave Table Bay on the same date, and to call at Madeira only on the way to Plymouth. The authorities themselves settled the question by allotting the honour to the *Mexican* as belonging to the senior Company in the South African service.

The incident gave rise to a good deal of mild speculation, if all reports were true; as the two ships were credited with a fairly equal control of speed.

Amongst our own passengers we had Sir Edward Strickland, Commissary General, and his wife, Colonel Cochran, Colonel Clark, Major Thompson, and a few other officers and men – an exceedingly vivacious and charming company.

During our meals we used to have the campaign fought all over again, and its failures and successes sifted very candidly.

It was quite an education to me. I took to it as a baby takes to mother's milk. In fact, I commenced to chronicle the more important records, in case that should happen which actually did occur, that I might be in a position to take prompt advantage of a dramatic opportunity.

As I have already said, the two steamers left Table Bay together, and ran almost neck and neck for several days, sometimes one having a little advantage and sometimes the other. Each morning at dawn the horizon was carefully scanned to see if the other vessel were still in sight; and when we did ultimately part company it was due to a slight divergence in our relative courses rather than to any difference of speed.

It was with a feeling of general disappointment, I think, that we did see the last of each other. Companionship of that kind at sea is always absorbing; but how much more so in our own case where we had so many interests in common.

In due course we arrived at Madeira. It was about 5 a.m., but boats were out before we anchored. Some one from our ship shouted out: "Has the *Mexican* arrived?" – and the answer came back across the water "No!" and then the music began. It seemed as if crew and passengers had agreed to prevent "navigating orders" from being heard.

---

[13] See No. 27 – he says there he's been told it wasn't the *Mexican* which was not yet built. It was probably the *Danube*.

No sooner had we anchored and received pratique,[14] than a representative of the *Times* newspaper scaled the bridge, notebook and pencil in hand, to solicit "copy."

Having heard of the victory of Ulundi, of Cetewayo's flight, of the war being over, and of peace despatches being on board the *Mexican*, he asked for all the information and detail that I could give him, so I handed him my "notes from Zululand," which I had kept in duplicate and introduced him to our military officers on board for confirmation of particulars.

So it came about that my records were cabled to London in extenso, filling over a column of the *Times*, under the heading of "Our Special Correspondent," and closing with the fascinating information that "Lord Gifford, the bearer of peace despatches, was following in the *Mexican*."

At this time, be it remembered, there was no cable service between Madeira and South Africa. All communication was by mail steamer, and consequently our news was of the utmost importance to the nation.

So far so good – but "every silver lining has a cloud." In order to keep everything straight and above board I put the duplicate copy of my "notes" into the ship's box for the office. This led to my being interviewed by Sir Donald, and getting a sound rap over the knuckles for assuming editorial functions. In future I was to limit myself to quoting from the papers where it was necessary to do so at all; and not to "provide" copy for others to quote. Alas! "the best laid schemes o' mice and men gang aft agley."

Never mind. To return to our muttons. Sir Edward Strickland was generally referred to as "Teddy" on board during the voyage Home. The wife of his bosom always called him so, and called him pretty frequently. He was rather partial to his pipe of Boer tobacco and a good historical novel, and used to inhabit my cabin – which was on the quarter deck – most of his time. There was a comfortable sofa there, and it just fitted him. He practically became part of it, and as he was a chatty and exceedingly amiable old gentleman he was somewhat of an acquisition.

Lady Strickland was disposed to retire to rest early at night – nine o'clock was about her time; and Teddy had to come along too. He might be comfortably ensconced with his pipe and tumbler of hot something alongside of him, which he called "sleeping draught," and her Ladyship would come to the door and say: "Teddy, it's nine o'clock." "Thank you, my dear, I'm nearly done." Another turn up and down the deck and a more emphatic announcement of the hour. "All right, my love." Still a few more turns, and a stern, "Teddy!" There was no gainsaying the

---

[14] A licence to enter port on showing a clean bill of health.

essence of command expressed in that short name – and the sorely harassed possessor, with a vicious *sotto voce* that sounded remarkably like "Otam," Zulu for "good night," would knock the ashes out of his pipe on to my carpet, finish his sleeping draught, and gallantly offering his arm with a cryptic smile that betrayed his feelings, would suffer himself to be led away to dream of authority over men, and horses, and wagons, and provisions galore.

When Sir Garnet Wolseley came out to take command it seems that he required all Departments to submit their accounts for his inspection. "Teddy" jokingly told me that when his turn came he just told Sir Garnet that his orders were to see that the men wanted for nothing, and that he had carried out his instructions.

Perhaps it may be possible to carry out such a commission with profit. I have heard that "Teddy" was a capable hand at bargaining, and that the Dutch farmers found him a hardish nut to crack.

Colonel Cochrane was a splendid man, braw, big, and bonny; and as sterling as his looks. I think he was of the Black Watch, but of this I am not quite sure. Thirty-eight years have worn holes in my memory that are past darning up. Anyhow, he might well be the pride of any regiment, and he was immensely popular on board. He gave us the pleasure of his company at my home in Acton one day to lunch, and to my dear wife's horror it happened to be "resurrection day," and she was quite unprepared to entertain so distinguished a visitor, but she was the only one who worried about it.

To describe one, however, is to describe all. Each in his way was equally pleasant in person and partnership, adorning and enlivening the usual tedium of a voyage at sea.

The *Mexican* arrived in Plymouth about six hours after ourselves, no doubt a good deal disappointed to have had their news forestalled by "the enemy," but such mishaps are of common occurrence, and belong to the fortunes of war.

On one of my voyages in the *Taymouth Castle* we took out four notable passengers – Dr. James Stewart of Lovedale, Charles Fairbridge, of Cape Town, and David – afterwards Sir David – Gill, Astronomer Royal at Cape Town, and his wife. Sir David, on the occasion I refer to, landed at St. Helena, en route for the island of Ascension, where he was going to observe the transit of Mars, for the purpose of establishing the delicate question of the earth's distance from the sun. Lady Gill afterwards wrote a very interesting book of "experiences" during their sojourn on the island.

[Strangely enough, we have this week received the sad news of her ladyship's death in Scotland last Sunday. – ED. *S.A.*]

They were a delightful group, and a very restful one. It was only necessary to sit still and listen, and grow wise upon any subject of

34

conversation that might be started. Gill upon astronomy, Stewart upon the Native question, and Fairbridge upon Law and every other subject under the sun (for he was a travelling encyclopaedia) made up an intellectual trio altogether different from the random chaff and badinage of the ordinary "smart set."

Sir David gave an interesting lecture on one occasion, the substance of which has appeared in print elsewhere; but one argument is worth repeating. Referring to the enormous inter-stellar distances in the heavens, he instanced that between "Alpha Centauri" and our solar system, the Centaur being estimated to be the nearest of all the fixed stars to our sun. It is of the first magnitude and is one of the pointers to the Southern Cross. Its distance is more or less correctly estimated at twenty billions of miles; but, he said, this conveys no intelligent idea of its meaning to the mind.

"To put it in another form. Supposing it to be possible to lay a railway from our sun to Alpha Centauri, and to start a train that should keep up a regular sixty miles an hour, without accident or stoppage, how long do you suppose it would take to reach its destination?" After various guesses had been made, beginning with three months, and ending, against an incredulous howl, at twenty years, the audience received a shock on being told by the lecturer that it would require "48,665,000 years" to complete the journey!

Dr. Stewart's strong point was the education and just treatment of the native races; the prohibition of the liquor traffic amongst them; the illegalising of the custom prevailing in some coast ports of paying natives at public houses; and making "Cape Smoke" part payment of wages on farms and elsewhere. He maintained that, provided the above were made indictable offences, and that three months' expenditure of the Zulu war were entrusted to him with a free hand, he would guarantee that there should be no native question and no native wars. From what I know of this remarkable man, I should say that he was not far wrong.

On arrival at Cape Town one or two of our more lively young fellows started ashore, to investigate and seek adventures, and they succeeded beyond hope and expectations.

In those days a sale was held every Saturday morning on the parade, behind the present railway station and post office. Our young men arrived on the outskirts of the crowd of prospective purchasers, and one of them, a tall Scotchman named Andrew Walker, craning his neck to see what was going on, caught the auctioneer's eye, and foolishly nodded to him. "Going, going, going at £4, going, going, gone! It's yours, Sir!" said Mr. Jones to our friend Walker, to whom, of course, as is usual in such circumstances, all faces were immediately turned; whilst a man led an ancient piebald horse up and demanded payment It was no use to argue. "You nodded at me, Sir – the horse is yours!" Amongst them our smarties had to make up the sum, and the halter was forced into Walker's unwilling hand, whilst a police officer who appeared to spring up from nowhere, ordered him to take his purchase away at once; and the disconsolate procession moved on. What was to be done? Suttaford's long-fronted shop was opposite them; so a sudden inclination to buy a necktie led them to the upper door, where they left the quadruped and entered, intending to walk quietly to the lower door in order to make a bolt for it. In the meantime the Centaur ambled up to the adjoining chemist's, and smelling at a drum of kerosene oil on the pavement, expressed his disapproval of the odour by deliberately kicking it over. The hullabaloo again attracted the attention of the ubiquitous policeman, who smelt a rat, and looking down Adderley Street, caught sight of our friends, and overtaking them, insisted upon marching Mr. Walker back again to the chemist's, who promptly gave him in charge horse and all; and as the Court was close by, and then sitting, he was ignominiously taken across and charged, his friends accompanying him to see the end of the play. Needless to say they had all been rather thirsty that morning, and were not perhaps as sedate as they might have been.

They arrived in Court just as a case terminated, and were called on straight away. After hearing the charge, the magistrate asked our friend his name. "My name is Walker,"[15] he replied.

"Take care, sir, this is not the place for buffoonery."

"I'm not joking, Your Worship – my name is Walker – Andrew Walker."

"Produce some documentary evidence to that effect."

After fumbling fruitlessly for some card or letter, he confessed that he could not do so. "But," he said, "I believe my linen is marked."

There was a titter in Court; but the Bench instructed the Clerk to make an examination, and the tail of the culprit's shirt was hauled out before an interested company of various colours, and after a good deal of pulling about, the Clerk announced that the letters A. W. did appear to support the prisoner's statement.

"What is your address?"

"The *Taymouth Castle*, Your Worship."

"Is the *Taymouth* in dock, Constable?"

"Arrived this morning, Your Worship."

A few more questions, and our friend was mulct in the cost of the kerosene and dismissed with a warning.

At the door of the Court stood a black attendant holding the spirited Arab steed, which then appeared to be fast asleep. The halter was again put into the reluctant hands of A. W. and Co., and they started off for pastures new. They offered the animal for sale at a "greatly

---

[15] A catchphrase.

36

reduced price"; they were prepared to "give it away," provided that they could secure a "comfortable home for the poor thing"; they wanted to "make a present of it" to anyone who would "be kind to it"; and at last tendered it, along with a sovereign, to a grinning Kafir,[16] if he would take it away and "bury it." All in vain! It clung to them like the measles; and they were driven at last to the expedient of leaving it at a livery stables along with a week's board and lodging, and a particular injunction to take care of it until they could make arrangements to send it up to a lady who loved horses of that colour.

Our friend carefully avoided the land after this until the ship sailed. I only heard of it later on.

---

[16] The word Kafir or Kaffir is now considered offensive but at that time it was simply intended to mean a black South African, perhaps specifically a Fengu.

No. 8.

IT was in the *Tantallon Castle* that we had the distinguished honour of taking Home from Cape Town King Khama, the grand old Christian Chief of Bechuanaland, along with his two brother chiefs, Bathoen and Sibili, to pay a visit to Her Gracious Majesty Queen Victoria of eternally revered memory. The King's Missionary Minister, the Rev. Mr. Willoughby, accompanied the party as secretary and interpreter.

This particular voyage ended on September 6, 1895, but even if I did not remember the exact date it would matter little, as I am not recording history, but just raking up reminiscences from the pebbles of the past.

Khama was a tall stately figure of a man, lean of flesh but great of soul, and rich in quiet dignity. I don't know how far he was able to understand our language, but no doubt it would be a great mistake to under-estimate his attainments. At all events, I never heard him express himself in English. His communications were invariably conveyed through Mr. Willoughby.

Khama had never seen the sea until he reached Cape Town. It was no doubt pictured in his own mind as a rather large and, perhaps, exaggerated lake. His face grew longer as Table Mountain melted into the purple shadows of a glorious sunset and nothing appeared to rise up ahead to take its place.

However, the old chief was too grave and too diplomatic to give expression to any fears that might be disturbing his brain – mingled as such fears were with the prospect of a loss of dignity and self-respect amongst strangers, by premonitory symptoms of internal, uneasiness quite new to his sedate line of life and experience.

I remember hearing a story once of a certain exalted lady in France who lay a-dying. Her Father Confessor entreated her to make the *amende honorable* in order to secure a first-class passage into the realms of bliss. With a weary and satisfied smile she assured him that St. Peter would never be uncivil to a duchess.

Neptune, however, had no respect for his Royal brother, for Khama had to submit to more or less solitary confinement in his limited cabin accommodation for several days before the Southern Ocean and his alimentary canal became reconciled.

Bathoen and Sibili succumbed, of course, out of pure loyalty to their paramount sovereign – *cela va sans dire*.

Sibili was a big, burly sample of his race – of imposing and prepossessing personality, evidently bent on having a good time, but just a little afraid to take the lid off. At first he was as shy as a girl; but he gradually acquired confidence and made many inquiries – always through

Willoughby – for he evidently understood no English before he joined the ship.

Bathoen was of medium stature and thick set. He was stern-looking and unbending; and, strangely enough, always suggested the Church to me, as though he should have been a padre. I suppose it was his solemn and superior air. He had much of the human oyster about him, and courted no familiarity. His particular tribe may not, perhaps, have adopted the native emblems of mourning for his absence, whatever his wives may have done. This is mere conjecture, and quite possibly the faulty interpretation of a sealed book.

On regaining his liberty Khama took in the sea from all points of view, subjecting every part of the horizon to his native penetration; but he grew more silent day by day, and about the Equator confided his fears to Willoughby that the "White Chief" had lost his way, and that there was neither mountain nor mark, hill nor hut, trail nor tree in all the vast wilderness of water, water, water everywhere!

On hearing this I sent a message to the King to reassure him, and to say that if he would come up on to the bridge at sunrise on Saturday morning (this was on Thursday) I should be able, by God's grace, to show him the two small mountains of Cape Verd grow up out of the horizon ahead and a little to the right, and we should pass five miles from them at or about 8 o'clock, before he should go down to breakfast.

At 5 a.m. Khama and Willoughby were there, and the morning was clear and splendid as usual in that region.

"No hills! I told you so!" If looks meant anything, speech was not necessary. Wait – the sun will rise at 6.

A few minutes before the orb of day drowned all the East in impenetrable glory, the faint blue vision of "The Paps" appeared – and gradually intensifying into purple reality, were gilded on their eastern slopes with a never to be forgotten sheen of radiance that filled all the essentials of a fairy landscape upon a fairy ocean.

I watched Khama as he stood, rapt in speechless worship, until the sun burst forth and asserted his all-embracing supremacy over land and sea, resolving cool dreams of joy and beauty into sober facts of tropic glare and heat, compelling all to seek the shelter of the awnings fore and aft.

Khama caught my eye, and with an apologetic smile sent Willoughby to express his thanks, and sorrow for his recent doubts and fears, assuring me that henceforth his confidence could never fail.

I told Willoughby that if I should receive a formal invitation to dine with His Majesty that evening, I should not be able to forego the honour. The invitation was duly received.

The three Chiefs and Willoughby had their own table in the corner of the saloon on the starboard side, with their own steward to wait upon them, and a very quiet and select corner it was.

Two days after passing Cape Verd a complaint was brought to me by Sibili, through the interpreter, that he had lost his nether garment. Inquiry elicited the fact that Sibili had asked one of the sailors to wash this particular pair of tweed trousers, and that the garment had afterwards disappeared from the drying line, no trace being left behind.

I found on inquiry that he had a waistcoat of the same material. This I annexed, and told Willoughby to impress upon the whole party the necessity of preserving absolute silence regarding the loss.

I need scarcely say that Sibili had another pair of bags.[17]

We called at Madeira the following day, and I got Blandy to cable for a detective to meet the ship at Plymouth. I was so horrified to think that a White heathen on board my ship should have been despicable enough to rob a Black Christian of his breeches! As Commander of the vessel I felt keenly that my honour was at stake. Such delinquency would certainly not pass unheeded in Bechuanaland, the Chief being in residence.

On reaching Plymouth an extremely sober looking gentleman introduced himself to me, as a passenger for London, first class. Khama and his party landed at Plymouth.

On the run round we arranged our programme. Orders were issued that on arrival in dock all baggage was to be strictly searched – no reason for this being given.

The tweed waistcoat, the key to our plot, was in the hands of our friend from Plymouth,

The search, of course, took time, and there was much grumbling amongst the men at the unexpected delay, until two of the quarter-masters came to me and very respectfully asked if they might know the cause of the unusual proceeding. Under a promise of silence, I told them.

Alas! they told me then, in confidence, that the lost garment had been stolen by one of the firemen and swapped at Madeira for a grey parrot, and that pirate and parrot had already landed and gone.

I asked his name; but this they absolutely declined to give, stating as their reason that no port in Great Britain would be safe for them henceforth as informers. A strange indictment surely.

However, the search went forward to an unsatisfactory finish, and thus closed Volume I. of the episode.

I ascertained Khama's address from the Passenger Department at the office, and went to pay my respects the day following. I found

---

[17] Trousers.

40

Willoughby in, and he unearthed Sibili from the smoking-room of the hotel. Having explained all that we had done and my regret for the failure of our scheme, I ascertained that he, Sibili, had purchased this pair of trousers and waistcoat at a second-hand shop in Cape Town for 25s. This sum I tendered to him, and after a little persuasion he accepted it. Finis of Volume II.

A day or two afterwards I received a note from Willoughby, begging me to call, as Khama wished to see me.

I went at once. The Chief received me courteously, but rather stiffly; and I was informed, through the interpreter of course, that he was displeased with me for having negotiated the above little business with his subordinate without his knowledge, and that I must be good enough to receive the 25s. back again from Mr. Willoughby.

I told him that I was unable to do this, as the theft had been committed on board my ship, under my command, by one of my crew, and that I had failed to discover the thief, or the stolen property.

Khama would have none of my reasoning. So I begged him to listen to a parable. (This I learned from Willoughby during the voyage.)

A certain trader, on his travels up country, had the misfortune to lose one of his pair of horses, and he was thereby hung up for repair. On inquiry, he was told that the chief of the tribe had some horses for sale; and he went to see him. The Chief recommended him a good nag, but the price was high – £30. The trader demurred. "The horse is a salted[18] animal, vaccinated against lung sickness, and is worth the money – you shall have a guarantee with it for twelve months – take it or not." The trader led away his purchase and resumed his travels. Three weeks afterwards that horse died of colic. Some months later on, the trader journeyed south through the same district, and the Chief sent for him.

"I have heard that the horse I sold you died shortly afterwards?"

"Yes. Unfortunately it did, for he was a fine beast."

"There's your money – £30."

"What for, Chief? He died of colic, not lung disease. Your guarantee was against hung sickness."

"That may or may not be so; but the horse died within such a short time, and the salting may have had something to do with it. He must have been a dead horse when you bought him. There's your money."

"Chief, you're an honest man. So am I. I will not take your money."

"Either you take that money or you leave my country, and return at your peril."

---

[18] It had recovered from a bout of the deadly "African horse sickness" and was now immune.

"Oh, well, if you take it so seriously I suppose I must submit to compromise. I will divide it with you."

"No more palaver. Here's your money – £30. Take it or go."

And that trader had to take it, because he loved him.

Whilst I was rehearsing my parable, Khama was a study. He never raised his eyes, but just sat with folded hands and without moving. After a short, silent pause, I added: "King, the Commander of a British mail steamer cannot afford to be less scrupulous upon a point of honour than even the Great Chief of the Bechuanas himself."

Then Khama stood up; and raising his eyes, with a gentle smile, held out his hand, and taking mine in his, he bowed with silent dignity, and through his friend thanked me for having come to visit him.

I learned afterwards from Willoughby that Sibili had spent the money I paid him for the lost continuations on the purchase of a malacca cane with a silver knob. Finish Volume III.

Before the party returned to South Africa, in another ship, I got the British and Foreign Bible Society to produce for me a beautiful copy of the scriptures (in Sesuto, I think it was) with "Khama" in block silver letters attached to the cover, which he very amiably accepted as a souvenir of his voyage Home.

Some voyages afterwards, I received from him a splendid wild cat skin carriage rug, which I have still – a right royal presentation. There is room in Africa, and otherwheres in this small world of ours, for many Khamas, unless I am much mistaken.

Tantallon Castle – Tony Haslett Collection

No. 9.

"CHICKENS come home to roost."

Just before leaving London in the *Warwick Castle* for Dartmouth, en route for the Cape, about the year 1882, I received a letter from a Mrs. Haldane, of Stirling, to this effect.

"My little girl Edna, 9 years of age, has been with her aunt in Durban for the last twelve months, and I am anxious to have her home again. We sent her out for her health, and she has entirely recovered I am glad to say. If you will be good enough to undertake a child of that age travelling alone, and put her into the stewardess's care, giving an eye to her occasionally yourself, I will cable out to my sister-in-law to secure her passage first class, and will myself meet the ship at Madeira, and return with her."

I answered this as follows: "I accept the responsibility with pleasure. No need to waste money on cables; a letter-telegram to sister will give her plenty of time. Meet the ship in London on arrival: never mind Madeira; wire me to Dartmouth."

Received reply: "Many thanks; am sending postal-telegram; *bon voyage.*"

On arrival in Cape Town I wired particulars to Miss Haldane at Durban, asking for reply to Algoa Bay. There I received a telegram: "Edna refuses to travel without me, and I cannot go; no use." I wired to Edna in return: "Will not Edna trust the old Captain? Mother will be so disappointed. Reply East London."

Wire awaiting me there from Miss Haldane: "Edna will go."

Wired in reply: "Bring her on board Wednesday, and remain with her until ship sails on Thursday."

This was done, and Edna got accustomed to the ship and to her future guardian.

We sailed as usual at 4 p.m. on Thursday. The ships did not cross the bar in those days, but were served by the *Lion* tender in the bay.

There was a bit of a scene when Auntie kissed Edna "Good-bye" and went over the side in the basket, but no change of front as regards the voyage.

As soon as the tug hauled off she caught hold of my hand with both of hers, and looked up at me through her tears as much as to say, "You have taken me away from my Auntie, and now you must take care of me yourself."

All persuasions of our admirable stewardess were unavailing; she would not leave me for a moment. We went up on to the bridge together, and I gave her a small mirror, and showed her how to heliograph to "Auntie" in the tender on her way to the shore. This was capital, and we got under way.

When out to sea, course set, and all clear, stewardess came to escort her to tea; not a bit of it. She would go to dinner with me – and she did.

Bed time came, so did the stewardess again. She was to sleep in the stewardess's cabin for the present.

I don't know what a kiddie's synonym for "See you hanged first" may be in words, but in action it was exemplified on this occasion with a nine years grace. "No thank you, I am going to sleep in the Captain's cabin."

Mrs. Sinclair, good old soul, looked at me with a whimsical air. "All right," I said, "make up my bed for her. I can take a stretch on the sofa when I want a nap." My cabin was immediately under the navigation bridge.

This being all satisfactorily arranged, Edna was persuaded to go along with the motherly old stewardess to be bathed and prepared for bed, and into my bed she went.

That night, off St. John's river, we had a heavy S.W. gale, and I was somewhat anxious about my little lodger; fearing lest the roaring of the wind and sea, as well as the violent motion of an empty steamer on the high head swell, might bring on an attack of terror and sea sickness, being all alone. So I had to jump down every now and then to inspect. But she never turned a hair. In fact, a leak developed from the deck above, and soaked one side of her pillow, and I carefully picked her up and turned her round end for end, without waking her.

In the morning it was fair weather again, and she was up on the bridge as fresh as a daisy at 8 o'clock, after the kind ministrations of Mrs. Sinclair – and said she didn't hear anything all night.

We arrived at East London on Friday, and amongst the few passengers who joined us there for London was Miss Florence Stewart, second daughter of the Rev. Dr. James Stewart, of Lovedale – one of the fairest of South Africa's fair daughters. N.B.– Later on I shall be able to show that I speak from a pretty varied and extensive experience – bless their hearts.

I introduced my little charge to her, and she very kindly undertook to mother her for the voyage as she had a cabin to herself by agreement on her father's account.

It was not, however, before we reached Cape Town, a week afterwards, that Edna was persuaded to leave her present perch. She flitted about, and became the mascot of the ship, but her homing place was always my cabin, and her chair my knee. When I moved around she was with me, to inspect cargo, or superintend the receiving or landing of passengers. When I went ashore, she had to accompany me – or I fear there would have been an explosion. But she took very kindly to

Florence, and before we sailed from Cape Town accepted the situation after a little scene and took up her night quarters with her new friend.

All day long she was in evidence; helping us to navigate – critically watching the observations – romping in and out of my cabin with two other equally mercurial mermaids she had adopted on board. The sailors, who as a class never call anything by its right name if they can help it, christened her "Dulcinea,"[19] with fine appreciation of classic literature that must have originated in the fertile brain of some smartie amongst them, the fruits of whose reading had not been erased by tar and sea water. It mattered little to her ladyship what they called her. They all loved her and would have played Don Quixote on her account against all the dragons and sea serpents in existence.

I don't think they would require to keep an inventory of their encounters. Serpents a many I have seen at sea, but a sea serpent – scarcely. Round about Sumatra, sea snakes, four to six feet in length, are plentiful; but popular superstition demands anything from a hundred yards up to half a mile long, upholstered with a magnificent mane, and fitted with eyes like the searchlights of a man-o'-war. I doubt that particular brand is very scarce.

In due time we arrived at Plymouth. I had warned Mrs. Haldane to keep in touch with the London Office regarding the time we were expected to reach the East India Dock, and I also sent her a wire myself from Plymouth to the office that I hoped to arrive at seven o'clock the following morning. It was in November – very cold and very damp.

We did arrive on the tide I had referred to, and were hauling round the pierhead from the river into the dock, when I was startled by Edna catching hold of me as I stood by the man at the wheel. She was in light attire – no wraps, no hat, no gloves, and thin shoes – on that miserable morning,

I knew that at such a time, and with her expectations, argument would be futile, even if I could have given attention to it. So I picked her up on to my knee with my foot on a rail, and buttoned her up inside my overcoat, with her sweet little face peering out through an opening under my chin. It might well convey the impression to an observer that the captain of the *Warwick Castle* must be very vain, because he wears so large and remarkable a breastpin in his necktie.

It just occurs to me that I have not attempted any description of my young charge. I have said that she was nine years of age. She was medium in height for her age, but very slight and delicate-looking; fair complexion, with grey eyes and brown hair. Full of spirits, and always on

---

[19] Don Quixote's idealised lady-love; Sancho Panza says she is actually loud, strong and stroppy.

the go. To my prejudiced eye she was just a perfect and beautiful little fairy.

As the ship neared the quay, out came a hand and arm pointing to the crowd on the wharf – and "There's mama! and there's papa!" and I could add there were sobs and tears of joy inside my coat, and for a moment the crowd looked dim; but the mother had already caught sight of the wee face in its strange setting, and the sobs and tears of joy were not confined to the ship. "All's well that ends well."

But what about the chickens coming home to roost?

Well, I received a very pressing invitation from Mr. and Mrs. Haldane to visit them in Stirling the next time I should be up north shipbuilding. But though I was in Glasgow several times on such business, it was twelve years before I could invent a decent opportunity to run over to Stirling.

I went, however, and took the chance of finding anyone there.

There was no need to make much inquiry. The Haldanes were well known, and I knocked at their door.

This was smartly opened by one of the smartest young ladies in Bonnie Scotland. One look, and, she exclaimed, "Great Caesar! Mother, it's Captain Robinson!"

Evidently I had not changed much; but my "breast pin" – well! No need for surprise. The flower had more than fulfilled the promise of the bud. But, is there perchance a grain of regret that the flower can no longer be the bud? Pause, and consider.

After lunch Mr. Haldane took me for a cruise around the town. In answer to his inquiry, I told him that I had only once before been in Stirling, and that it must be about twenty-five years ago; but that occasion had been indelibly stamped upon my memory by what I have always considered a remarkable and most unusual act of courtesy. I had to change trains in Stirling on my way South, and had three mortal hours to wait.

Looking up at the grand old Castle, I dropped into a chemist's shop, and asked if there were any possibility for a visitor to gain permission to look over it.

"Possibility," said he, "Aye is there? Mary," through the door behind him. "Shut up the shop – I'm going to show the gentleman over the Castle; if anybody wants me, I'll be back in twa' hours. Come awa."

"But, my dear Sir," I protested.

"Hoot man – haud your tongue. and come awa – there's no sae muckle business but what can wait."

And that good man, who was evidently a keen enthusiast, and had the stirring histories connected with the Castle and surrounding country at his finger ends, took me round, and indicated all the points of interest visible from the tower; and on our return to the shop would not even allow me to purchase so much as a bottle of scent – but insisted upon my sharing a bottle of ale with him, because I had the bad taste enough to refuse "whusky."

And – I said to Mr. Haldane – I have always possessed the bump of locality, and this is the street, or I am much mistaken, where the chemist's shop was, and it should be just round that corner. And there it is! I said, as we came upon it, and there is the little door at the back.

"Strange coincidence," said M . Haldane. "Look at the name over the window."

"Haldane & Son."

"He was my uncle. He died years ago!"

Warwick Castle — Tony Haslett Collection

No. 10.

I HAD not been very long in command of Donald Currie's "Castle" steamers before it occurred to me that a good deal too much of the shareholders' money was being squandered upon a good many unfruitful and cynical gadabouts.

Sumptuous luncheon parties, generously furnished with every variety of stimulating moisture from cocktails and champagne to curaçoa, with unlimited supplies of expensive cigars to enrich the post-prandial mocha, were practically the rule in Algoa Bay, voyage after voyage; and never an occasion passed without a number of the so-called guests having to be hunted for, persuaded, helped, and often dragged out of bar, smoking-room, or passengers' cabins, and bundled down the companion ladder into the tender, in order to enable the ship to get under way.

On more than one occasion such gentlemen have been discovered fast asleep in some corner after the steamer was at sea, and had to be landed at the next port.

Entertainments are all very well, perhaps, as a lure for freights and passengers – but at best, it was only the fathers who carried away the plunder with more or less grace and stability; the mothers very seldom had a show in, and the children never.

It occurred to me that here was a celestial opportunity to strike out an original line upon a basis of vastly reduced expenditure, but greatly enhanced appreciation and innocent enjoyment, that would most certainly not limit the chances of company emoluments, but would lay the foundation of loyal adhesion to the flag at the right end of a new generation, without loosening its hold upon the present.

Not for a moment, be it generously understood, was the thought connected with advertisement or profit; but still, as an absent agent in the interests of the firm, I could not afford to allow any benevolent novelties of my own to compromise the *status quo ante*. I felt sure before starting on the new tack that I was heading for a safe channel, and subsequent events have solidly endorsed this view. Many hundreds of South African colonists, Dutch and English, have to-day a loving memory of the pearl-grey steamers with the rosy funnels engraved upon their hearts, who otherwise would have known nothing whatever about them, or I am a stupid fabricator of doubtful romances.

To give anything like comprehensive effect to my future programme, it would have to be something more than local in its application, and this would necessarily entail railway service. So before doing anything else, I paid a visit to the Traffic Manager in Cape Town, and unfolded my scheme to him, requesting a ruling that would apply generally *ad valorem* of distance.

48

He very kindly entered into the subject, and turned up all the different class regulations applying to favoured passenger fares that could be found in print. None of these, however, were favourable enough for my purpose. I must justify my new departure to Sir Donald by an unusual concession on the part of the Colony, or I might fail to persuade him later on to "foot the bills," light though they would be as compared with the usual orthodox extravagance.

After much friendly sparring, I managed to convince him that as the railways were Colonial property, and our prospective guests were Colonial children, whom we were proposing to entertain on board our Castle steamers at our own expense – hoping thereby to combine instruction with pleasure – it was his graceful opportunity to provide the young people with the means to so desirable an end.

Ultimately, he agreed to furnish first-class corridor carriages, sufficient according to numbers, for their own private use; to bring them through from their point of departure to the pier or to the ship's side, as the case might be, and to take them back again, at a nominal charge of one-third of a single third-class fare for the double journey.

This generous rule held good in every case from that time forward in Colonial ports, and was admitted by the authorities on the Natal lines because the Cape had created so excellent a precedent.

Preliminaries having thus been satisfactorily arranged, no time was to be lost. My first idea was to invite girls' and boys' schools alternately; but, unfortunately, the boys themselves knocked the bottom out of that plan. Everything in proper order, however – ladies first.

I am not going to enter upon any wearisome repetition, but shall ask permission just to sketch out our general plan of campaign, in order to encourage others to follow on, and act the part of fairy godfathers in bestowing unlimited pleasure upon the young people of the Colony, who have hitherto been so much neglected in the mail steamer ministrations. From every possible point of view it is worth the doing, and it most certainly carries no financial loss in its train. Besides, I have read somewhere that "It is more blessed to give than to receive." The author of the quotation probably meant what he said.

Before leaving Cape Town Homeward, I paid a visit to the "Good Hope Seminary" – reposing peacefully in the lap of Table Mountain – and invited Miss Morton, the charming Lady Principal, to bring all her young charges (over nine years of age) on board the ship in dock on our return, to spend the afternoon with us, and have some fun. In order to invest the prospect of the visit with some degree of amusement and pleasurable anticipation, a prize list was drawn up for competitions according to taste and ability, each one to choose her own subject. Four verses of poetry, or one page of prose, or a pencil sketch, or a drawing in colours, or a small specimen of needlework, plain or ornamental. I want to make it clear before going further, that the cost of all prizes came out of my own private purse, and not out of the main hatch. This was the tax I paid with pleasure upon my own delight in their enjoyment.

On the appointed date, the ships being once more in Cape Town, Miss Morton marched her forces down – 84 strong – and they were ceremoniously received at the gangway, and escorted to the upper deck, which was screened off, and decorated with flags and plants, &c. The band was enthusiastically grinding sweet sounds and such officers as could be spared from duty, along with any passengers remaining on board, were invited to help in entertaining the visitors. There was some merry dancing, and parties were told off to inspect all the interesting details of the steamer – the bridge and navigating outfit, the enginerooms and stoke-holes, the galleys and bakeries, &c. The officers explained the mysteries of steering, heaving the lead, "shooting the sun," correcting the compass, and keeping the look out. The engineers put them through their catechism on the subject of boilers, cranks, shafts, steam, pumps, propellers, coal consumption, &c. The Knights of the Saucepans gave them practical instruction in the profound secrets of their culinary art, drilled the more daring ones in the triumphant composition of an omelet, and stood by, trident in hand, whilst they ate it, explained the secrets of the automatic bread mixing and baking machinery, &c., all of which being more or less new to them afforded no end of amusement, and a considerable amount of useful information that would invest many of their subsequent book studies with the reality of experience.

Like master, like man! I was particularly fortunate in having loyal and sympathetic officers of each department with me on these occasions, who laid themselves out to make the visits something more than mere holidays; and they *were* more.

After tea the prizes were awarded, the awards being settled beforehand by some of the ladies on board, to whom the girls were strangers, and from whom all names were withheld. This function was invariably attended with keen interest and appreciation.

The last prize, a quite unexpected one, nearly always ended in a salvo of cheering and clapping of hands. It was the most valuable of all the awards – a really first-class album, on the flyleaf of which was already engrossed, under a blank, for the name of the fortunate winner, "Awarded to her on the unanimous proclamation of her own school fellows, as being the most amiable and beloved of them all."

A beautiful incident occurred on one of these particular occasions which I must try to render. Holding up the prize, and explaining the conditions of award as usual – constituting the whole school their own judge and jury in the case – I called upon them to name the fortunate recipient, and two names were vociferously and persistently proclaimed.

A show of hands was called for each candidate, and the count was equal! So I asked the two nominees kindly to step forward, and they joined hand in hand and stood before me amidst a universal dead silence. Having complimented the school upon the possession of "two most amiable members," I said to the girls before me – "There is only one way to settle this most interesting question, and it must be done by yourselves – which of you two is the more admirable in character?" and the instant and simultaneous reply from both was "She is," pointing to each other! God bless them both. I fortunately had a duplicate copy of the album with me on board intended for another occasion, so was able to give them each one.

This was the only instance of the kind I ever had. It is quite wonderful, I think, that a hidden and probably unsuspected public affection should find generous and universal expression at the click of a sudden challenge. I found this to be absolute in the case of every girls' school and ladies' college that we had the privilege to entertain on board. There was never any hesitation, nor whispered consultation beforehand, but the verdict was spontaneous, immediate, and glad.

This fact surely illustrates the strong undercurrent of magnetic influence that refined natures inevitably must and do exercise upon their surroundings – no doubt quite unknown to themselves.

One of our particular features at each of their gatherings was the group photograph; a pleasant reminder to each of our guests of a happy day spent on board ship. A professional photographer was always engaged for the purpose, and we fortunately had no failures.

I find I still have twenty-five of these fascinating sets, and a clear recollection of at least six or eight more – representing some 1700 of the fair sirens of the sunny South – Dutch, English, and Huguenot – the most precious gems of golden South Africa.

It is no small honour that is resurrected in a retrospective glance through the telescope of Time, and to reawaken memories of the abounding and far-reaching pleasure of those glorious days of privilege. It was worth going to sea for.

Of the schools, some were from a distance. For instance, two even from Grahamstown to Algoa Bay, the "D.S.G.," and I think the "Wesleyan"; two from Maritzburg to Durban Bay, "St. Ann's" and another; one from Cradock, "Rocklands"; two from Wellington to Cape Town, the Huguenot Seminary, and another; three from Stellenbosch to Cape Town, &c.

In the case of "Rocklands," Cradock, the party left by train about 10 a.m., arrived at Port Elizabeth at 8 p.m., went off to the ship in a dead calm by full moonlight, dined, danced, and slept on board. Fun and frolic all next day, and train back from Port Elizabeth about 8 p.m., arriving home pretty tired in time for their breakfast.

51

Our next *fête* was to have been from Graaff-Reinet; but I was transferred to the home service that voyage, and this, unfortunately, fell through.

It would serve little purpose, perhaps, to go into further details of our arrangements on board for general interest and amusement. Programmes were provided for everyone, and handed to them as they came on board. Stewardesses were in attendance continually. Nothing was neglected.

I think I must claim indulgence, however, just to mention one remarkable case that was outside of my own management. Everyone who navigates the South African coasts knows that the weather at East London is liable to change from hour to hour. We arrived there one morning at 5 o'clock, from Natal, in a dead calm, with smooth water – a perfect day. I sent a letter off by the early launch, inviting St. John's School to come on board, and saying that I would meet them at the pier at 11 a.m. and take them to the ship.

At 7 a.m. a change came over the scene. A south-westerly wind and swell sprang into existence, and developed. A passenger remarked that my plan had miscarried. I replied, "We shall see." He went ashore with me, and we had to hold on pretty tight as we crossed the bar.

"You would be a brute," said he, "to take children off at such a time." I asked him how long it had taken to change the weather. "Two hours," he replied. "Well then," I said, "it may take two hours to change it back again: 7 to 9 – 9 to 11." He gave me a look of supreme contempt and admiration. I went quietly behind the boathouse, and held up 60 disappointed children to the "Clerk of the weather" – children who never could get such an outing in consequence of the meteorological uncertainty of the region. I confess that I trembled; but I took them into the launch at 11 o'clock, calming the fears of the principals, and by the time we reached the bar, the wind had gone off with the swell, and everything was as smooth as it had been at 6 a.m. And so it remained until the party returned to shore at 4 p.m. As soon as I saw that they were safely over the bar and into the shelter of the river, I devoutly returned thanks to the "Clerk of the weather," and said we can now resume the reading of this morning's suspended warning, and take what is bound to follow. At 6 o'clock that evening the storm broke, and for 12 hours it was magnificent.

No. 11.

IN my last paper I said that the *fêtes* held on board at the South African coast ports were originally intended to be for girls and boys alternately, but that the boys had themselves "upset my apple cart."

Our first "boys' reception" was in Algoa Bay. I forget how many there were, but I soon found out that there were too many to look after. They evidently wanted no one to show them round. They were like ants, hurrying about in all directions, and appearing to have no object in life except to get into mischief. Whilst two or three of them were on the forecastle head tinkering with the releasing gear of the second anchor, and others were playing experiments with the compass on the lower bridge, a third party of prospectors discovered the steam whistle lanyard, and before anyone could prevent it commenced kicking up a shindy that very nearly brought off the police boat and the fire engine. Some of them commenced climbing up aloft, but that did not worry me, for there was a day when I commenced doing the same thing myself.

One youngster of an inquiring turn of mind, wondering what the deck ventilators were for, and judging them to be eligible openings for young men, was hanging down one of them to a dangerous extent, with a view to further investigation, when another monkey came along, and, seeing two legs dangling outside, was tempted to give one of them a friendly nip as he went past.

The act was disastrous, and might well have been fatal. The spontaneous kick-up that naturally followed the little joke over-balanced the unhappy recipient, and he disappeared head first down the ventilator! Providentially, it led only into the 'tweendecks, where they had been rolling a number of loose bales of wool; and the boy tumbled amongst these and was none the worse for his fall.

Not so the delinquent, however. Seeing what he had done, and fearing the worst, he set up a howl that brought a small crowd together at once, and might have led to a general wailing – but that the victim himself came butting in like a billy goat to punch the head of the "cad who had nipped his leg!"

Since then all our ventilators have been fitted with iron crosses just below the opening. Strange that this simple plan should not have been adopted long before, as a check to burglary, as well as a protection against accidents.

All attempts to marshal the lads into groups, for the purpose of giving them little lecture parties at the various points of interest, were a failure. They wanted to get into the boats, to try on life jackets, to scratch their names on the bright work, to pull the flags up and down, and in fact to do generally just what we did not wish them to do.

I was glad when they were all counted carefully into the launch to return to *terra firma*, though I must say they gave a hearty expression to their feelings as they steamed away from the ship's side.

The second attempt of the kind was in Durban Bay, where a school came off and displayed precisely the same characteristics as those of Port Elizabeth, but went one better for Natal. What a scare we had!

Two or three of them got down the engine-room and into the tunnel aft; and, frolicking about, a boy about 12 or 13 years of age fell into one of the engine oil tanks, and very nearly lost the number of his mess. The yells of the rest brought the engineers and men along, and the lad was fished out more dead than alive, rubbed down, undressed and put into a hot bath, thoroughly washed, and rigged up in a small steward's outfit, and sent ashore to his mother – clothes to follow when cleansed.

I vowed then that I would never have any more boys' schools on board the ship, and I never did. "Boys is pison." There is too much of the monkey about them for sober seamen.

On one occasion only did Sir Donald speak to me about our "picnics." I showed him some programmes, told him of the Colonial railway concession, and gave him a sketch of our proceedings. I think he approved; at all events, he made no demur but just shelved the subject with a smile. The bills were never commented upon, which alone showed that they were not considered exorbitant.

Before consigning the subject of the schools to the limbo of forgotten lore I must mention one situation that I found myself entangled in. Our receptions on board the ship led to my receiving invitations from various quarters to "come and give a lecture to the school" upon such subjects as navigation, astronomy, sailors' yarns, &c.

On one occasion I was persuaded to go from Port Elizabeth to Grahamstown for this purpose. I took a train that landed me at my destination about 6 p.m., and had to catch a return train that was to leave Grahamstown at 8, or remain there overnight, which I was not at all anxious to do. So everything had to be "rushed" in order to fit in.

At ten minutes to the hour "Good byes" and "Good nights" were hurried through, and I raced off.

The door was shut before I realised that the night was uncommonly dark after the brilliant lights of the room: but I had no time to call a halt and ask them to "send a gleam across the wave,"[20] but just trusted to instinct and ran for what looked like the gate to find myself locked in the loving embrace of a wacht-en-beetje[21] bush!

---

[20] A line from the hymn "Let the lower lights be burning".
[21] "wait-a-bit", so-called for its hooked thorns.

To stimulate endeavour the station bell could be faintly heard ringing a warning to hurry up, and I fought that bush to get through in spite of the bayonets and failed.

Dragging myself back by the sheer force of despair, torn and bleeding, I found that it was not a hedge at all, but just a bush in a bed; and sight having by this time improved the landscape I found the gate and made tracks for the station as fast as two muscular "bridge legs" would carry me, spurred along by hearing the second peal of the station bell, and tumbled into the train as it was upon the point of starting, breathless and exhausted.

I was alone. Having administered first aid to the wounded to the best of my present ability, I climbed into one of the canvas shelf beds and promptly went to sleep.

I dreamed that I was surrounded by angels in radiant drapery accompanied by a subtle and not unfamiliar aroma; and can clearly remember being sleepily surprised that celestials should discuss such mundane matters as pork and beans, and even laugh at the mention of them: alas!

Suddenly the clatter of something falling beneath changed the tenor of my dream, and peeping over the edge of my pew I fancied I discerned two less angelic, but more substantial forms, feeding on thick ham sandwiches and having a bottle squeezed in between them, bearing a label that looked like "Dewar."

It gradually dawned upon me that my vision was materialising in a sadly unpoetical manner. But how came these creatures here, when, and where? I know I was very tired. The train probably pulled up at some place without awaking me: but how did these two get in without seeing me? And now – what to do?

Pondering over this exceedingly knotty problem, the train commenced to slow down, and we ran into a small siding. My guests hurriedly bundled their wraps and things together, and climbed down on to the low platform.

"Ladies," I thoughtlessly exclaimed, "you have left your tumbler behind you!" One astonished look, and both exclaimed: "It's a man!" and fell into each other's arms with a peal of hysterical laughter. The train moved on; and left them still rehearsing. I was saved.

The fact is that, being an exceedingly warm night, accentuated as it was by my muscular exertion at starting, I was half undressed and using my clothes for a pillow – under the impression that a night train was a through train, and that I should not be disturbed.

I was reminded of a pleasant evening, spent with Mr. and Mrs. D. C. Andrews under the shadow of Table Mountain, when he and Lachlan MacLean were co-agents of the Union-Castle Company in Cape Town.

When the time came to go, Andrew asked me to see another of his guests, a lady, as far as the railway station, seeing that we were both going so far in the same direction.

It was a long walk and a glorious night – such a night as no one ever sees except in richly-endowed South Africa. The heavens brilliant with iridescent stars; and the atmosphere so marvellously limpid that the unassisted sight could discern, and in a sense appreciate, the relative positions of the nearer and more distant orbs.

To pass out of Mrs. Andrews' hospitable drawing-room, illuminated by its two handsome pedestal paraffin lamps with pink silk shades, into this celestial panorama of secret and silent eternity – made one instinctively thank God for eyes to see and drink in such majestic visions of illimitable magnificence.

How marvellous the thought that our little planet floats suspended amidst the brilliant galaxy of celestial glory – rushing along at the rate of 18 miles per second in its own little orbit; *plus* the incalculable impetus of our solar system in its stupendous revolution around some still more distant centre, and so *ad infinitum* – claiming an integral though comparatively insignificant part in the universal cosmos. We "look up" to the heavens, and forget that the heavens are all around us. But so it is. Our friends at the Antipodes are looking up also but in the opposite direction.

The attempt to describe the transcendent glories of the South African skies at such seasons can only result in impertinent failure; even now I feel that what I have written is almost an insult to the great Creator and all-wise Governor of such infinite wonders. The fact is that language utterly fails – and wordless worship poorly meets the need.

Carried away by my own inspired ignorance, I gave my companion a lecture on astronomy as we walked along on our way, pointing out all the principal stars by name, and showing her how to find them by angular reference to one another, &c., until we reached the railway station, where I left her to ponder over her lesson, and dream of the great unknown beyond the reach of sight – the sphere beyond the stars.

Mr. Andrews asked me the following day if I had fulfilled his commission, and seen his friend into the train? I assured him that I had done my best to interest her on the way down by a dissertation upon the heavenly bodies, and their use to us at sea.

"I am sure," said he, "she would thoroughly enjoy that, as she is an astronomer's daughter!"

Well, never mind, accidents will happen. There are worse misfortunes at sea.

In the year 1882 I took out Mr. Nelson, the astronomer, when he first went to Natal. It was the year of the great comet – never to be forgotten in its supreme and commanding magnificence. As we went down through the southern tropics it used to rise about 2 a.m., and at the zenith of its beauty it measured over 60° of arc! It was dreadful in its grandeur.

I used to call Nelson at his own request on each occasion; and he invariably appeared with a black waistcoat tightly buttoned over his white night shirt, the tails fluttering in the frolic breeze – a comic object to pay court to our royal visitor – and a royal visitor, indeed, it was.

It is a pure fancy of my own – an ignorant conceit, no doubt – that these celestial mysteries describe the links between abysmal systems.

To come down, however, from the clouds of conjecture to the level of exact mathematics, may I venture to suggest that the vast majority of even well-educated people utterly fail to enjoy the magnificent marvels of Creation, of Law, and of Government, for lack of thoughtful observation and study – of opportunity, also, no doubt?

Let me give one single illustration of my meaning.

In the good old sailing-ship days, when voyages often ran into years and chronometers were little better than superior clocks, it was essential that we should have some means of ascertaining Greenwich time at sea, since longitude in time is measured from the meridian of Greenwich.

We have such a means. The moon we are all so fond of is the seaman's clock. Its movements in orbit are so miraculously exact that our astronomical experts tabulate its distance from particular stars, and from the sun, for every three hours, and add accurate tables for computing the intervals for every second of time, and calculations are made every four years in advance.

By these means an unhappy ship that has lost her way in the Pacific, Atlantic, or Antarctic Ocean, through failure of her chronometer or neglect of the captain to wind it up (which has happened after a birthday celebration before now), careful observation of any of the distances referred to above at once gives the required time at Greenwich (dependent, of course, upon excellence of instruments and accuracy of measurement); and the vessel can proceed rejoicing on her isolated way until the captain has another birthday.

No. 12.

I THINK it was about the year 1883 that a strange and altogether unaccountable mortality fell upon the fish around the South African Coast. We were there during the height of the epidemic. I never heard any authorised expression of opinion upon the subject.

The cod on the banks of Newfoundland suffered a somewhat similar visitation a good many years ago, but on the South African Coast it affected all the fish, great and small alike, the whole way round from Saldanha Bay to East London, and perhaps further. I cannot tell from personal experience. I was credibly informed that the beach was strewn with dead fish of all description wherever men were found to take note of the fact. On our way round to the eastward the sea stank abominably. It was of a dirty green colour and sparkled with scales in a remarkable way, besides being very frothy and dull in sound.

In Cape Town Dock the atmosphere was actually poisonous. We were under instructions to keep disinfectants liberally distributed throughout the ship, and there was an official plan formulated to drench the dock itself with carbolic; but this, of course, had to be relinquished for want of sufficient material.

I was in the *Roslin Castle* at the time, and we had lost two blades of our propeller on the way out. These we replaced in Cape Town Dock, and for some reason the diver had to go down to the dock-floor. When he returned to the surface he informed us that at the bottom he had actually been standing up to his waist in the midst of a conglomeration of dead fish – not a wriggle amongst them.

This might well be, for in attempting to put one of the small Indian transports into the dry dock of that date, the greatest difficulty was experienced in getting the pontoon gate into position. It was so blocked with fish that the pumps choked, and could not produce a vacuum to draw the gate to. Various expedients had to be resorted to before they succeeded in placing the ship upon the blocks.

After she was so placed, and the hampered pumps had reduced the water to a low level, Cape Town came down to see the sight. Nothing less than personal experience could convey the impression of it. Streams of carts and wagons commenced at once to load up and convey for distribution over the surrounding lands tons of free fish manure, before public health should be affected.

I repeat – I never heard any authorised expression of opinion upon the subject, far-reaching as it was, and of such an important nature.

In these days of super-scientists, the uninitiated had better hold their peace; but in the absence of all legitimate light, even a blind man may hazard a shot in the dark without fear of doing much harm. Is it at all likely that the earth, in a submarine eruption of some kind about the neighbourhood of East London, may have given off poisonous matters that have thence been distributed by means of the Agulhas current round the coast westwards to Saldanha Bay? I can think of nothing else – and conscience at all events is quite clear – for my opinions will hurt neither fish nor the fancy of wiser men. Still, the whole question must remain one of very great interest. [Our worthy friend has doubtless stumbled on the correct explanation of the wholesale slaughtering of the harvest of the sea, but the submarine eruption was further away than East London. Java and its neighbouring isles were that year desolated by a series of violent eruptions from about two-thirds of 46 volcanoes, beginning with Krakatoa, casting up immense quantities of lava, mud, ashes, and fragments of rocks, darkening the air for about 50 square miles. Mountains were split up, some disappeared, and many new craters were formed. Rumbling noises were heard about August 25, and violent eruptions of Krakatoa took place on August 26. There was much submarine disturbance, and an immense "tidal wave" destroyed Anjer and other places. The lighthouses in the Straits of Sunda were swallowed up, and new volcanic peaks appeared, rendering navigation highly dangerous. The loss of life was estimated at 35,000. There were great atmospheric, oceanic, and electrical disturbances for thousands of square miles. In November and December of that year intensely red sunsets and after-glow, and very red sunrises, were seen in England and other parts of the globe. They were attributed by Dr. Meldrum, Dr. Norman Lockyer, and others to the volcanic dust projected by the eruptions of Krakatoa. – Ed. *S. A.]*

Some years afterwards, on the way from East London to Natal, we were witnesses to a vast mortality of quite a different nature. We steamed through eight miles of drowned locusts, in a belt that we estimated at four miles in breadth and at least a foot in depth, running parallel with the coast line. This calculation was not guess work – for the belt was bright brown in colour, with clearly defined edges, on a calm afternoon, and in smooth water. The noise of cleavage as we raced through them resembled that of running through dry leaves on a gigantic scale. We could not but congratulate Pondoland on its deliverance from so formidable an army of desolation. I wonder what brought them there. I feel sure it was not a case of *felo de se*. Perhaps there are some Christian natives in those parts of South Africa.

Since we are started upon a novel line of reminiscences, I feel disposed for this once only to keep the fish, flesh, and fowl of South Africa in evidence.

To turn to another case. In 1884, when I relieved Alec Winchester in the *Norham Castle*, we had a strange – and I think I may venture to say, unique experience.

59

My most excellent chief steward came to me one day with a very serious complaint, that quite a large number of bottles of champagne had been ullaged[22] and spoiled; and he blamed – Rats!

With sparkling originality, I asked him how many legs his rodents had? He looked hurt, and said: "No. I think you will come to the same conclusion as myself if you will accompany me to the wine room." I did so; and was convinced.

All our wines were stowed, head outward, upon lines of racks sloping upward from the back just sufficient to prevent the vibration or movement of the ship from displacing them. Along the edge of the racks, under the corks of most of the champagne bottles, we found cork dust accumulations, the corks themselves twisting out on one side of the wire only, the other side having been engineered away by teeth and claws, after the strings were first bitten through, until the effervescent contents commenced to seep out, to the intense enjoyment of the scientific Johnnie Rat for a few minutes, and the consequent degradation of the whole bottle of royal liquor.

The thing was as clear as daylight; and the cunning plan – the clever economy of labour in working on one side of the cork only – was very remarkable.

But how did the rascals diagnose the contents and their effervescent character? None of the still wines were tampered with. Strange instinct surely.

I told the chief officer about our investigation, and he exclaimed: "Oh! that accounts for the mad revelry of the brutes on deck every night. We have come to the conclusion that all the rats on this ship are gone mad. They are doing calisthenics and dancing tangoes all over the place, even on the bridge deck. The milk in the coconut is easily accounted for."

The losses were really so serious, and a check upon them apparently so hopeless, that on returning to London the wine and store rooms were gutted out regardless of expense. The professional rat-catchers went in for a regular slaughter of the innocents – they had to give up counting them – but they cleared the ship for the time, and we had no more "educated mechanics" to reckon with.

In the meantime, however, we were approaching Natal.

On our arrival at the anchorage the tender came off for the mails and passengers. Just as she was about to leave I called to the Captain, and asked him to make inquiries for a cat for me, as we were infested with rats, and might be held responsible for damage done by them, not having a puss on board. Our dreaded liability was diluted wholesale the following morning by the advent of no less than eight able-bodied

---

[22] The level had gone down.

mousers – the Captain of the tender himself contributing a gaunt yellow calamity, in a hamper, with a tail like a boat hook, the last joint having been dislocated at right angles by an accident of some kind. The chorus set up by the legion of nocturnal musicians on finding themselves unexpectedly turned adrift on the deck of a ship for the first time must have put the fear of purgatory into every tipsy rat within reach of the sound. The big butter-cat with the crooked caudal made a rush upstairs and stowed himself away under the standard compass, defying all persuasive invitations and offers of dainties to dislodge him. However, he did not affect the compass, so he was left severely alone, to recover from the indignant mortification of false imprisonment at his leisure.

I don't like to volunteer information before it is asked for – but as a good deal of interest hangs upon the knowledge, I wish to remind my readers that our mail steamers had no actual communication with the shores of South Africa, except in Cape Town Dock. In every other port all business with the land had to be transacted through the medium of tenders or cargo boats – always in daylight.

During our voyage Home on this particular occasion, there was a distinct reduction of rodentary frolics on deck. This may have been due to the unhealthy neighbourhood of a Thomas Puss of the yellow persuasion, or otherwise – probably otherwise; or our feline battalion may have succeeded perhaps in arresting some of the more venturesome of the revellers.

The rat catchers in London did the rest, as I have already stated.

We completed our usual term of three weeks in England, and again started through summer seas for the golden sands of fair South Africa, and in the ordinary course of events, once more anchored behind the Bluff in Durban Bay – quite unprepared for evil tidings – for a sad tragedy that coincided with our advent.

We arrived too late in the evening for communication that day. The tender came alongside the following morning for mails and passengers; and the Captain took me all aback by asking how I had managed to land the yellow cat that he gave me on our departure from Natal last voyage; that would be 11 weeks ago? I was sorry to have to confess that I had never seen poor puss after the day we sailed, and had quite forgotten all about it until that moment.

He in turn was greatly surprised, and told me that the beast had appeared in his garden early that very morning and had killed another of his fowls, and that this criminal propensity had been his motive for getting rid of it when I asked him for a ratter.

"Are you sure it is the same cat?" I asked.

"Oh, there's no doubt about the scamp," he said, "but he'll kill no more fowls of mine. At first I did not connect the animal with its past history – it was so much bigger and thinner, ragged and torn; with glaring eyes and a slinking gait – more like a savage beast than a domestic cat. It had evidently been left to forage for itself on board, and appears to have been living on starvation diet; but how did it get ashore since last night?"

"My dear fellow," I replied, "that creature never came from us. Supposing, for argument's sake, that it was with us; a cat's homing instinct would stop short at jumping overboard to swim three-quarters of a mile, during the night – even were there no strong current to carry it away. No doubt you have had a stranger to deal with."

"Make no mistake," he said, "I can't forget that old Tom, with the crooked tail, in spite of his bedraggled appearance – and besides, he knew me too."

"Well, what are you going to do with it?" I asked.

"Do with it! Why bury it; I drowned the beast."

This aroused my interest afresh, and we proceeded to compare notes; the results of which were as follows:

That cat left Natal on board the ship – there is no manner of doubt about that point. If it managed to land in a cargo boat at East London, it had 250 miles across country to get back; if at Algoa Bay, 400 miles; at Mossel Bay, 600; or at Cape Town, where the stage with the shore offers every facility, and the only reasonable opportunity since leaving Durban, it would have to traverse some 900 miles of country as the crow flies – over hill and dale, desert and river; fighting its own battles, hunting its own game, finding its own water: and finished the performance in ten weeks! That is to say, from the date of our arrival in Cape Town from Natal to the date of our arrival again at Natal after making the voyage Home and out again.

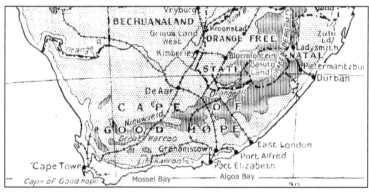

If all the facts are as stated, and suggested, what a pitiful, heart-rending finish to so heroic a performance! Poor Pussy! [The gallant Captain has evidently overlooked the possibility of the cat boarding at Cape Town Station a train bound for Durban.– Ed. *S.A.*]

To fly off at a tangent for a moment in obedience to an ancient memory – from South Africa to North America – from steamers back again to sailing ships – is perhaps not too far a cry, with another catastrophe as a sequel to the diversion. We were homeward bound from India, and had run short of provisions, either through parsimony, or inexcusable carelessness on the Captain's part. We had got down to cadging from every ship we met after crossing the Equator, and were actually reduced to half allowances of biscuit and a pint of water per day for the last fortnight before reaching Falmouth. Even the Captain's cat had to be satisfied with the same spare diet; and used to "mieau" round the deck at night time in melancholy protest at the shyness of the wary rat; until a big French sailor named Fouché, who should have been on the "look out," knocked it on the head, skinned it, roasted it in the galley, and ate the whole of it there and then, and sent the skin in a parcel to the "old man" as a present! [23]

Norham Castle – Tony Haslett Collection

---

[23] It seems likely this was JC's second voyage in the *Orient*. She arrived at Falmouth from Calcutta on 29 Jan. 1867, after a total voyage of over 14 months, "with crew sick". The Captain was Wolfe.

No. 13.

RING a-ding, a-ding, a-ding. Second bell. Any more for the shore! Hurry up! Steam blowing-off, drowning lesser sounds; 4.30 p.m., Wednesday; Cape Town Dock; *Dunottar Castle*. Homeward bound, inquisitive crowds watching last cases of gold hoisted on board; passengers anxiously picking out their own baggage; doubtful-looking stranger prowling after anybody's baggage; dockmaster and men singling up moorings; distracted mother rushing around asking everybody if they had seen her little girl; general impression of a hive of human bees at swarming time; band playing "Home, Sweet Home"; everyone shouting and nobody listening; visitors and friends blocking the gangway whilst they kiss and cuddle one another again and yet again – handsome young man, taking courage by example, wishing to supplement legitimate farewell after the same manner, gets young lady's muff shoved in his face; usual waving of handkerchiefs and exchanges of last instructions and messages from shore to ship and from ship to shore. Ring a-ding, a-ding, a-ding – Captain on the bridge – out gangway – somebody left on board – up again – anybody else? Down with it – good-bye, good-bye. Let go for'ard – hold on aft – slack away – let go! Slow ahead port; half speed; stop port; slow ahead both. Chaos exhausted; silence everywhere. Table Mountain astern; old ties severed to make room for new; gong sounds preparation for dinner; all interests self-centred; decks cleared; next course!

Everyone's first anxiety was to ascertain who they were to be "stabled" with; hoping the fates may have been propitious for themselves by putting a spoke in the wheel of others at the last moment before sailing. All such temporary hopes and fears soon give place to mutual satisfaction, and the germination of lifelong friendships, which last till the end of the voyage.

On coming down from the bridge I was hailed by a tall, dark man, and my barometer went down with a slump. "Well, Captain, here I am again." "So I see," I replied in tones more frigid than friendly, I fear; and as I was passing on he said: "You don't seem pleased to see me, Captain?" I turned on him, and candidly said: "I had rather see a picture of the Devil on board the ship."

"Ah, Captain," he said, "forget and forgive. I am quite changed from those days. I have been hanging over the edge of Hades too long to forget the pictures on the screen as the clock ticked off the last rehearsal;" and, passing his arm through mine, he said softly, "I am really sorry I ever gave you cause to complain – don't give me away – and you will see that I am not playing the hypocrite."

And I wish to say that Mr. L— was true to his word. His was a notable example of inconsiderate and relentless mischief-mongering spoiled by a glimpse through the gates ajar. He used to be always hatching fresh plots for setting sober people by the ears – thoroughly enjoying their vexed discomfiture, and his own jokes, as he called them. Now, everything was changed indeed. Still in delicate health – poor chap – he was mostly his own company, and occupied much of his time reading.

I must sling one old chestnut at him since it was one he slung at me, and then I will "give him away" no more.

He was one of the cleverest conjurers I ever saw at sea, and on several occasions he gave illustrations of his skill that were quite past finding out. He was far too wise to reveal his secrets, and would "red herring" a troublesome inquirer by saying, "My good fellow, it's perfectly simple when you know how."

On the occasion I refer to he had announced himself on the programme of an evening concert in the following terms: Professor L— will perform a miracle. His miracle was a somewhat audacious one, and well calculated to awaken suspicion that I was indirectly blackmailing my Passengers in the Cause of Seamen.

His turn having come round, he stepped forward with professional sangfroid, and rolling his sleeves up to the elbows commenced to entertain us with accounts of the various Royal Families before whom he had performed this particular *coup de théâtre*, and their astonishment at the brilliant display. Then, calling upon the stewards present to bring him something in the shape of a cash box and a salver, he was promptly supplied with a silver cake tray and the "Seamen's Friend" empty money box – both having evidently been provided for the purpose beforehand.

Expressing his entire satisfaction with these properties, he said he should require ten sovereigns, and sent a steward round with the cake tray for contributions. As these supplies appeared to hang fire, he called the cake tray, and dropping a sovereign into it which he took out of his own pocket, raised a laugh by saying he didn't think there were nine sovereigns among the whole audience.

Now try again, he said, and take this pencil and paper and mark down the name of everyone who appears to be. solvent.

Rattle, rattle, rattle – that's right – two more – good – one – that'll do. Now please watch me very carefully. You see, my arms are bare; no hanky panky; I take the box in one hand, and holding it out at arm's length, I pick up a coin with the other, and – listen – I drop it into the box and shake it up; right – there all right – repeat operation – two, three, five, ten. All in. Pass box round please – shake her up – all satisfied – yes. Steward, take the box up to Captain's cabin, lock it up, and bring me down the Captain's stove pipe hat -- I know he has one – saw him coming on board wearing it – then we will develop our miracle.

65

In the meantime, please hand me along those things I asked the Chief Steward for. So, thank you – a basin of flour, a jug of water, some currants and raisins, three fresh eggs, a pat of butter, some sugar and a pudding cloth, as well as a galley spoon, a candle and a stick, and a box of matches. Thank you. Ah, here comes the hat. With your permission, Captain – thank you.

Without more ado, and without the pretence of waiting for the permission, this audacious miracle worker proceeded to empty the whole of the above groceries and the cloth into my "Lincoln and Bennett,"[24] and vigorously mixed up the compound with the big spoon – enlarging meanwhile upon the astonishment that was in store when, the cake being made and cut up, each subscriber would find his own particular coin in his own particular slice.

Then lighting the candle, which by the way was an ordinary engine room dip, he lifted the poor head gear up with both hands and commenced to sway it about over the flame by no means clear of the tallow, till the light was fairly rubbed out by the no longer immaculate beaver, and having apparently satisfied himself that all was well, he rolled the "miracle" out into a soup tureen on the table, amidst a storm of laughter.

It was a fearsome sight. The lining of the hat belched out as the unwholesome-looking mess exuded, and the impudent performer scooped out the residuum with the long spoon, replaced the lining, and handed my best Sunday hat to a steward to be returned to the Captain's cabin, with the remark that if I would provide myself with a "new tile"[25] and send him in the bill he would of course pay it.

After this humorous bit of by play, he coolly informed the audience that something had evidently gone wrong, and that he could only attribute the failure to the ship's eggs.

In reply to a rather sharp inquiry as to the missing sovereigns he referred the lenders to the captain, in whose cabin the box been placed; and added – as for my own coin, I shall leave it where it is, in the sailor's poor box.

Those were the days of bluff in Johannesburg, and L——'s miracle was treated as a joke with a sequel for the rest of the voyage.

Two of the subscribers came to me afterwards and complained that they were had. I quite agreed with them that they had been victimised under false pretences, and offered them the box and the key to enable them to recover their coins, because I could not remove them myself from a missionary box, having had no hand in placing them there. My offer was gracefully declined. I may add that the new hat did not

---

[24] Quality hat makers based in Piccadilly.
[25] New hat.

materialise; but I still survive, and admire our good conjurer's consummate cheek. Peace be with him wherever he is.

Of course L— had to run the gauntlet in the smoking-room after it was all over, for his contemptible failure and swindle. But he somehow carried the day as usual by maintaining that he had fulfilled his contract, and that the ten pounds into the sailor's box inside of five minutes was a fairly good miracle, all things considered.

And how about the "Old man's" hat – what had that to do with it? Do with it! Gosh – it had everything to do with it. Why it was under cover of his discomfiture that you fellows didn't come down too heavily upon me – aye? Never mind, boys, it was in a good cause.

That voyage will remain ever memorable to me by a foolish joke I myself perpetrated upon my trusting passengers, never for a moment anticipating the close place I was going to find myself decoyed into.

My good friend, the late W. H. Rogers, of Kimberley and Johannesburg, had sent me a case of extremely interesting and valuable samples from the mines of both places. This is a parenthesis.

We were passing the Bijouga or Bissagos Islands, which lie off the Gold Coast; and it is customary to take a cast of the lead now and then, as their currents are strong, the Islands low and invisible, though only about 20 to 25 miles distant, and the water shoal – anything from 20 to 30 fathoms at a reasonably safe offing. Passengers always congregate to watch operations at such a time. It is perhaps an interesting break in the monotony of their daily routine, or perhaps there is an unsuspected sympathy with something harder than the water that separates them from it; they want to know how far it is from them.

A mischievous spirit led me to my sample case, and, selecting a pretty bit of gold quartz, I suggested to Cassidy – my dear old chief officer – that he should take it in his hand and quietly press it into the tallow at the base of the lead as he lifted it over the rail after taking a cast. This he did so cleverly that no one noticed the action; and in turning the lead up to examine the character of the "bottom" it had brought up, all eyes bulged out with excitement. A cry of "Gold! gold!" was set up, and a rush made to me, begging for an exact calculation of the ship's position at the moment of sounding. In fact, several of the men commenced to dance and shout with agitation – they were sure they had struck it rich – and Gold Coast eldoradoes blotted out all their reasoning faculties for the time being. I tried to pacify them by saying that "someone" was bluffing them. It only made the matter worse. "Look at that," said one man, who had managed to possess himself of the sinful sample; "is that gold, or am I a lunatic?" I said: "You go and ask Cassidy why he stuck that into the 'arming.'" "No, no, no; we saw the lead lifted in, and as soon as it was turned there it was, as clear as daylight." I said again, "You take my word for it, you are being hoaxed."

By this time people came hurrying aft from all parts of the ship, and made the confusion worse. There was nothing for it but a public and humiliating climb down, so I confessed that I had given Cassidy the sample for a joke. A kind of lull followed for a moment, and all eyes were fixed on me, when one keen prospector said: "Captain, you are too clever; you want to peg-off that claim for yourself. But, look here; if you can locate the find and are on to form a small company, do it now. I'm sportsman enough to back you up."

This raised a laugh at my expense, but broke the excitement up and gradually cleared the air, though I fancy my sporting friend and a few others thought I was worth watching. I made the matter ludicrous the next cast by giving Cassidy a Donald Currie uniform button to experiment with in the same way, but he managed to stick it into the arming this time before dropping the lead; and when it came up, keen eyes watched carefully for any juggling, and were for a moment astonished to see the brass button and sand mixed together in orthodox fashion. A smart American lady remarked that no doubt there were lots of them about, but that the bottom of the sea was not paved with that kind of advertisement.

It is wonderful how average humanity is amused with small things in small places – even upon the mighty ocean.

Dunottar Castle – Tony Haslett Collection

No. 14.

IN the summer of 1880 or thereabouts we sailed from Dartmouth in the *Warwick Castle* with the mails for South Africa and a fairly good passenger list. On examining the latter after we had got fairly away, I noticed two coincidences of a somewhat interesting nature. They were a Mr., Mrs., and Miss Robinson in the first class, and also a Miss Warwick, so that both ship and commander were, in a sense, duplicated, and I was curious to see how the representatives should turn out.

I was not kept waiting long. We got "under way" at noon, and having cleared the land and shaped a course for ten miles off Ushant, I went down and joined the company at lunch, the weather being beautifully fine.

It is the usual custom at the commencement of a voyage for the purser or chief steward to submit a passenger list to the captain, in order that he may see whom he would choose to sit beside him. He may have personal friends amongst them, or there may be some with a claim to seniority, or with a special letter of introduction, or of influence, &c.; and, after all, the commander of the ship is invested with rank as well as authority for the time being, and is, consequently, an important individual *pro tem.* and likes to have his own way, though he may, perhaps, have to clean his own shoes and use his pocket handkerchief for a dinner napkin when under the orders of the Admiral of the Home Station.

On this particular occasion I found the top seats right and left of my table already occupied and amply filled. As I reached my chair, a lordly sample of Semitic opulence rose on the left, with his serviette tucked into his collar, and his soup spoon grasped in his hand. "Happy to meet you," he said. "We are namesakes, and that is why I take these seats. This lady" – pointing his spoon across to indicate his *vis-a-vis*, a portly double-breasted edition of himself – "is my wife, Mrs. Robinson; and my daughter, Rachael, is next to her."

Of course I acknowledged the introduction with due formality, and we sat down.

The saloon was fairly full, and my friend's rather loud voice and emphatic manner attracted attention and raised a smile here and there.

But it is strange how quickly one settles down to unexpected environments on board ship. The sympathetic feeling of fellowship in reliance on the safe side of a steel plate may partly account for it – more perhaps than one is apt to imagine; but quite apart from philosophical deductions, there are rainbows in every shower if one is fortunate enough to occupy the correct point of view; and human nature invariably possesses admirable traits even amongst the least promising of its examples, given time and opportunity for their expression.

My namesake, in spite of a certain tendency to drift into financial matters on most occasions, wasn't a bad old fellow on the whole, and his daughter Rachael was undoubtedly one of the most beautiful creatures that have ever gemmed a ship under my command. Subsequent experience proved her to be as sweet and gentle in disposition and accomplishments as she was charming in person. She sang like a prima donna to her own accompaniments on the guitar, and was always ready to respond to a request. Her repertoire was varied and delightful, and her treatment in each case altogether artistic.

Such at least was the opinion of all on board, ladies as well as gentlemen. On fine tropical evenings, on deck, if you wanted to find any particular person, especially amongst the young gentlemen, you had not far to seek. I shall make no attempt to describe her, beyond hazarding a guess that her age may have been anywhere between 18 and 20.

The ship's namesake, Miss Warwick, was a dear little old-fashioned lady that we all very soon learned to love. She was not very far short of half a century. Some of us were soon taken into her confidence, and learned that she was going out to be married, that her *fiancé* had gone to South Africa thirty years before to make a home for her, and that they had never met since that time! She always carried his photograph in the bosom of her dress, and willingly and lovingly showed it to any of us when asked to do so. I can see it now. A good-looking young man of five and twenty or thereabouts; apparently of the farmer type with a large check bow straight across his tall collar, and his black hair well oiled and brushed forward into a stiff horn over each ear for the particular occasion. It was most pathetic. Confiding little person – she would just draw the card out, and croon over it, and return it to its sanctum after pressing it to her lips with her arm around it, apparently quite oblivious of the fact that thirty years may have wrought its changes between the then and the now of her youthful Adonis, even as they must have affected her own looking glass.

Very naturally, remarks were made amongst the passengers, who looked forward to an amusing denouement on our arrival at Cape Town; but I made up my mind (and held my tongue) that they should be disappointed if I might be fortunate enough to forestall their expectation, *D.V.*

I did forestall them. My cabin in the *Warwick Castle* was on the quarter deck. In those days we used to berth our mail steamers in the inner dock. We arrived in the Bay at 7 a.m. on this particular trip, and after getting alongside the quay and ringing-off the engines, I hurried down from the bridge, took Miss Warwick into my cabin, and told her to remain quite quietly there whilst I found her *fiancé* and brought him along to her privately.

"You have shown me his likeness, you know," I said to her, "and I don't want anyone to witness so sacred a meeting."

She clasped both my hands in hers and than thanked me with tears in her voice as well as upon her cheeks, and once more drew out the tragic little presentment of Auld Lang Syne to show me, before I went off on my quest.

The gangway was being hauled up, and the crowds on the wharf were eagerly awaiting their opportunity to greet friends on board who were lining the ship's side three and four deep.

Looking along the pier towards the stern, I picked out an unmistakably anxious figure dressed in a suit of drab fustian, with a slouch felt hat over grey hair and bearded face, dodging about here and there along the side, seeking amongst the strange faces above the rail for the only one that had any interest for him!

"That's my man for a dollar," I said to myself; and neglecting all personal greetings for the moment, I made my way down to my quarry, who was just approaching the gangway.

"Mr. Metcalf, I believe?"

"Yes," he replied.

"Come with me."

As we turned the corner towards my cabin, a trembling face was peering out of the door gazing around and beyond me and my convoy; and when she did see me along with an utter stranger approaching she retired quickly out of sight. At the door I merely said: "Mr. Metcalf, you will find Miss Warwick within," and I turned to leave them alone – but in turning I could not help seeing two vastly astonished people for a moment. I mounted guard outside, greeting my own friends the meanwhile. It was only for a few minutes, however – when the pair came dancing out arm in arm, gazing fondly at one another, having bridged over thirty years of anxiety and surprise in less than five minutes of regenerated trust and affection. Bless their hearts. I understood from her, if I remember rightly, that he had been farming in the Free State – struggling against persistent adversity, until quite recently, when he had sent home for her to come out and crown the home he had at last secured for her.

I have only once before known such an instance of double-barrelled constancy and consummation – and sad to relate, that one turned out a miserable failure after all. It was in high society, and stretched from bonny Scotland to Central India.

Let us hark back to the interrupted sequence of our errant reminiscences.

At this time I had not yet discovered that South Africa produced the finest grapes in the world. Nor do I know now whether the later supremacy of their vineyards reached back as far as the year '81. I considered the muscatels of Madeira the *ne plus ultra* of all vines, and this was the Madeira season.

Wishing to give some of my friends at Cape Town a supreme treat, I got Blandy, at Funchal, to send me a number of choice bunches on board, and had them carefully suspended by the stalks in a cool store where they could touch nothing and nothing could touch them; and each day I examined them and removed any doubtful berries.

We had an invalid lady amongst our passengers in the first class, who used to be helped up on deck in fine weather, and snugged up in a lounge chair against the after hatch skylight; a sad wreck, and a pitiful case. She spoke to no one, and only closed her eyes and moved her head if any one spoke to her. Poor thing.

It struck me one day that a few of my grapes might be refreshing to her, so I cut down a bunch and took it to her myself, begging her to try a few, and telling her how good they were. She thanked me with a wan smile, and tasted one or two now and then until only the skins and stalks were left; and I was vain enough to be happy as the experiment was repeated day by day with the same result.

I mentally apologised to my friends at Cape Town, and felt that they would not have me do otherwise.

The last bunch was just consecrated to the good cause when an amiable old Scottish lady put the seal upon the sacrifice by saying: "Man, Captain, I'll never cease to admire your charity as long as I live."

"My dear madam," I replied, "you wouldn't have me do less, I am quite sure, for a poor sufferer like that, under my care, too."

"Weel, maybe, maybe: but d'ye no ken what she's suffering from?"

"No," I said. " Do you?"

She smiled and said: "I thought everyone on board knew that." And, taking me by the arm, she whispered: "She's tipsy all day long; go and look behind her chair now."

I went, and saw a large bottle of champagne, half empty, and a tumbler. Returning to my friend, I said: "After all, that proves nothing; she may require the stimulant. I'll see the doctor."

I did so, and was a good deal surprised to hear from him that there was nothing whatever the matter with her, except that she was rather too fond of champagne, and, being very hysterical, was a difficult case to deal with.

I consoled myself with the new reading of an old saw – a goose and his grapes are soon parted – but what's the odds so long as somebody else is happy. I just asked the doctor to act the part of friend as well as physician to the poor creature, knowing that she could not be in better hands.

On arriving at Cape Town, my respected namesake received news that induced him to continue his voyage round the coast with us as far as Algoa Bay, which was supposed to be our destination. Amongst our coastwise passengers received on board at Cape Town were four officials connected with the Portuguese possessions on the East Coast, one of whom was evidently a man of senior rank and breeding. He was an uncommonly handsome and distinguished looking person, more Spanish than Portuguese in appearance, I thought, with the patrician manners and courtly bearing common to the aristocracy of either nation.

It was somewhat strange for such important people that not one of the party appeared to understand a word of English. The leader, however, spoke French fluently; and as I myself was fairly conversant in those days with the "English French as she is spoke" – having been for some time in the P. and O. Mediterranean Service[26] – we were able to exchange civilities in that language; and on such frequent occasions as I found myself getting out of my depth, there was always some duty that required immediate attention – whilst I went and turned up the dictionary.

We managed by that means to worry along in quite a friendly manner. I liked him, and was grieved that, for want of practice, I was so unequal to the favourable opportunity to maintain the credit of the British Mercantile Marine with these distinguished foreigners, as we call them.

As I have said in an earlier paper, British seamen were never linguists. With them the whole world is either English or Dutch. May not this very sweeping classification have derived its origins under the shadow of Scripture, where all are either Jews or Gentiles?

---

[26] 1868-9 on the *Poonah*.

I suggest this with all reverence – for our seafarers have or had a good deal of the old Bible buried away under their rough and careless exterior.

Fortunately for our passengers, as well as for ourselves, we had a bedroom steward who could converse in Portuguese – a most unusual circumstance – and he was told off to act as valet and factotum to the Colonel and his friends during the trip.

My portly namesake was himself innocent of any language but English, strictly business English; but he was not shy by any means. We were scarcely well out to sea before he nailed our new arrival and commenced to enlarge upon the wonderful Eldorado we were coasting along; the glittering possibilities and auriferous certainties of the immediate future awaiting the brave and open-handed investor.

His patient and courteous listener bowed and smiled his acquiescence in the unknown. He pointed to the picturesque shore-line – it was a brilliant morning – and to the beautiful sea, with signified and quite intelligible admiration. Then, with another salutation, he politely indicated a desire to be introduced to the "Pearl of Warwick" who was industriously occupied upon embroidery work of some kind; and, taking advantage of a temporary ebb in the old gentleman's well-meant flood of information, he politely suggested a promenade to the resigned Rachael.

One of her hitherto devoted cavaliers very jealously complained that though the Portuguese had no tongue for English, he was at all events well endowed with an eye for beauty, the fair Rachael being the attraction.

It certainly did appear to be a case of first-sight-Kismet! The indications were unmistakable, and I am bound to say I detected no sign of resentment on the part of the Syren. She understood nothing but English, so limitations were equal.

But when did Mars fail to salute Venus for want of means? What were eyes made for, supplemented by hands in dumb show? How expressive and comprehensive they can be at times, even where language is no bar!

These are grains of philosophy that I have garnered up from ancient and musty volumes of long forgotten lore; and I suppose there is a certain amount of truth in them. At any rate, all appeared to be plain sailing.

Unable to converse in the ordinary manner, not a little may be effected by signs. But a sigh! – which is by no means uncommon at times to either sex – what a dynamo of light and power that silent syllable releases! It knocks the stuffing out of all doubt, and renders diplomacy nugatory. It breathes a full powered interest almost as tenderly as an unabridged edition of Webster's Dictionary.

The world, too, is always kind under such circumstances; and the rest of the passengers gave them plenty of room to themselves, and apparently took no notice of them.

Papa Robinson appeared to he quite reconciled to the prospect of a Portuguese son-in-law, and kept mama at a safe distance for fear of obscuring the issues by uncomplimentary comparisons. Really it was all a very funny and dramatic day-and-a-half at sea.

I am sorry that in the sequel I have to play the unkind part of a marplot, but it is surely no fault of mine if people will jump to hasty conclusions and build castles in the air for other folks to live in.

On reaching Algoa Bay, the Portuguese Consul came off to greet the new arrivals. He at least had the use of his tongue and could speak English fluently.

The result of a very short interview with him induced papa cancel his passage to Durban, which he had booked with the Purser.

I wonder why?

No. 15.

"LET sleeping dogs lie " is no doubt sound advice within certain limitations. Like many other hoary maxims, it is based upon mysterious possibilities too varied for anything beyond abstract admonition. This particular one depends a good deal upon the "dog," and the conditions of its somnolency,

I have no wish or intention to awaken dormant memories of past controversies; my dog is a good one, and his dreams will not be unpleasantly disturbed by a friendly kick.

Let us draw a veil over the last five years of crimson wickedness – the wretched fruits of higher criticism and apostasy on the part of a highly civilised and so-called Christian nation that has permanently wrecked the peace and prosperity of an entire planet – and hark back to Anno Domini 1900, when I was in command of the *Kildonan Castle*, H.M. transport No. 44, during the South African misunderstanding.

We had been engaged since the very commencement of that unhappy episode in carrying whole men out and pieces home – 2500 at a time. In December of that year, the ship being in Table Bay, the entire trooping accommodation was elaborately renovated for the purpose of conveying the "Guards" and the "Greys" back to England. Embarkation was all arranged and the regiments ready, when a sudden and unexpected order was issued to take the ship round to Simon's Bay at once. A rumour was started – with or without cause, who shall say? – that a conspiracy was on foot to release the prisoners of war at Simon's Bay; and we were ordered round to receive them all on board and to remain at anchor under cover of H.M.S. *Doris.*

Now, the Boers are not a nautical race. They are strongly prejudiced against sea and ships. Their old traditions of long, miserable, and often compulsory voyages to South Africa, in small, unsavoury, crowded galleons – marvels of discomfort – had not lost any of the disagreeable associations connected with them, but on the contrary had fermented in the process of time, and become historical bugbears.

When the time came for the embarkation of these terrible prisoners, I "called all hands," and begged them continually to remember whilst we had them on board that these men were not breakers of the law, but honourable opponents who had bravely fought for freedom, and were for the present martyrs to their cause; that we ourselves, by considerate kindness and courtesy, might in no small degree contribute to a better understanding in our mutual relations when the war was over. This resolution was enthusiastically adopted and thenceforth loyally observed by all classes on board.

The embarkation itself was an event to remember. There were many old men as well as mere boys amongst the number – about 2400 if I remember rightly. They struggled up the gangway in single file, laden with an endless variety of household gods, the majority of which must have been utterly useless to them – besides food, rugs, beds, and ordinary luggage in amazing quantities. One could not help wondering how prisoners of war could do combatants' work and be captured with such stores of impedimenta, and still cleave to them through thick and thin. One man had a folding table and two ordinary kitchen chairs amongst his property.

They were, of course, relieved of all this superfluous stuff as soon as they came on board. It was carefully labelled and put down below, until the owners might be transferred to other quarters later on.

But how shall I describe the miserable, woebegone, unclean, and dishevelled captives themselves? Traditional prejudice and abhorrence of the sea and ships were plainly depicted upon every despondent and melancholy face. Poor creatures; some of our firemen even were in tears as the procession of sorrow passed them by. I confess I was no exception to the public sympathy, coming so soon after my exhortation to the men. I don't think our guard of soldiers on duty could have made many bull's eyes for the unmartial moisture of the first few minutes.

It was, however, a very short time before a revulsion of feeling swept over the whole scene. The first batch having been paraded, roll-called, and relegated to their respective quarters, the rest, as they came alongside the ship, were greeted with shouts of astonishment, appreciation, and delight that wiped away all tears and trouble, and raised a pandemonium of questions and answers over the bulwarks, and through all the ports along the ship's side, mingled with laughter and bye-play that robbed us of all further anxiety on behalf of our guests.

It was wonderful. I don't understand a word of Dutch; but that made no difference – every voice and action spoke volumes.

Now let me say, with pride, but without ostentation, that our great *Kildonan Castle,* H.M. transport No. 44, was a picture of comfort and convenience in every particular, and as clean as a lady's drawing-room – a credit to the Cape Town authorities and to the crew.

No wonder that the revelation to "our friends the enemy" – after the unwholesome experiences of prison camp ashore – led them to adopt a vastly different opinion of the sea and ships as soon as they realised the luxury of their new surroundings.

On the following morning the metamorphosis was complete. The begrimed, barberless, hopeless, and despondent victims of the fortune of war were absent without leave. In their room we were favoured with the original number, but of smart, well-groomed, responsible and representative men of every grade of South African Society. There were even four ministers of the Gospel amongst them, and certainly no one would have suspected it when they embarked. It is astonishing what a difference a comfortable wash and a shave, *plus* a decent suit of clothes, make in a man – not only in his personal appearance, but in his self-respect and general bearing. I always feel a a bit of a toff myself when I get a pair of clean cuffs on.

We had a guard of some 200 soldiers on board, including the colonel and staff, who regulated everything with the most perfect skill and gentleness. As a matter of fact, our honourable prisoners of war turned out to be the most peaceable, orderly, and lovable company of foes that one could wish to meet. There was never a hitch anywhere. No single case of "discipline" during the whole six weeks.

They were told off into sections and messes under their own chosen officers from the beginning, and these were in most cases well known citizens of the Transvaal and Free State – admirable men. We soon learned to love them all, and the whole ship became a hive of busy bees, all working for the public weal.

About the second or third day after embarkation, I had a deputation of leaders praying for leave to hold daily services on deck. The Colonel very kindly agreed with me to permit this at 9 a.m. and 4 p.m. The result was a revelation – to me. They had three meeting places: the forecastle head, the bridge deck between funnels, and the after deck – the two ends and the middle of the ship – and all three were running simultaneously.

Now the Boers are very fond of singing, and all their hymns are of the "Old Hundredth" type sung very slowly. There would be about 500 or 600 stalwart male voices at each of the meeting places droning out these grand old-world Psalms, sometimes all three together, but by no means the same songs; and as my cabin under the navigation bridge was over all, the combined efforts were really amazing at times, melancholy to a degree, but so real and devout that one could only rejoice in their enjoyment, and my word they did give tongue when they a struck a fine deep note! It made Simon's Bay vibrate with religious fervour.

We used to have our own Sunday morning and evening services in the saloon for the soldiers and crew at 11 a.m. and 7 p.m., and the alleyways used to be crowded with our friends at the open windows.

After the second Sunday I had another deputation, petitioning for permission to attend our own services. Poor fellows, they were not satisfied with their full allowance of three meetings daily. So I interviewed our good-natured colonel again, and again he agreed with me, to allow such of them as understood English to be present on Sundays, morning and evening; one side of the saloon being reserved for soldiers and crew, and the other side assigned to our guests – a graphic picture of worldly strife dissolved and mingled in gracious fellowship under the standard of "One God and Father of us all."

Our saloon, of course, was limited in size compared with the numbers who sought for admittance, but about 200 of them used to pack themselves in like sardines in a box, the alleyways and windows being still commandeered to their fullest extent.

I cannot tell what test applicants for admission were put through by their captains, but quite a number of them could speak English of sorts, and some, I think, understood more than they were inclined to show.

An instance of this occurred in my presence one day. Amongst other amusements and occupations started for their entertainment, we set them to work fishing. This would appear to be an almost unknown art amongst Boers generally, and the initial successes caused extraordinary excitement. I was pioneering the proceedings amongst a dense crowd at the after end, when a handsome Cape salmon was good enough to act "leading lady" in the play to the utter astonishment of the onlookers, who shouted something about "slang, slang" which I am told is Dutch for "snake." At first no one would touch it; but when told that it was good to eat and that it was not "slang," everyone craved for a line and started right away. One big Dutchman, who could not speak a word of English, commandeered a line, baited his hook very skilfully, and almost immediately got a determined tug. "Man, yon was a big ane" he exclaimed, lustily jerking up his line – quite forgetful for the moment of his Transvaal origin.

He was not the only stranger amongst them by a good many. Before our six weeks' experience had slipped away, quite a number of "foreigners" had betrayed their native colours; but, of course, no notice was taken of such renegades, beyond perhaps a little extra cold shoulder; they were paying the penalty of their transfer of allegiance.

Fishing continued to be a popular occupation until subsequent events disgusted the fish and drove them away to more salubrious localities.

Before leaving Cape Town we had taken in sufficient Natal coal see us home and back again; 1200 tens of this was in our main hold.

Now, please do not credit me with any intention to give a good dog a bad name. At the time I am referring to – 1900 to 1901 – the coal industry in Natal was in its infancy. The supplies were, of necessity, from surface workings, and the results were poor in quality and bad in character. There was a tradition amongst us all that it would burn nowhere except in the bunkers, and the numberless instances of spontaneous combustion on board ships carrying it decidedly justified its evil report. No doubt the mines got down to *pukker* seams long before this; and, moreover, they have unlimited areas to draw from.

Revenons. – About a month after arriving in Simon's Bay our ventilators, which were painted white outside and red in, began to assume a leaden colour, and to emit a disagreeable odour, which at times almost "appeared to be visible." Suspecting mischief, I signalled our guardship, *Doris.* A party of inspection came on board from her, and after a more or less cursory examination, and the placing of several thermometers upon the surface of the coal, they pronounced "All well, and no need for alarm."

The following day, odour was stronger, and colour deepening. I signalled again. This time the Naval coal expert from the harbour came off. Thermometers showed atmospheric temperature only; other indications were pronounced natural during such warm weather. After warning me not to be so fond of starting doubtful rumours, our delegate left the ship somewhat brusquely.

More and more convinced that we were in for trouble, on the following morning I opened up the batches and drove an iron slice six feet down into the coal, and lo! it came up red hot five minutes afterwards. A gang was sent down with shovels to dig a hole. They had not gone down more than three feet when they turned up "red."

Up went the signal, "We are on fire." And off came a party of Naval officers and engineers prepared to court-martial me apparently; but when we gave them visible evidence, there was an unmistakable scare, and a volley of orders to flood the hold, close the hatches, block the ventilators, stop every opening, and they would send a naval detachment on board to assist at "fire stations" in case of emergency. N.B. – The thermometers still registered honest atmospheric temperature.

It is always easy to be wise after the event. Fire requires air; being low down, it drew air through the surface of the coal in sufficient volume to keep the surface temperature normal.

A capital mistake was made in the order to hermetically close all hatches and openings, and simultaneously to flood the hold. Naturally, steam was generated below in vast quantities, and the result was – what we ought to have foreseen. I was on the upper bridge at 5 p.m., taking the evening bearings by compass, when a tremendous and terrifying rumble below occurred, immediately followed by an explosion and a roar. Hatches, tarpaulins, coals, steam, black sludge, and flames shot up as from a volcano to an incredible height, and scattered in every direction. I had the full benefit of the exhibition, and for a short time subsequent events interested me no more.

However, I was not hurt, and – praise be to God – with 2800 men on board the ship, no one else was one penny the worse.

(To be continued.)

The episode of the Boer PoWs is told in Marischal Murray's Union-Castle Chronicle 1853-1953, *and also in Laurens van der Post's* Yet Being Someone Other – *his mother's cousin was one of the PoWs. He says that he himself sailed with "Holy Joe" once.*

Kildonan Castle – Tony Haslett Collection

No. 16.

IN our last number we closed with an account of the explosion on board the *Kildonan Castle* in Simon's Bay.

It is obviously superfluous to remark that the noise, coupled with the display of flying hatches and tarpaulins, and surmounted with the canopy of black and white smoke and steam crowned with brilliant sunshine, brought the naval authorities off again to the ship without any further signalling.

It was impossible to investigate at the main hatch for some time owing to the scalding steam rolling out in volumes.

When the worst was past, fire hoses were got to work upon the coal surfaces; and gradually men, with towels round their mouths, got down for short periods, relieving one another, to extend the water service over the whole.

This kept the steam and the heat at unbearable density, and seeing that lanterns absolutely refused to burn under such conditions, it speaks wonders for the devoted men who worked in the stifling and pitchy darkness, though it were only for a few minutes at a time.

Several of them had to be pulled up in a half collapsed condition – none were allowed to go down without being "roped," for fear of failure.

After a couple of hours of this outrageous struggle against the combined forces of fire and steam, *plus* the deadly fumes of coal gas, indomitable pluck and endurance scored an obstinate victory. Men were able, under the hoses, to shovel coal into baskets to be tipped overboard. But they were literally digging out fire, and were in imminent danger all the time of getting badly burned.

The floods of water, however, gradually overcame the combustion, and by the time we had thrown about fifty tons into the sea orders were given to discharge the rest into lighters, which were to be alongside as soon as possible.

It was this partly consumed gassy coal that was jettisoned which disgusted the fish in our neighbourhood, and brought one important branch of our poor captives' amusements to an untimely period.

To their eternal credit let me proclaim the fact that I was waited upon by a deputation of their officers at the very commencement of our trouble, freely offering me the services of able-bodied volunteers in relays of two hundred at a time if they might be of any use to us! Dangerous prisoners of war! Downright good fellows, every one of them. I had to assure them, with many thanks, that, should occasion arise, I would not hesitate to accept so valuable and friendly an offer.

The fire having been effectually extinguished in the flooded hold, lighters were brought alongside, and the whole of the remaining coal was discharged, and sold at a big loss, of course, by the authorities. It was not all damaged, but it was too dangerous to risk a diagnosis with a view to retaining the good stuff on board. Natal coal was bad enough dry – wet, it would have been past hope. The ship herself was none the worse for the conflagration; the combustion was in the body of the coal itself, and not around it, strangely enough, so we had every cause to be thankful.

The result of the fire was, I believe, regretted by everyone. We were to return to Table Bay and tranship our friends to two smaller transports as soon as our discharge should be finished, and in the meantime, alas and alack, we received news of the death of our beloved Queen Victoria, of ever blessed memory!

That took us all by surprise and broke the whole ship's company down. It was remarkable. A cynic might have thought that everyone had lost his own mother. "Our Friends the Enemy" read the signs aright, and sent their two leading men to me to express the sympathy of all their ranks with our crew and nation generally! That was the climax! When I announced the message to the Colonel and the crew, it was like rivetting the fetters of friendly relations that had grown up between guests and guards; and all the conditions being considered, I submit that, as an act of grace, it would be bad to beat.

What a poison fanged serpent misunderstanding is!

The old sailor's axiom that the world is made up of English and Dutch is perhaps an inspiration after all. British and Dutch! What could we not do if barriers were removed?

If our six weeks' experience meant anything to thoughtful minds, it carried conviction that we were supplementary the one to the other; and that the South African struggle was a lamentable affair from both sides of the line.

I knew Dr. Reitz[27] well. He was a passenger with me on more than one voyage, and I was happily instrumental in doing him a service on a certain occasion which he was pleased to appreciate far too highly.

How earnestly I pleaded with him for the exercise of his influence to tide over the trouble that was looming large at the

---

[27] Francis William Reitz, State Secretary of the Boer South African Republic.

time. I still have the grand old gentleman's last letter, in which he takes me to task for being an Englishman,

General Joubert[28] and his vrouw also made a voyage with me once; and what a cheery, jovial old fellow he was; never more happy than when playing "musical chairs," or joining in some other innocent frolic amongst the young people. None of them ever caught him out in their games, he was far too slim[29] for them. And how he used to roar with laughter when his manoeuvres were successful. It was a comedy. The old lady would stand and look on with a scowl of disapproval on her dour face, wrathfully indignant that her Piet should play the goat amongst the kids of an English steamer. Dear old wife – she was at a disadvantage – not being able to speak English.

But to return to "our Friends the Enemy."

Dutch painters have held their own amongst the artists of the world, but I fear they have not transmitted their genius to all the Boers of South Africa if ours were a fair sample of the profession. I was presented with three water colours as souvenirs, done on board, which I value exceedingly on account of the kind-hearted limners rather than for any startling artistic merit in the productions themselves. I keep them still in memory of that fascinating six weeks' experience of the fortune of war.

But I have many other mementoes of various kinds, given to me by the amiable and industrious mechanics; one of them, a model of a "Cape cart," is quite excellently made; and considering that a pocket-knife appears to have been his principal outfit in the way of tools, it is quite astonishing.

We had to keep them all supplied with wood, nails, tin, wire, paints, twine, canvas, &c.; in fact, the ship's stores were drawn upon for every imaginable thing in order to keep the men pleasantly occupied. I spent a lot of time chatting with them and watching them at work; it was quite an education. It was like being amongst a lot of happy school boys.

When we returned to Table Bay and transhipped them all to the other two transports allotted to them (I find that there were 3000 of them), they climbed up into the rigging, and on to every available paint of vantage, and cheered the *Kildonan Castle* to the echo – breaking into one of their grand old Dutch Psalms of Praise that was taken up by both ships with one accord, until their voices faded away into the glorious sunset of a calm summer evening as they steamed out of Table Bay.

---

[28] Commandant General of the SAR.
[29] Sly.

It was a trial to the feelings. Very touching – one almost felt inclined to think that even warfare is no exception to the rule that lights as well as shadows are common to every thing under the sun.

I should like to add that the gloomy prospects for next Harvest-home lay heavily upon the hearts of our guests. There was a reasonable fear that the seed would fail, perhaps be utterly destroyed, and that a fresh start would be difficult and disappointing.

A conversation upon this subject with some of our leading men led to a *"Kildonan* Fund" being raised, to be supplemented by any of our own friends at Home who might sympathise with the movement, for the purchase and transmission, after the war, of as much seed, of their own selection, as the results of our puny efforts could provide and pay freight on. It went out in due course for distribution without any trumpets to celebrate its insignificance, but with many a prayer for blessings upon it, "for who hath despised the day of small things?"

After the departure of our prisoners of war, the ship was taken in hand by the authorities in Cape Town for an overhaul of damage by fire; but as I have already said, it was the heart of the coal that had been in a state of spontaneous combustion, the surroundings had not been affected; about 600 tons had suffered. The whole 1200 were, however, discharged and a new supply taken in.

I may say, *en passant*, that we had two more "heatings" on board before reaching Home, but both were in what we call "pocket bunkers" which discharge into the engine room, so we could deal with them separately and effectively. We must have struck a particularly warm hearted vein of Natal coal that voyage. Such experiences, happily, are quite things of the past.

In the meantime, the ship was converted into a floating hospital for the homeward conveyance of 1400 "casualties," a curious commentary upon her recent inhabitants.

The authorities certainly made a first-rate arrangement of sick wards throughout; it was a picture of comfort, if such a term be appropriate to the case, and reflected credit upon the designers not only for their plans but for their consideration of the wounded heroes and their attendants. Every cot was the separate possession of its occupant, who could be ministered to from every side. It was wonderful how they managed to fit up for so many, and to do it so conveniently.

But oh! the wood! the stacks of beautiful clean planking that were absorbed in the preparation! It makes my mouth water to think of it in these days, when I cannot get even one plank to make a box big enough to keep my spare money in!

How I did glory in that floating hospital! It was so clean, so well planned, so beautiful. And when the ministering angels came on board and took charge – what a scattering of comfortable little beds, and bales of blankets and sheeting, &c., took place and how different everything looked when they had put the finishing touches to their gracious preparations.

N.B. – All the devoted women who have been performing such marvels of mercy (during the recent years of world war, amongst the mud and discomfort, the dirt and the stench, the sights and the sounds, the heat and the cold, as well as submitting to the lack of everything in the shape of refinement – the music and poetry of domestic life – these gentle creatures, of whom a forgetful country is not worthy – should every one be decorated with a gold bar-brooch, bearing the one word – "INASMUCH" – in simple raised letters, for most surely they have fulfilled all the conditions to the bitter end – God bless them.

Our poor pieces of suffering humanity were tenderly brought on board and stowed away in their little cots. What a pathetic procession it was; and all so patient and silent – scarcely a murmur amongst them.

What is it that comes over our soldiers at such times. It appears to be a point of honour amongst them never to grouse, however sharp the anguish; but just to take the blanket between their teeth and bear the unbearable – suffering for others!

I took full advantage of surgical permission to be amongst them whenever duty admitted of it; and I love to think of the lessons I learned there. It was a great privilege.

I think I must just tell one short story on account of the majestic and reverent ignorance of the subject. We had a young soldier who had been shot through the lung, a nice looking lad of 22, whose strange name was Rosey. Complications of every kind had supervened upon his wound, and he was brought on board in a moribund state, quite unconscious, and remained so for several days. The surgeon in charge frankly pronounced him a hopeless case.

I frequently sat beside him, and silently watched the flickering spirit apparently struggling for release. It seemed so sad – this boy – a stranger in strange surroundings – wounded to the death, and unconsciously holding on to life by a mere thread; no loving mother or other relative to smooth back his tumbled hair; and a narrow gleam showing the "gates ajar" between the Now and Then!

86

I think it was our fourth day out, as I sat there in the afternoon, his eyes partly opened with a new expression. He appeared to wonder at the white deck and beams above him, as though faintly trying to brush away the cobwebs of dreamland; and closed them again with a tiny frown of baffled thought.

I signalled to a passing angel, and she came, and bending over him, tenderly smoothed his pillow and laid her hand upon his forehead – and the weary eyes again were opened, but upon a fairer view than a white deck and unsympathetic beams. "O woman – in our hours of ease!" and so, to the good surgeon's surprise, a new life was born by the Sphinx of forlorn hope, and sanctified by a first impression that miles of ocean would never dissipate.

Wonders will never cease. By the following afternoon, not only had reason reassumed her power, but the fever and delirium had disappeared before her gracious rule, leaving a motionless recumbent figure as though as in warm white marble of a silent and beautiful boy; a wounded hero withal.

One more day and he could speak a little and listen eagerly when spoken to. I asked him his name. Rosey – William. Mother? Yes. Father? No. Home? London, Bermondsey. Other relatives. One sister, married. All this I took down for possible future reference.

Now comes the incident I referred to. "Rosey, do you love Jesus?" A blank stare, and then, "Who are you gettin' at?" " I want to get at you, Rosey." With a deep sigh, he replied, "Jesus ain't for the likes o' we." "Who is He for then?" "He's for the gentry – not for the likes o' we!"

That spiked my gun! I was appalled. But he was in earnest. It was easy to call his attention to corrections from Scripture, and Rosey seized the life line like a drowning man.

When he was leaving the ship he grasped my hand, and with a tear in his eye he blurted out: "Captain, you have given me a hard job; you don't know what life in those slums is! Goodbye!"

Good-bye, Rosey – good-bye; a Friend goes along with you.

No. 17.
A GHOST STORY

I'M going on strike.

It has become the fashion nowadays to "down tools" of any and every kind on any and every imaginable pretext under the moon – which itself, by-the-bye, suffers under the imputation of Bolshevism; and I don't see why I should not be in the fashion myself – so I am going on strike – for change of air and scene.

Change is nearly always good – sometimes it is essential. To me it is essential now. I've made so much out of gilt-edged securities in South Africa lately that I have decided to risk a plunge into Australian Bendigoes for the pleasure of a new sensation.

I have not been to the little island since the early seventies, so I don't suppose I should find my way about at first, because from all accounts things have "growed" like Topsy out there since then. But I want to go back a bit earlier still, into the late fifties, when Melbourne was a scattered settlement of tin shanties and canvas hotels on a sandbank, and Sydney was quite a respectable small town. I was a little brass-bound midshipmite on the crew list of the finest passenger sailing vessel in her day and generation – Dunbar's *La Hogue*, Captain John Williams – one of the best, if not the very best that ever commanded a ship – dear old "Holy Joe" as he was called.

We were moored alongside the Circular Quay in Sydney Harbour on November 5, 1858, and had been "celebrating" as usual. Elated with sundry and divers pyrotechnic displays and other seasonable and sensible ovations a few of us were – but hold; before going further, in order to turn on the lime-light effectively, I must pull up the curtain and unroll surroundings.

The *La Hogue* was a beautiful frigate built ship, painted after the prevailing fashion of those days with a line of black and white ports and a white stripe along the upper bulwarks. She was 1331 tons register; large then, but pretty small as compared with the vessels of to-day. She was a poop ship – that is to say, her passenger accommodation was above the main deck, aft, and it was 100 ft. in length; with the cabins running along each side of the saloon and across the stern. At the fore end of it, the doors at each side opened directly on to the main deck.

Just between these doors there was a small hatchway that led down into what was generally known as the "midshipmen's hole," and we carried 12 of these ornamental and aspiring navigators in that ship, besides third and fourth mates; all of which stamped her as a vessel of the first class.

Just inside the saloon doors a stairway led down into a passage on the lower deck running along the centre, with steward's store-rooms on either side and across the stern, much after the plan of the saloon. At the fore end of this passage a door led through into the region of the midshipmen's quarters. This door was always kept locked, and the key was in the steward's custody lest the midshipmen might tarnish their smart uniforms and fair fame with raisins or other attractive dainties. Needless to say, the suspicion that prompted the jealous guardianship of this key was a permanent rock of offence and bone of contention between the midshipmen's hole and the steward's pantry. They naturally desired that the means of communication should be under their own charge as responsible guardians over the owner's property.

The chief steward rejoiced in the name of Broughton when on shore, but on board the ship he was only known as "Whiskers," because he wore these facial adornments á la "Dundreary," though Lord D. had not yet seen the light in those days. He was really a very gentlemanly-looking man, a relative of the captain's; fairly tall and slender, of quiet, unassuming manners, and, bar the key, much respected. He had a pantry man and a scavenger boy to his staff.

There was one other person I must portray as being a somewhat important actor in the events that follow – the second mate, Mr. Goddard. He became chief mate the following voyage, and eventually captain of the *La Hogue*, and of the *Parramatta* later on. He was about 40 years of age, a tall, loose jointed kind of figure, with an inclination to stoop and to shamble in his walk. But he was a good chap. Unlike the steward, his hirsute ornaments resembled two small bath sponges, one on the centre of each cheek, under an assertive mop of dark brown hair, that gave him a very picturesque appearance. He had a peculiarity of speech which was quite a monopoly. He prefaced nearly every remark with "urra, urra," and, when excited, it was "tut, tut, urra, urra."

Let us return now to November 5 on board the *La Hogue* in Sydney Harbour. We had been celebrating the date in the usual popular manner. Most, in fact nearly all the ship's company had gone up town to help others to celebrate. The captain and first mate, Mr. Elmsley, were amongst their friends; and the second mate was in charge. Three of us midshipmen were in our den, smoking strong tobacco and bracing up exhausted energy with hot rum punch; for I am grieved to say that in those good old times midshipmen as well as their elders had their rum ration regularly served out once a day, and twice on Saturdays and special occasions. Our dear old captain was a total abstainer himself, and I don't think he knew that we had it.

Anyhow, there we were, at the witching hour of night, in a state of noisy excitement, enjoying ourselves, when "Whiskers" suddenly made his appearance in our midst, with a face as white as chalk, and in a stage whisper asked whether we had seen or heard anything! No – what is it? "There's a ghost, in the store rooms!" "Gracious goodness! How do you know?" "Oh! come with me. I dare not go alone; and there is no one but the second mate on board."

By this time we were all fairly frightened. We held a hasty council of war, and decided to ascertain first of all whether any of the crew were on board forward. No one would volunteer to go alone, so we all four went, sticking close together, and found the butcher (so called because he fed the fowls and prepared them for table) and the sailmaker both asleep and very drowsy. We soon sobered them with the awful news, and all six of us crept aft and found Mr. Goddard in the saloon reading "Tristram Shandy" under a solitary dim night lamp.

"Sir, sir, 'Whiskers' says there's a ghost down below in the store rooms!"

"A what?" Down went the book, and up sprung the mate. "Tut, tut! – urra, urra! there are no such things as ghosts!"

"But, sir, pray come with us and let us see."

"Tut, tut. Go and see what it is yourselves, and come and let me know. Robinson, you stay with me."

"Please, sir, come with us."

"Urra, urra! what a lot of cowardly fellows. Go at once and see what's the matter."

"Whiskers" had by this time lit a candle lantern and we were all looking like a group of ghosts ourselves in the dim light. At this moment a weird, indescribable sound was heard from below, followed by a faint knocking. and we all cuddled one another and chattered our teeth loose.

To make matters worse, the second mate reached over the table to turn the lamp up, and – turned it out! So there we were, with a horn candle lantern in the dark saloon, unable to see one another's complexions.

For some time we clung together, listening in deadly silence, and just when someone was going to whisper a remark, that awe inspiring sound was heard again from the bowels of the ship aft, followed by the same tap, tap, tapping – and again silence. It was dreadful. A whispered consultation took place, mingled with endless tuts and urras, and we made a start for the stairway to the storerooms, "Whiskers," carrying the lamp, shoved along in front by the rest, and Mr. Goddard in the rear with a musket in his hand which he had reached from the rack of the saloon. "Urra, urra – go down with the lamp and look around," whispered he.

"Here, please take the lamp, sir, and lead the way."

"Tut, tut, don't be so foolish. Go on down."

"Well, all come close together, closer still" – (This was all carried on in stage whispers, of course.) Inch by inch we pressed one another half-way down the stairs, when that truly alarming and utterly unaccountable sound occurred again! There was no shame about us – we just fell over one another up the ladder into saloon again – in total darkness – the candle had been put out!

"Anybody got a match?" Yes – fortunately "Whiskers" had a box in his pocket.

It was an undoubted fact that the cause of all this midnight dismay was totally unprecedented and unexplainable. The actors in it were not such timorous donkeys as one might be led to suppose. The circumstances and surroundings – the witching hour – the "otherwise" dead silence and utter darkness of the great ship's lower deck, and the absence of any other living soul on board all combined to excuse the fears of these four men and three boys.

On regaining the saloon, another serious council of war was carried on *sotto voce*, which only added terror to the nightmare. The conclusion endorsed by all was that something absolutely must be done, since total failure to ascertain the cause might perhaps lead to bitter remorse when the mystery should be unravelled. So each one undertook to stand shoulder to shoulder with "Whiskers" and the lantern supported by a man on each side in the van, and the three midshipmen close behind them, the rear being covered by the second mate and his gun. Moreover, all vowed to stand firm and still should the ghostly lamentation recur whilst the party were reconnoitring. Accordingly, we formed up, and commenced to descend very slowly down the ladder, and then halted to close our ranks more compactly. This done, as there was still no sound, we encouraged one another to advance step by step along the gloomy passage towards the stern, with frequent soft tut, tuts and urra, urras from the rear, until we had covered half the distance to the transom storeroom, when that sepulchral agony seemed to take form and fly at us from the very doors.

One moment to stand and shiver, and human courage degenerated into a wild stampede. Out went the light again, and in the darkness the second mate got mixed up with the gun between his legs at the foot of the ladder, and all the party climbed over him in their panic. I tremble to think what tragedy might have followed had that gun been loaded. But, indeed, the weapon would not have been there I feel sure, had it been so, for I am persuaded that Mr. Goddard would not have pressed the trigger against a mosquito if he saw it biting him, great soft hearted sailor that he was, let alone carry a loaded carbine in a crowd even with a ghost as the objective.

Well, no one no was seriously hurt in this *débâcle*, but in spite of the circus, the mate's urra, urra, at the indignity he had suffered, gave rise to a shade of amusement which distinctly improved the morale of the company.

The lamp having been re-lighted, all joined hands in a solemn league and covenant to go boldly forward and open that door, come what might; and to that door we marched in the late order without a sound on our own or on any other part. "Whiskers" reached forward from the front rank, and bungling the key into the lock, bravely turned it and threw open the door!

Nothing but darkness visible! A faint "urra, urra, I told you so" from the rear rank, and in a whisper, "hold the light lower down. What's that on the deck – that black thing?" Everyone gasped and clung closely together, as that graveyard dirge resounded again, and the "black thing" seemed to move, and knock, knock, knock on the deck.

Looking back across the ages I will maintain against all detractors that, at this moment, given conditions and surroundings, the courage of that little band of seven – three of whom were mere boys, one a " jemmy dux," or butcher so-called, a steward, and an old sailmaker – the courage of that little band cannot be impugned. They stood their ground manfully, and tremblingly upheld one another during that that dreadful solo.

"It's something alive," we whispered round. Inch by inch they drew into the doorway, until the ghostly candle light revealed – the Captain's retriever, Bob, lying flat on the deck, but what! in place of his proper head, he had a tin face! Fear was cast to the winds, and an examination was hastily made which explained the whole mystery.

"Urra, urra, go to the saloon sideboard and bring a couple of spoons as quickly as you can find them in the dark." The dog was nearly dead; but everyone was fond of old Bob. It appears that "Whiskers" had gone to the storeroom in the afternoon to get something for the officers' supper, and had cut into the top of a 6-lb. tin of (what we used to call) "soup and bully" with the can opener; and having taken out what he required in a basin, he left the tin standing on a case and retired – not being aware that Master Bob had followed him into the storeroom and was shut in.

The rest is a matter of course. Bob approving of the savoury odour, found the flavour to match, and after wolfing a pound or two as a sample, went to sleep and no doubt dreamed of more. The dream materialised later on, and the contents getting lower invited a deeper quest, which was comparatively easy, as the opening was just large enough to admit his face, and the hair offered no resistance to further investigation. Not to be baulked in the completion of his atrocious act of piracy, it became necessary to wriggle one ear inside the jagged edge of the tin; and as this cut the other ear it also had to be manoeuvred in – and the ghost was there!

No getting out; every effort increased the difficulty – the rough edges cut into the skin, and swollen jaws supervened. This stopped free breathing, of course; and the poor beast was suffocating inside the deadly trap, and creating the hideous noises that scared the ship and brought relief at the very last moment.

With the handles of the two spoons and a volley of urra, urras, Mr Goddard and the steward worked the ears out, and gradually, bit by bit, helped the poor swollen face back to open air. By that time Bob was to all appearance the canine member of a past generation – but a little rum, and some loving "first aid" to the wounded brought him round; and to show him a "bully beef tin" after that, skinned his teeth – amiable as he was by nature.

No. 18.
ANOTHER GHOST STORY

The La Hogue outside Sydney Heads about 1860

A FEW days after the incidents recorded in the last paper the weather was, as usual, glorious in that glorious climate during their summer season, and Port Jackson – or Sydney Harbour, as it was generally called – was a perfection of earthly Paradise. It was wonderful. As a harbour, there is no place in the wide world like it. Entirely landlocked, it is entered from the Southern Ocean by a narrow opening between cliffs some two hundred feet in height, the channel turning at almost right angles to shut out the undulations of the sea, so that in fair weather the surface of the water is like a beautiful lake. It is not a bay, but a succession of bays all round in every direction, almost every one of them deserving to be called a separate harbour, and amply fulfilling all the requirements. In the days I am referring to – in 1858 – these beautiful bays were timbered down to the water's edge with a marvellous variety and wealth of character and colour. In fact Sydney Harbour was, and no doubt still is, Fairyland on a magnificent scale.

The conveniences of the port at that date were of the crudest, of course. In these days of luxurious ease as regards shipping requirements, it raises a smile to recall makeshifts that we were quite satisfied with at the time, and looked upon with the greatest satisfaction so long as our particular ends were served.

There was no hurry in those days; no necessity for it. Everything was undertaken and carried through in a dignified and orderly manner;

and what could not be done to-day was naturally postponed until a more convenient season – to-morrow or next day.

This system had much to recommend it. There were fewer breakdowns in health as well as in material. Suicides were very scarce. Newspapers were few, and dealt mostly with facts. Bibles were on every table, and were for the most part badly thumbed. "The Days o' Auld Land Syne" were no bad days at a' at a'. Demonocracy had not shaken the fleas out of its mane in '58.

But I'm afraid I am moralising at the expense of my friends.

A few days after the incidents recorded in our last paper, the port water boat came alongside the *La Hogue* to replenish our empty casks for the voyage home. She had a fascinating little dingey alongside of her, about six feet long, with a badly broken stern, and an old oar blade to scull with. I looked with covetous eyes upon that little boat and lay low.

During the dinner hour I waylaid the Captain of the water barge, and asked if I might have the dingey for a while, and he earned my eternal gratitude by saying that I might have it as long as I liked!

I wanted nothing further and "casually" forgot to ask leave for the afternoon, for fear of any timorous objection on the part of my respected seniors. So hopping over the side and down a rope into the barge, I embarked straight away, and commenced to scull across the circular quay.

My programme was to round the point into Wooloomooloo Bay, where rock oysters were as plentiful as blackberries, and to take back a consignment that would mollify the officers for my having taken French leave.

I must call a halt now in order to explain a certain meteorological phenomenon not uncommon in Sydney Harbour during the summer season. When the day is unusually brilliant and beautiful, a squall of great violence, that is locally known as a "Southerly Buster," sweeps down upon the devoted port with blinding clouds of sand and dust from the interior, followed some hours later on by a deluge of rain that shuts out all visibility, and exhausts itself into a dark, hot, and heavy dead calm. As a rule, scarcely any indication is given of its approach, unless the barometer may show signs. Perhaps it does, I cannot tell.

Anyhow, I had no barometer in my broken-sterned argosy. I was gathering oysters for the Corporation. But about three o'clock "I was led" to look up, and saw what I knew to be a danger signal in the sky. Not a moment to spare! Away I went for the point as hard as my poor scull would drive the little cockle-shell through the calm water, and I got round into the circular quay and in sight of my ship when the awful storm broke, and twisted the raised stem of my poor little dingey right round before the tempest! No time to pray! One look, and I saw that the only possible hope of deliverance lay in reaching a schooner that was lying at anchor about five hundred yards away, and right in the track of the storm. Those on board had seen me, too; and in less time than it has taken me to describe the fateful situation I was hanging on with the muscles of despair to a rope thrown to me, which I managed to fasten, I know not how, around the after thwart of my little skiff, grabbed in the hands of the schooner's crew, and pulled on board just as she sank under my feet.

Of course, I was soaked and capless. Strangely enough, I remember thinking during that terrible bid for life that the storm fiend seemed to be combing the startled waters into froth with a million rakes, and screaming with anger that my little coracle should fly along like a feather before the blast, though the foam and spray over the stern covered us in the savage endeavour to fill her and bring our audacious career to an end. The noise was deafening. The voices of the hurricane were sublime.

Don't suppose that we felt ourselves safe on board the little coasting schooner. With both her anchors down and a full scope of chain out, she yawed to port and starboard, backwards and forwards, straining desperately at her moorings, taking more than spray over each bow as she raced from side to side, and heeled heavily over each way according to the veer. The whistling of the rigging added to the general uproar, and the eyes of the crew, as well as of the Captain, were constantly turned to the ever-increasing surf upon the hungry rocks astern, distant only about half a-mile.

This was sixty years ago, and I am here to-day telling you the story, I believe, for the first time. How little we think of our blessings! And yet, perhaps, there is something behind our great events which "gives us pause," lest we might tread too lightly upon Holy ground.

It was between three and four in the afternoon when I was yanked on board the *Pearl* by those loving sailor hands, and sent down below to get a change. No leisure for story telling. We all kept on deck watching, watching, watching. Was anything but anxious duty to the ship occupying the thoughts of those brave Colonial sea-dogs during that wordless watch as they laid their hands upon the cables before the windlass every now and then, and gazed over the stern between whiles? "There's a sweet little cherub that sits up aloft to look after the life of poor Jack." He was surely looking after them that night.

All things change – the better for the worse and the worse for the better. By eight o'clock the hurricane had subsided into a steady gale, and anxiety on board the schooner was so far allayed that they could confidently argue that as the cables had held on through the first they could easily do so to the last; so we went down below into the sailor's forecastle and chatted until I, at all events, fell asleep.

I was roused up at 4 a.m. It was then dead calm and very dark. The schooner's "market boat" was going ashore, and they were going to take me with them.

On making a trial we found my little ship was still fast by the rope, and we pulled her up and turned the water out of her; but, alas, the scull oar had gone with the gale. I got into her, and the market boat towed me astern and alongside the water barge, which was moored to the quay. Of course, everyone was fast asleep, so I hitched the dingey to the quarter where I had found it and slipped round quietly to my own ship.

In the dark I fell over our stern moorings, and scraped my face rather badly against the rough hawser, causing some rather free bleeding. I was a good deal hurt, too, but made no sound, beginning to feel rather guilty.

The night watchman was no doubt brewing himself some coffee in the galley – so I went down quietly into our den, and turned in just as I was, drawing my curtain silently, and fell fast asleep; I was quite done up and dead tired.

Horrible dreams of drowning, and sharks, and seaweed shrouds and mourning relatives seemed to be mixed up with murmuring voices and the odour of coffee; and, half awake, I heard someone say: "Poor little beggar; what awful news for them at home."

Without realising the subject of conversation one little bit, I just drew my curtain back and quietly asked who they were talking about.

The bursting of a bomb amongst them could not have created a greater diversion. With abject terror and profane exclamations the whole mess vanished, over the long table and under it, anyhow to reach the door, capsizing their coffee, and leaving me alone.

Still quite unconscious of playing any leading part, I turned out and poured myself out a cup of coffee, which I was quietly enjoying when the chief mate, Mr. Elmslie, followed by the second and all the mess, came cautiously to the door and looked in!

"Is that you, Robinson?" I stood up and saluted – "Yes, sir."

"When did you come on board?"

"At 4.30 this morning, sir."

"Where have you been?"

"On board the schooner *Pearl*, in the Bay, sir."

Then turning to the rest, he said: "Robinson's ghost is certainly covered with blood, but I think he is otherwise material. I'll report to the Captain now, and he will no doubt go into the matter after breakfast."

By this time I was pretty sorry for myself, and yet, and yet – well, it was difficult to decide quite, whether there was not just a shade of satisfaction in having played the leading part in so amazing and tragic an experience. All's well that ends well – but it had not ended yet for me –

so there was still an element of doubt to be cleared up. Had I known everything the shade of satisfaction would have been still more ghostly.

However, there was nothing to be gained by meeting trouble two-thirds of the way, so I had a good wash and removed the sanguinary records of my fall, and after getting the doctor to administer "first aid" with a few inches of sticking plaster, had some breakfast by way of preparation for my court-martial.

In due course I was sent for to the Captain's cabin, and found the good "old man," the chief and second mates, and a stranger in semi-uniform awaiting me.

All looked very grave, and I am afraid I felt a good deal like wilting. What follows is from a deeply engraved memory that still retains the essence of the interview.

The Captain did all the questioning.

"What have. you done to your face, Robinson?"

"I fell over the stern moorings in the dark this morning, Sir, coming on board."

"Where were you coming from?"

"I came ashore from the schooner *Pearl* with their market boat, sir."

"How came you to be on board the *Pearl*?"

I told him the story briefly.

"Why were you in that dingey – did any one give you leave?"

"I asked the water barge master, and he said I might go in her."

"What was your object in going so far away?"

"I went to get some oysters for the cuddy and for our mess, Sir."

"Did you ask any one on board for permission to go?" I hung my head. "Did you tell any one on board what you were proposing to do?" Still no answer.

"Now listen to me. When that dreadful squall struck the Bay, the water barge owner came to the chief officer in a state of terror, and told him that you had borrowed the broken boat and had gone round the point into Wooloomooloo Bay. Consternation prevailed. Warnings were sent round to all ships to keep a sharp look out for you. The harbour master, who is here present, on being informed of what we feared, deliberately, and contrary to his better judgment, decided to risk himself and a double crew to pull round the point and search the Bay for you, and they were away in that howling tempest four hours, and with difficulty returned, thoroughly exhausted. The master of the water barge is in a state of utter wretchedness. On board your own ship, from stem to stern, the anxiety and strain have been indescribable. I myself have not been in bed; with you upon my mind, I have had other work to do. What have you to say for yourself?"

The tears were running down my cheeks during this summing up of my case. I could only plead the sudden and altogether unexpected storm, and express my bitter regret that I should have been the cause of so much anxiety to everybody. Turning to the harbour master, I blurted out, "Oh, Sir, I thank you and the crew of the boat for your goodness, and hope you will forgive me."

"Good lad," said he, "you can do no more, but never take liberties again with sunny weather in Sydney Harbour."

Addressing the chief officer, the dear old Captain said: "I suppose we must leave the matter where it is. The boy has had a salutary warning that will last him a lifetime. Robinson, you may go. Don't forget that you have some one else to thank for your deliverance."

I bowed low and backed out of the cabin, hesitating what to do next when I heard the Captain say, "Poor little chap, I could not be too hard upon him, he is so innocent!"

The poor little chap was innocent in those days. I have often thought since, when those four words recur to me – alas, what a wreck of what might have been, and what was certainly Divinely intended to be! I am an old man now: am I voicing similar regrets on the part of others besides myself?

No. 19.

I WAS once in a fix whilst going down Channel in the *Warwick Castle*. We were on our way from London to Dartmouth in winter, and after passing the Sovereign Light Ship about 8 p.m. we ran into a dense fog with syrens and horns all round to cheer us up. It was quite calm, and freezing hard; the drippings from aloft falling upon rails and decks, not to mention ourselves, like snow sludge.

I cannot help thinking now that sailors must be made of jolly good stuff to qualify them for an "all night out" on such occasions; and they are pretty frequent up North.

On this particular voyage we had crawled down as far as the Ower's Light Ship, to the east of the Isle of Wight, when I heard a distant horn a little on the port bow. Sounding our own, I listened, and there it was again. This call and reply was repeated several times, and the other ship appeared to be almost ahead; so I ported a bit to give her more room, and called again – but she still appeared to occupy the same relative position. We ported some more, with the same result.

Concluding that she was bound round the east end of the Wight, and was therefore crossing our track, I ordered the helm a' starboard, and brought our ship round several points. But lo! the answer to each of our calls came from the same relative position still, and the other ship appeared to maintain the same distance from us. I was quite at a loss – so I stopped our engines in order to give our friend a fair field and enable us the better to diagnose the situation. Call, and soft answer, remained the same.

I called to the "look out" on the forecastle head to keep his ears open for the horn ahead; and he replied that he heard none; but, he added, I think it's the cow that you hear, sir! She moans every time, the foghorn sounds! N.B. – Our cow box was lashed in the port fore rigging, at the break of the forecastle.

"Go forward there, one of you, and give that cow a smack over the head with a broom stick every time she answers our whistle."

And so it was. That wretched creature gave us all a bad half-hour, but the remedy was effectual. It sounds funny that the swell commander of a Cape mail steamer should be doing his level best to navigate round his own dairy in a thick fog.

We had a passenger on board at the time who used to write stories in one of the Church papers, I forget which, over the *nom de plume* of Christopher Crayon.[30] I was relating the cow incident at breakfast the following morning, with perhaps a little poetical

---

[30] James Ewing Ritchie.

embellishment, and this gentleman asked my permission to use it for one of his articles, and he did so use it.

A few years afterwards our venerated chief had a luncheon party on board the new steamer, *Dunottar Castle*, in dock. My bluff old friend, Captain Webster, was in command. We were all yarning, as usual, and I related the cow story against myself, to the amusement of our surroundings. When I had finished, Webster, in the most public and candid way, said, "Robinson, you're a dumb liar. I read that yarn before you were born." He was about ten years my senior.

There was rather "a pause in the proceedings," and guests wondered, perhaps, where the duel would take place.

I asked Webster whether he remembered the name of the writer, and he said he did. It was Christopher Crayon! "Yes," I replied, "you are right. He was a passenger with me at the time. Please apologise."

"Oh, well," he said, with a laugh, "if that is so I take it back," and there was no quarrel after all. Sailors are queer fish. I simply remarked that I was glad to find that he read a Church paper, and he accepted the polite impeachment.

What a host of mixed memories the thought of fog conjures up. I really think I must keep the horn blowing a little longer.

Homeward bound in the *Warwick Castle* in 1881, the year of the Great Blizzard in England, we struck fog off Finisterre and had to "feel" our way home across the Bay and the Channel to Plymouth with the aid of the lead and "dead reckoning." It was terribly anxious work. It is quite useless to try to explain the difficulties of such navigation – there are so many influencing items that have to be reckoned with. Suffice it to say that the seaman's "sweet little cherub" over-ruled all for our safe arrival.

It may perhaps be interesting to take a general look at the programme. Given as follows: To proceed absolutely blindfold over three or four hundred miles of ocean, crowded with shipping, across the ebbs and flows in the chops of the English Channel, and pick up the sound signal of the Eddystone Lighthouse, nine miles outside of Plymouth, with the Lizard to the left of you and the Start to the right of you, and the "lead" to give you the depth of water; with your nerves and muscles on the rack after forty or fifty hours on deck at a stretch, and the terrible knowledge that there are some hundreds of human lives depending upon and implicitly trusting the Man on the Bridge! I pity that man who himself has not someone higher still to trust in.

Well, on this particular occasion we had reached a spot where we expected to pick up our objective. It was midnight, calm and smooth, thick as a hedge, and as black as ink. The engines were stopped, and all ears were on the alert.

Suddenly, the fog seemed less dense for a moment and again closed down. Jump to the chronometer! Again less dark for a moment: Time! And again: Time! Eddystone Light! Thank God! We could judge that it was somewhere abreast of us to port, and not far off; so with all confidence we shaped a course for the west end of Plymouth Breakwater and picked up the light. Strangely enough the fog was much thinner inside than out, and we got to anchor safely and blew our signal to the shore.

Not being expected in such weather it was some considerable time before we had communication, and 4 a.m. when we left Plymouth on our way to London. The dense fog had thinned a good bit by that time under the influence of a stiff N.E. wind.

Seven of our gentlemen passengers had elected to run round in the ship. James Searle was one of them; and, I think, Fred Blaine was another. I forget the rest. We had also our Dungeness pilot on board who had joined us at Plymouth.

By the time we rounded the Start it was blowing a gale, and snowing hard. Fog is bad enough; but with it the weather is generally calm, and if you can't see you can hear. But snow is frequently, as on the present occasion, accompanied by wind, and you can neither see nor hear. Snow at sea is the sailor's greatest enemy. A gale of wind plus a snow storm reduces seamanship to zero.

By 10 a.m. with us it was blowing a heavy gale and the snow was continuous in blinding sheets. Our London pilot, Alexander, came up on to the bridge after breakfast, and I shouted into his Sou'-wester: "What do you think of it?"

"Not fit to turn a dog out into," said he.

"I am making for the lee of the Wight to anchor," I said.

"The best thing you can do if you can find your way there," said he.

We struggled on, and providentially met nothing on the way, at all events, nothing within sight or hearing, until about 7 p.m., when the sea began to get smooth. This was the indication we were looking for, and we let go our anchor in 12 fathoms, veered to 105, and lay still!

What a relief! But how it did blow, and freeze, and snow!

Finding that the tide and the wind kept the ship steady on taut cable, we set a strict watch and actually went down to have some dinner. One hour earlier, this would have appeared to be a ridiculous impossibility. After dinner, and a careful look round, our passengers and pilot went with me to my room on the quarterdeck, where we lit a lot of candles and nine pipes, and had a jug of coffee royal to warm us up a bit, dressed up as we were in great coats and comforters. We were pretty closely packed, but made no complaint on that score.

We had no steam heaters in our ships in those days; it was like being in an ice house everywhere.

The decks were quite a foot deep in snow when we came up from dinner, with heavy drifts round all corners. But at 11 o'clock the ship was more like an iceberg than a steamer. The wind had abated, and we were swung round to the ebb. I made an attempt to open my door at that hour, but a snowdrift had practically sealed us up, and we had to apply force in order to squeeze out. It was still snowing heavily; but at midnight it fell dead calm, and, as if by magic, the clouds drifted away to sea like a long white fog bank under a brilliant moon and clear sky, and we lay like a huge wedding cake floating on a silver sea, with St. Catherine's and the Needles lights about equal distances to right and left of us – "For His mercy endureth for ever!"

All hands were piped up to clear ship; but it was 2 a.m. before we got under way and proceeded up Channel.

We were the first ship to get up from Gravesend to the docks for two days. Everything that had been afloat was driven ashore along the river banks, and the river itself was completely frozen over from Gravesend up. A number of smaller vessels that had frozen out below the Nore followed up in our wake as we plowed along, rending the fields of ice with our stem, making a great noise of crashing and banging in the process, for the ice appeared to be about 4 ins. thick.

Our own outward bound steamer, *Dunrobin Castle*, was hung up at Gravesend with a broken steamchest owing to the dreadful frost.

On arrival we found London snowbound, and traffic by road suspended. I quite forget how I got home to Acton, but I found that we had been snowed up, and communication had to be effected by means of chairs from the first floor window down the drift to the road. It was an arctic scene and situation.

But I am reminded of another fog, 6000 miles from the Bay of Biscay, that did not result in a howling blizzard of ice and snow, with train service suspended and telegraph lines on the ground, but which had a remarkably dramatic sequel nevertheless. It was during the war in South Africa.

I was in the *Kildonan Castle*, H.M. Transport No. 44. We arrived in Table Bay one morning about six o'clock, with 2600 troops on board, the weather being very hazy, and the Bay crowded with vessels of all descriptions. I counted 70 myself, but there were more. We anchored off Moulle Point, and signalled our arrival. One poor fellow, a soldier, died after we brought up – the only one we lost during the voyage.

The Port boat came off after breakfast, blowing his fog-horn, because it was getting very thick. Having received pratique, I reported the death, and requested that arrangements should at once be made to land the body for burial. This was agreed to as necessary, and the launch returned to attend to the business.

By the time he reached the dock the fog had closed down dense and white as milk, so that we could not see our own funnels 50 ft. away. The chorus of ship's bells near and far in the calm, fog-bound bay was quite remarkable, and continued for three days and three nights without intermission!

We waited patiently for the return of the launch, keeping our ears open for any indication, but all in vain.

The third morning the surgeon and commanding officer came to me and asked what was to be done? After anxious consultation it was decided that we must bury at sea.

It goes without saying that I dare not move the ship, so the "office" must be performed by means of a lifeboat.

Let it be understood, first of all, that no "committal" must take place inside of 15 fathoms, and we were anchored in 8. A chart of the bay and approaches was laid out, and a position marked upon it with a cross upon it for the "launch." The course from ship to the cross was laid off, and the distance measured. The lifeboat was fitted with a compass, and a patent log, as well as the chart, and a lead line. A special signal by foghorn was fixed upon, which was to be sounded every half minute exactly from the start until the return of the party. The second officer and boat's crew who were to go, accompanied by two military officers, were put through a rehearsal of the programme.

The body was duly placed in the boat, and the funeral service was conducted on board immediately above; and as the firing party and the buglers made their "salute," and sounded the "Last Post" on the forecastle head, the ambassadors of death departed on their mournful mission.

They were immediately lost to sight; even alongside the ship they had been but dimly visible from the deck, but the regular splash of the oars continued audible for a long time in the breathless calm that prevailed, and gradually died away into silence.

Our prearranged signal was religiously observed, and a tense and dramatic quietness pervaded the whole ship during the interval of sound.

I confess that I was extremely anxious myself. The conditions were so unprecedented. I knew that every human precaution had been taken, and that we had only done what was right and necessary; but the minutes dragged along with leaden measure – five, ten, twenty, forty! Hearts were thumping painfully; every ear was strained to the uttermost. A solitary boat, with nine men and a corpse, shut out from all audible or visible connection with a living world, upon a formless waste of secret waters! The mind conjured up all kinds of horrible possibilities.

Whispers here and there – listen – I think – I think – I'm sure – hush – it's fancy – no – don't you hear? I do – Yes! – and at last! After forty-five long-drawn minutes we did faintly hear that welcome rhythm as it gradually became audible to all – and a spontaneous cheer went up from 2000 throats that must have encouraged the still invisible members of that devoted band to a realisation of safety and renewed effort.

What a great relief it was to us all when we received them safely on board!

On questioning the second officer (whose name I cannot recall, I am sorry to say, though himself I remember perfectly) it would appear that we were not alone in conjuring up weird fancies. When they had reverently committed the body to its watery grave, it seemed for a moment to stand up in the fog and look at them; and though they pulled away manfully, the impression remained that they were glued to the spot unable to get clear of the dread vision, until they picked up the sound of our special signal, and heard the cheers of the soldiers on board.

"Pray never send me away on such a duty again," he added; "I would almost rather be buried myself!"

No. 20.

WHAT a crowd! and what a glorious day! and what a wealth of beautiful plants and flowers! and music! Well, the Band was doing its best – and none can do more than that.

Amidst this brilliant maze of life and light, where art and science mingled with sweet sound and Nature's fragrant gifts lent sad delight to breaking hearts around, I stood observant – until named I turned – and lights grew dim and tone and colour fled. All else suspended, startled vision earned full recompense instead. As when some soft effulgence haloed round with loyal rays concentric all absorbs of outward things – so she, with locks unbound and shy half-veiled orbs; and on mine ear there stole in accents mild the dreamy semblance of a distant prayer: "May we intreat your interest in this child and leave her in your care?" Yea, be it on my head, my lips replied; while conscience, trembling 'neath a trust so great – upon thy heart it shall be, inly cried, as low I bent to Fate! Too eager time my transient joy has sapped; too well my vow has borne the unequal strife! alone, how cold; the last dear love-link snapped that bound my soul to life.[31]

Don't be alarmed, gentle reader. I'm not a flirt. This little bit of sentiment was only written in the album of one of my many fair wards, who was going out to South Africa to be married, to record my admiration for her decorous and amiable conduct during the voyage. It was 36 years ago. She was a very beautiful girl of 19 then: a handsome middle-aged lady now, no doubt, somewhere in the giddy Continent. Her maiden name is hidden in the above paragraph.

I don't know what my brother Commanders may think of such commissions, but to me it was always a kind of nightmare to be asked to take charge of girls going out to meet their destiny abroad, so many of them seemed to think the voyage and the novel surroundings a delightful opportunity for a last fling.

It is a strange trait of nature under such circumstances that young men, as a rule, pay more marked attention to young women who are known to be engaged than to those who are free; perhaps because they think they are safe with the first, whereas they might get entangled in the meshes of the eligible maidens. Perhaps also the romance of a pre-arrangement may awaken the instinct of inquiry as to the why and wherefore of the absent member.

Young folks forget also that on board ship they are of necessity thrown together as they never are elsewhere. One day at sea is about equal to a year on shore on so that it needs a genuine love and a loyal

---

[31] This strange paragraph is actually a six-stanza rhyming poem.

memory to counteract the distracting magnetism of hourly homage on the part of an attractive novelty unconsciously wearing his or her best Sunday-go-to-meeting manners within the sacred sphere of influence. I think it was the great Dr. Chalmers who said something about "the expulsive force of a new affection." Could any words in our comprehensive language more aptly apply to the situation?

How strange it appears to us – that each young person is launched upon the sea of life without any knowledge of the art of swimming; and they have to learn by personal and often bitter experience what their fathers and mothers have been unable to teach them.

It is no easy matter for a stranger to sit in judgment, let alone teach the young idea how to shoot. No two temperaments are alike. No two observers occupy the same point of view. The faulty finds defects in every mirror. We can only fall back upon the ancient law of charity, which thinks no evil and hopes for the best.

It is such thoughts and fears as these, based upon a few queer little episodes of past experience, that have rather scared me when the request, so frequently uttered, has been repeated. Of course it is impossible to refuse such appeals. To whom can the anxious father or mother apply but to the captain of the ship that their darling is to travel by – unless they have friends amongst the passengers? And what responsibility does the acceptance carry? I take it that the request is not a bald formality, nor yet an empty compliment. I have generally turned to the young lady in question and asked whether it is her own wish that I should assume parental care of her – during the voyage – or whether she looks upon the matter as a mere introduction and manner of speech. The reply was nearly always an index to the outlook.

I am not going to sling ink at random over the few incidents that have marred the white pages of the past; but let me just give one or two simple illustrations of happenings that have worried me at the time. It will not hurt anyone, for I shall give no names; and anyhow they are ancient history.

A young lady of good family in the Midlands was specially commended to my care by her father and mother and uncles and aunts. She rejoiced in a hyphenated name, and was going out to Natal to be married. It was in the *Warwick Castle*, and our destination was Algoa Bay.

During the outward voyage I did all I could to make her feel that she was cared for, and I thought that all was well. We were well on our way to Cape Town when an elderly gentleman asked me whether she were not going out to be married, as it appeared that she had transferred her affections to a military officer on board, with whom she was flirting rather freely.

I had noticed nothing, which plainly indicated that I was a poor hand at guardianship; but being warned I soon discovered that I had been very much asleep. A favourable opportunity offering, I asked her whether it were not unwise to permit marked attention to be paid to her on board, seeing that all knew she was going out to he married? My astonishment may be imagined when she actually put her thumb to her nose, and spreading her fingers out, said: "Mind your own business; I can look after mine."

"Of course," I replied, "you are no longer under my care." She laughed and left. I sent and asked the gentleman to come and see me, and explained the situation to him. He denied that there was any serious understanding between them, and said it was only a little *quelque chose pour passer le temps.* "It must stop," I said. "Very well; stop it is," he replied.

The next day we arrived at Cape Town, and he went ashore. The lady went on with us to Algoa Bay, and transhipped to the *Melrose* for Natal.

A fortnight later on she returned by the *Melrose* from Natal, and came on board of us to select a cabin for the homeward voyage. I asked if her husband were going with her, and was not surprised to hear that she was still single, and had changed her mind on meeting her *fiancé* in Durban. I recommended her to book her passage in the *Garth Castle*, which would follow us a week later, as she had been rather talked about on board; and she took the gentle hint and disappeared from my horizon.

Once again. Quite a large party – the head of our firm being one of them – came on board in England to see a young lady off, who was to be married to a gentleman holding a Government appointment at Cape Town. I was sent for, introduced, and requested to act as guardian during the voyage to a tall, handsome, aristocratic looking girl, about two and twenty years of age.

Our chief came to my room afterwards and told me to take her alongside of me at table, and to do all I could to make her voyage an enjoyable one. He said she and her fiancé were the links between two important county families, friends of his, and that great estates were involved.

Having received such a charge from such a source, I treated my ward as I would my own daughter, and we got along famously. After crossing the equator a concert was got up amongst the passengers, and my princess was announced on the programme for the first song in the second part. She was highly trained and had a beautiful voice. I was in the chair that evening, and the saloon was crowded to hear her.

When her turn came, I rose and announced what I knew to be the event of the evening, but there was no princess. The stewardess was sent to her cabin to notify her, but she was not there. I was just upon the point of calling for the second event, when a gentleman passenger came to me with the princess's compliments and regrets that, having a headache, she would not be able to sing that evening!

"Who gave you that message?"

"She, herself."

"Where is she?"

"On deck at the stern."

"Sit down, please; I will go and see her."

I went: and in the dark as I stepped quickly towards her, she turned sharply round and threw her arms round my neck! For a moment only – and then collapsed in a deluge of tears and sobs. It was my turn now; I took her in my arms and talked pater familias to her. I managed to persuade her that she was in danger of making an awful *faux pas*, but that so far no one on board was any the wiser – "so run down, my dear, and sponge your face, and take your part bravely; we will suspend further conversation until to-morrow."

I hastened down and announced her coming, and in a few minutes she came in and took the audience by storm most pluckily, and retired afterwards to her cabin.

After the concert had ended, I also retired to my cabin and sent for the gentleman. I may as well introduce him at once. A shortish perky-looking young fellow of the Jockey type; a great sportsman on board, and able to sing comic songs, and carry more than his ration of whisky without a lurch.

He came, in a defiant spirit, not quite sober, but still able to converse.

"Sit down, please. I have ascertained this evening that you have been poaching upon another man's preserves. How? You are, I am quite sure, aware that a certain young lady who is under my care is going out to Cape Town to be married."

"Well?"

"Is that, in your opinion, a gentlemanly procedure?"

"All's fair in love and war."

"Would you be equally complacent to another if your own sister were in question?"

"Well, it depends."

"Does it depend upon your claim to be a gentleman?"

Silence – and then the whisky began to run down his cheeks, and there was evidently some tender essence hidden beneath his jaunty exterior. He promised at last to cease his attentions if I would promise not to give him away.

So ended the interview, and chapter one; and I kept a sharp look out, assisted by a keener one in my good, motherly old stewardess.

In due course we arrived at Cape Town. It was 8 a.m. Breakfast-time. My ward was absent. Under the circumstances of our arrival, packing up, and all that kind of thing, I waited for her, chatting with our parting guests.

"A gentleman to see you, Sir, at your cabin."

"All right, steward." I found him standing in my cabin, very pale, and evidently much moved. Salutations over, he introduced himself, though I had easily guessed who it was. A tall, handsome well-bred man about 30 years of age, the very beau ideal of a gentleman.

"I have come on board to welcome a lady passenger by your ship, Miss —, to whom I am engaged to be married; and she refuses to see me! Can you throw any light upon this surprise?"

"Before we we go any further," I said, "excuse me for a moment whilst I go and see her myself. Please sit down."

A trembling voice said "Come in," and I entered. My princess was standing, dressed ready to land, pulling a white kid glove to pieces in a state of great agitation. " Mr. —, who is in my cabin, tells me that you have refused to see him – surely some mistake?"

She hung her head and muttered that she had changed her mind. I seized her by the two shoulders, face to face. "Do you really mean to say that you have allowed that insignificant little whisky drinking mountebank to come between you and that splendid young Apollo who is in my cabin? Have you so far lost the sense of your own beautiful personality that you should contemplate so great a sacrifice?"

Tears and sobs were for a few moments the only response. Then: "Spare me, O spare me, you are prejudiced against Mr. —, and don't know how good he is. I cannot help it!"

"Now, listen; you are my daughter for the time being, by request of your parents and friends in England; and I shall exercise my right whilst you reconsider your altogether unaccountable and mad resolve. You shall not leave the ship without my permission. Any attempt to do so would only lead to an undignified and compromising disturbance. I will come and see you again later on, my dear; let me recommend you to seek counsel from Above in the meantime."

On reaching the deck, I found, on inquiry, that the sporting gentleman had gone ashore. I gave strict orders that he was on no account to be allowed on board again without my permission; I took the good old stewardess and the chief officer into my confidence on the other's account.

In my cabin I found the anxious but dignified *fiancé*. Without giving her away too much, I told him that she had evidently lost her head for the moment in a board-ship caprice, which I hoped we should be able to disarm. "But," I said, "are you quite sure you are willing to overlook such temporary disloyalty, and to hold me clear of all blame if I intervene successfully?"

"More than willing," he replied. "We have known one another from childhood, and have been engaged for over two years. I love the ground she stands upon."

I told him what steps I had taken for the present, and recommended him to go away and bring some special lady friends down with him at once to greet her and stay to lunch on board, but to keep his own counsel.

A former chief steward of mine was manager of the Royal Hotel. He came on board just then, and casually remarked that Mr. Sporting Johnnie had been in and engaged two bedrooms and a sitting-room, and that he was none too sober.

A short time afterwards there was a controversy at the gangway, and the poor chap demanded to see the captain. I went ashore, and, leading him away, showed him how he had gone behind his promise to me, and how impossible his behaviour was. He was tipsy and noisy, and claimed that he was "a man," and had a man's feelings, and he loved the girl – and the whisky ran down his cheeks like rain.

I pitied the poor beggar from my heart. I had no idea that he was capable of such deep feeling, even in his cups. Looking him straight in the face, I said: "You claim to be a 'man'" – do you also claim to be a gentleman?"

"Yes, I do," he replied.

"Then," I said, "you will take the first train to Johannesburg, where you are going, and so play a true gentleman's part in a spirit of self-sacrifice that you will never regret, knowing that by almost wrecking the lives of an engaged couple you have been nearly forgetting that you are the gentleman you claim to be."

Sobbing his heart out, he blurted out that it was a cruel thing, but he was a man and a gentleman, and he would go to Johannesburg and never come back.

"Now," I said, "you are the man I take you for. Good-bye!"

"But, Captain" – between his tipsy sobs – "mayn't I go on board and say good-bye to her?"

"Most certainly not. Good-bye."

I was a guest at the wedding in the cathedral on the day following, but I did not go to the breakfast at – – .

The luncheon gong

Concert on deck

**Postcards of life on board published by the Union-Castle Line
between 1900 and 1914**

No. 21.

NO, I'm not a pessimist; only a bit of a philosopher.

Quite true that the last paper appeared to deal mostly with failures; but really they were nothing more than contrasts. Life at sea is not made up altogether of disappointments; there are rosy sunsets as well as showers of rain; golden dawns as well as gales of wind; and we cannot shut out one without reducing the other. No one loves the lower level less than I, but without the deeper shades the higher lights would lack speciality.

I've had a fair share of both during my 30 years in command of Castle and Union-Castle mail steamers. What privileges I have enjoyed! Thirty years of pre-eminence and sole responsibility upon God's beautiful ocean in all winds, all weathers, without cross or casualty. "For His mercy endureth for ever!" How little I have deserved so large a share of immunity.

We were launched upon the subject of "wards in chancery" in our last paper, and drifted downward by the force of gravity into the regions of melodrama; but the downgrade has its limits, and the ascendant is the rule.

Brides a-many I have sailed with – to the Sunny, Golden South; but I once took out the future inspiration of "South Africa" herself[32] – a merry, winsome maiden, who, with or without her own knowledge and consent, was generally known as "Sunshine" on board the ship, never having been seen without an infectious smile upon her bonny face and a sunny twinkle in her laughing eyes. No wonder the top line on the title page had to be added since then.[33]

What a wonderful asset inherent amiability is. It lifts up everything and everybody within its radiance, and nothing but cussedness can resist its influence or doubt the purity of its service. I suppose that all mankind, masculine and feminine, likes to be loved, and instinctively hungers for it; and yet the vile ego within fights against the weakness of betrayal and finds refuge in scorn.

Amiability is a thing that cannot be assumed or imitated. A churl trying to rake up warmth from a cold heart in order to kindle a glow upon his frontispiece succeeds only in looking like a bull pup with a stomach ache, and fails even to awaken the sympathy that the corkscrew-tailed beast would.

---

[32] Mary Augusta Powys who married the editor of *South Africa*. See No. 23.

[33] "Largest circulation of any South African newspaper."

It was very early in the eighties, and, I think, on board the *Pembroke Castle*, that I first met Lady S. A. – nearly 40 years ago – and "Her bright smile haunts me still," as the old song has it. We had quite a nice little company of travellers with us that voyage; one or two of whom have become notables since then, and are pillars of the Southern tentacle of the Imperial Octopus. Mr. Henry Juta, as he then was – now the great judge Sir Henry – was one of them.

It amuses me when I think of it, and I expect it amuses him also to think that he once played the prank of "Counsel for the Defence" in a mock trial by jury on board the *Pembroke* that voyage, with Lady Sunshine for his junior, the captain being judge – than whom a greater burlesque of the wig and gown could scarcely be found.

The case was based upon the assumed theft by a depraved ruffian – a very harmless looking gentleman – of a set of false teeth belonging to a deeply aggrieved but otherwise smiling sufferer. The teeth were on view in court, the set having been skilfully carved out of a turnip, but by mistake evidently intended to fit a cow and not a human being.

Well, what's the odds so long as you're happy. Small things please large minds in small ships on the mighty ocean. The procedure was at all events dignified and correct, and the pleadings *pro* and *con* foreshadowed the stately future in embryo.

I hope I shall not be indicted for *lèse-majesté* should Sir Henry come across this revival of a buried frolic.

The finding of the Court was never reached. The Junior Counsel in her "defence" surrounded the case with such a glamour of injured innocence and attractive personality that the Judge's spectacles required constant attention, and his notes got into arrears. There is no telling how it might have finished, but a sudden squall of wind and rain struck the ship at the critical moment and the judge promptly fled to take charge of another case which was very much more in his line.

He was accused afterwards of having forgotten to disrobe before making so hasty a retreat from the Bench to the Bridge – but this requires confirmation.

Our court case reminds me of a somewhat similar antic on board of another ship, when Henry Dickens, afterwards K.C., the son of Charles the Great, was a passenger with me.

Amongst other amusements inaugurated, a poem competition was set going, with a prize as incentive. The verses I sent in were adjudged the best; but one disappointed competitor started the report that the lines were not my own, and that I had fraudulently submitted a bogus attempt to snatch the prize.

A court case was called, and Dickens was judge. Two clever attorneys were counsel *pro* and *con*, and I was the prisoner in the dock. Dickens as judge in his summing-up was really magnificent; and I felt myself to be the meanest creature unhanged. I am not at all sure that many others of those present were not similarly impressed.

In his charge to the jury (a disgracefully packed one of saucy girls and young bounders), the judge called upon them to decide whether I had written the lines out of my own head, or had dishonestly copied them from a production of the brains belonging to the Captain's boy. It was a foregone conclusion. The verdict was: "Guilty, without extenuating circumstances."

There were tears – crocodile's – upon many faces during the Bench's eloquent and impassioned exhortation to the prisoner to turn over a new leaf and keep it clean for the future. The Sentence of the Court was – that I was to receive the prize there and then, and hand it over to my cabin boy with many apologies for my trespass before the whole session.

With a police officer in uniform on either side of me there was no other course open but to obey; and I have never felt quite honest since.

To return, however, to the voyage of the *Pembroke Castle* and Lady Sunshine.

I have an idea that women are women's best critics. I have another idea, that in this most people will agree with me. When girls run after some particular one, and pick up her fan, and hand her things, and pay her little quiet attentions – be sure that the recipient is a "Kimberley White."[34] Lady Sunshine was generally the centre of a little group of devotees on deck, and though perhaps the youngest amongst them, it was wonderful how she used to mother them all.

It was a repetition of my own early experience. My dear wife was a passenger on board ship, a young girl going out to join her married sister in Australia,[35] and all the other ladies on board used to worship her. It was quite extraordinary. This set me thinking; and I was thinking still when she joined the angels eight years ago; and now I know, and am looking forward.

Among the fair ladies on board the *Pembroke* was a handsome Viennese named Elsa, going out to be married also. She shared a cabin with her friend Sunshine, and passed most of her time in confidential rhapsodies anent her future Adonis, who was also Viennese, and was settled down to farming in the Free State.

She was of an imaginative and romantic disposition, and held animated converse with her distant lover gazing at the stars, fully persuaded that he was constantly and similarly occupied. She could speak

---

[34] A superior kind of diamond.
[35] There is a fuller account of this on page 214.

English fairly well, and on moonlight nights used to gurgle along by the hour for Lady Sunshine's benefit, apostrophising her beloved Emil.

Her timid little mother and *gouvernante* were passengers also, her guardians during the voyage; but they could speak no English and were rather forlorn, sitting apart very silent and gazing back across the waters towards their beloved Homeland.

Elsa was a nice, simple girl in spite of her sentimental bias, and was very circumspect on board, and true to her *fiancé*. She had quite a shipment of elaborate and expensive furniture and outfit of every kind for her new home in the Free State – a veritable white elephant in a farmhouse.

The great Emil had promised her in his last letter to camp out on the wharf at Cape Town, in order that his noble form should be the first object in view when the steamer arrived, making the grand old Table Mountain sink into insignificance.

The morning came! No Emil! Strained vision and aching hearts on board! Table Mountain, however, was there all right. Great consternation! Such twitterings on the part of the little chaperones – such loudly expressed despair on that of Elsa!

Lady Sunshine in her sweet charity endeavoured to pacify her, telling her that all would be well, – but no! She herself must go at once and look for her missing lover; and go she did, in a ramshackle Cape Town cab, driven by a picturesque Malay in a conical and comical straw hat, and no trousers.

They had not been long gone, when a bronzed and shabby-looking man, with a very dirty and unshaven face, came on board – the great Emil! The little mother and *gouvernante*, assisted by Lady Sunshine, explained to him the unexpected absence of his beloved, and advised him to wait. He was keen upon returning to look for her – when fortunately the cab arrived on the scene, and Elsa, pale and weeping, got out.

"Emil is here!" we all called out at once. She bounded up the gangway, saw him, hesitated, and shrieked out "That is not my Emil!"

To make a long story short, she absolutely refused to have anything to do with the poor man, and went into her cabin and banged the door in a storm of hysterical sobs, leaving us all outside to comfort the miserable Emil. Somebody – I think it was Lady Sunshine – was struck with a brilliant idea. Emil was sent off instantly to get bathed, washed, shaved, have his moustache waxed, get into a smart, ready-made suit of clothes, and return when he was made up – as soon as possible.

In a very short time he appeared unrecognisable, and the wisdom of the suggestion was manifest. A strikingly handsome Emil came to claim his beautiful bride. (N.B. – What a mortifying reflection it is that a man depends so much upon his clothes! When the youngster was just

116

starting from home for his first Eton term, and his loving mother reminded him that clothes did not constitute the gentleman, he replied, "No, dear mother; I know. It's the hat." – *Punch*. Nevertheless, clothes are a most important item. There would be a good deal more democratic equality in rank and estimation if all the world ran about in *puris naturalibus*. Form and bearing would be Royal insignia then, and *vice versa*.)

We got Elsa to open her cabin door, pushed Emil in, and awaited developments.

After dramatic moments, broken sobs, and a soulful silence, out came the pair hand in hand, looking rather sheepish, but very happy.

We all agreed that an immediate wedding was the diplomatic move to make, so we all accompanied the party to the Cathedral, saw them securely tied up, drank their health and everlasting happiness at a champagne lunch, and felt that we had earned a few days' peace, which we enjoyed on our way round the coast to Natal.

I heard some time afterwards that Elsa did not take kindly to the rough life in the Colony, and the happy pair took flight and returned to Europe to be absorbed.

There were no grounds for temporary hitches and diplomatic scheming when we reached the Garden Colony; everything went off as merrily as marriage bells, and I am happy to say they have been ringing the changes ever since – and long may they continue to chime the meridian ascendant.

It was in November that we arrived in Durban Bay, and anchored on a glorious afternoon. What a beautiful panorama was unrolled to view as we rounded the Bluff; and how all the looking-glasses along the Berea were set going, flashing welcomes to the new arrivals. It was grand.

Even to old *habitués* at such a time, Durban, the magnificent, is a veritable dream of peaceful repose. What must it mean to the heart-beat of a receptive bride-elect – who, for the first time, wonders, and drinks in the golden promise with the homing instincts of her sex?

But it is no business of ours to chronicle events of too tender a nature for presumptuous pens to outline, however much pleasure there may be in moralising upon the environments.

I shall never forget my own impressions the first time I arrived and anchored in that highly-favoured corner of creation. I wanted to do nothing but sit down and study the picture; and that is a considerable time ago. I cannot remember the year, but it was before the Point Railway was laid, as it is now. The funny little "train service", from the Point to Durban was a crooked, lumpy little bit of track laid on what they called mushroom sleepers, like inverted saucepan lids on a large scale. These were just laid on the sand, and carried a narrow gauge of metals over lumps and hollows at various angles and elevations, which necessitated a very slow advance to prevent the queer little engine from leaving the line.

It did leave the metals one day when I was a first-class passenger in a kind of cattle truck, and we had to tramp along over the sand. It was a tiring process, but we thought little of such things in those primitive days; we had not been spoiled by luxurious and extravagant conveniences.

There were only two or three houses, very small ones, too, between the Point settlement and the end of West Street; and West Street itself was very thinly furnished with mansions.

Now, I wonder, what year that may have been! I think it was about 1874 or 1875. Durban was small and scattered then, and the Berea was mostly woodland and very picturesque.

It seems to me, judging by my own personal experience alone, that South Africa must have sprung up from Genesis· to Grandeur in a very short time and at a great rate. Cape Town itself, when I first visited it, was a settlement of flat-roofed houses with broad stoeps in front of every one of them reaching to the roadway, and having no footpaths or pavements. It used to be a common saying, too, that a man could easily find his way blindfold from the primitive little dock to the post office in Adderley Street by the smells on the way. The present purity of the atmosphere speaks wonders for the engineering enterprise of the last few years. But I am getting off my track, and expect I shall be having the witch doctors after me to smell me out if I don't stop.

Stop it is.

The two next pieces seem to be JC's tributes in fiction to powerful men who had helped him. Rowbotham is JC, who lost his wife to a stroke in October 1913, and his youngest son and daughter, as described, in November 1914. This piece appeared in the December 20th 1919 issue, the fifth anniversary of his children's deaths but is apparently set around 1916. His oldest son Charles Douglas served as a Major in the North Staffordshire Regiment during WWI.

In this piece he thanks the chairman of the Union-Castle Company – at that time it was Sir Owen Cosby Philipps who became Baron Kylsant, but the physical description sounds more like Sir Donald Currie.

In No. 23, JC is evidently thanking the editor of South Africa *(Edward P. Mathers) for accepting his memoirs for publication; then he resumes his reminiscences with a celebration of Christmas with royalty, the Duke and Duchess of Connaught, on board the* Armadale Castle *in late 1905, the year before he came ashore.*

No. 22.

LADEN WITH CHRISTMAS GREETINGS TO OLD AND YOUNG

The head of the Firm sat alone in his private office at the end of the Board table with his back to the fire, having in front of him several piles of important-looking documents and letters, and the usual outfit of the busy man; but at the moment he was leaning back in his chair linking and unlinking his fingers, evidently absorbed in contemplation.

His eyes were directed towards the nearer of the windows overlooking the street, watching the feathery snowflakes in their millions falling silently and softly – there being no wind – and gradually but surely filling up all the sills and copings with pure and beautiful little drifts. It was a fairy winter scene, though in one of the noisiest of London's unquiet streets.[36]

He was a robust, elderly man, with grey hair and beard, and projecting brows that gave his dark eyes a deep set appearance; but this only accentuated the evidence of profound calm and quiet power, the secret of his gracious disposition; a man to be depended upon, and to be trusted, but not played with.

Returning to the matters in front of him, Sir Percy Oldham passed a number of papers under review, and pausing at one in particular, he touched the electric bell at his side, and, a uniformed attendant entering, he quietly said: "My compliments to Mr. Chase, please, and ask him to see me." The manager came in immediately, bringing a still further parcel of documents, and with a bow took the chair beside Sir Percy.

"I see by this statement that our old pensioner Rowbotham has had an accident of some kind."

"Well, it's scarcely an accident, Sir Percy; but a little too much energy in gardening at his age has led to internal trouble that called for an immediate and serious operation."

"Has anyone seen him – I mean from ourselves?"

"Yes, sir. Mr. Waldron went down on hearing of his illness, and tells me that he found him in a deplorable state at home. He interviewed his doctor, who said that he would have to return to hospital, and probably undergo a second operation."

"I think it would be a better plan for him to go into the nursing home which is under the superintendence of the surgeon who performed the operation. Please arrange this at once. See that

---

[36] The Union-Castle office was in Fenchurch Street.

he has the best quarters available, and that he wants for nothing; and give instructions that he is to remain there until the surgeon can give him an absolutely clean bill of health. Let no expense be spared. By the bye, was he not in some trouble a year or two ago?"

"Yes, sir, he lost his wife suddenly, and his youngest son, an officer in the Navy, and his youngest daughter, a hospital nurse at Cape Town, all within a few weeks; and you were good enough to send Mr. Pickford down to make inquiries as to his consequent expenses and financial position, which resulted in your passing a cheque for £100 on his account."

"Ah, yes, I remember. Poor old fellow. He has had a lot of trouble. Well, please arrange this nursing home matter for me, Mr. Chase, and keep me posted upon the result. It will be a sad Christmas for him – and for many more, I am afraid."

"Rowbotham's eldest son has been serving on the Continent since the beginning of the war."

"Thank you, Mr. Chase."

Suddenly the church bells near by commenced ringing the Christmas chimes – ding dong, ding dong, ding dong, ding dong – and the old man leaned back in his chair again, and once more indulged in reverie.

> Hark! merrily peal the Christmas chimes,
> The old, old story ringing.
> Hail clamouring tongues, your brazen rhymes
> Are ever heart's ease bringing.
> Your praise rebounds from Heaven's own gates
> With songs of angels blended;
> Where He who trod this earth awaits
> The flock that once He tended
> Sweet Christmas bells! your cadence sounds
> Rich music in our ears.

On reaching home Sir Percy heard his wife at the piano singing a Christmas Carol; and before removing his outer wraps he went into the drawing-room quietly, and stooping over her saluted her with a loving kiss. She was so startled by the unexpected assault that the Carol stopped on "B natural!" and jumping up, she returned the compliment with a rosy smile; then laying her hands on his shoulders she asked, "Why this delightful ebullition of Auld Lang Syne?"

Taking her lovingly in his arms he said, "I can't tell why, sweetheart, but I think the bells have inspired me this evening with a clearer vision of the bright beyond; and your voice as I entered the house seemed to suggest the reality of angels on this as well as on the starlit side of the Christmas proclamation."

"Well," said she, "is Percy also amongst the prophets? Praise to the Holiest in the height! I, too, have been magnetised into life this day as I have never been before. Evidently the double effect is based upon a common cause – and it must be a very happy one. Now be quick, dear, or you will keep dinner waiting. The gong will be sounding directly."

Ding-dong, ding-dong.

One of London's great lawyers was standing before the fire, in his private sanctum, with one foot on the fender, holding a letter in his hand, and apparently in deep thought. The same beautiful snow was falling in similar feathery flakes and unostentatiously but remorselessly covering over every lodgment of the houses in the court; but not a sound was heard without, except the occasional muffled rumble of a distant cab ploughing along through the snow-smothered streets.

He was a tall, handsome man with dark hair and eyes, clean shaven, of good colour, and with a kindly all embracing expression that made clients feel that they were under observation by a first rate man. He may have been about 45 or 50 years of age.

A knock at the door, and a clerk looked in and announced: "A gentleman to see you, Sir." There was a very cordial greeting when the caller entered, an elderly man, and evidently an old friend of Mr. Joseph Elder's. After the ordinary compliments and exchange of news covering some months since they last met, Mr. Elder referred to the letter in his hand.

"It is rather a strange coincidence," said he, "that you should drop in just now, as I was reading this and figuring out the next move. You remember the £25 you sent me some months ago to use in any case of need?"

"Yes," replied his friend.

"Well, I have an old client away down in the country who has got into debt with his banker; and he wrote asking me to try and get him a job of some kind that would enable him to put in a bit of war service for the country, and help to pay off this debt; but he is over 75 years of age, and though hale and hearty, I could get no one to look at him. I have known him many years and have a great regard for him. He is a pensioner, and the inflated war expenses have rather submerged him. Well, I thought it was just the kind of thing you would approve of – so I added another twenty-five to yours and sent him a cheque for fifty, with a nice little letter. By return of post I got the cheque back again, along with a polite note of thanks, and an intimation that it was service he asked for, not subscriptions. I followed his lead by sending the offending cheque back again, telling him not to be too thin skinned, but just to pay it into his bankers and say no more about it. And now, here it is again by return of post! And he asks whether we have no 'Red Cross' or 'King's Fund' in London, that we are seeking to waste our money in this way! What am I to do with such a client? He says I am the queerest sample of a legal adviser that he has ever collided with."

With a laugh, his friend replied: "Let us send it back again, and tell him it is a Christmas present from friends of his who wish to be *incog.*, and that they will be extremely hurt if he still refuses their little seasonable offering."

Ding dong, ding dong, ding dong, ding dong.

Break gently to the breaking heart
That Time means not for ever:
That friends shall meet, no more to part,
Beyond the shadowy river.
Console the poor, with care opprest;
And beckon toil-worn mortals
To Him who gives the weary rest
Within the pearly portals,
Sweet Christmas bells – your joyful song
Dries up the mourner's tears.

On reaching Mr. Elder's house the two friends were met in the hall by the hostess, who flew to meet her husband without noticing their visitor, and with happy tears exclaimed: "Oh, Hubbie, look at this! What do you think – I have received a wire this afternoon from the nurse at the hospital in France, saying that they have found the bullet at last and have removed it, and Jack bore the operation well and is pronounced out of danger. Oh, listen to the Christmas bells. How they do express my gratitude for this wonderful and unexpected mercy! Last week struck down and condemned to die – and to-day he is alive again!"

Introducing his friend, Mr. Elder explained that Jack was his wife's only brother; and folding her lovingly in his arms he pressed his cheek to her forehead, and murmured: "Sweet Christmas bells, sweetheart!"

"I, too," said his friend, "feel their influence this evening as I have never felt it before since I was in my teens! I wonder why?"

Ding dong, ding dong.

LADEN WITH CHRISTMAS GREETINGS TO OLD AND YOUNG

Scarcely beyond a stone's throw from them in Great Babylon the influential Editor of a great periodical sat before a vast pile of literature and reference books of every description, with a big waste paper basket alongside his chair and a large slim business looking pair of scissors and long steel paper knife beside his pad.

He was smiling to himself, not unkindly, over a letter in his hand from a presumptuous aspirant after literary honours, and soliloquising occasionally as he read it over a second time.

"Humph. Oh, I dare say. I ha'e my doubts. You would – would you? All very well, and yet – perhaps – perhaps – Oh! I see; it's pot-boiling he's after, not notoriety. That argument applies to a good many scribblers, I doubt. I'm not sure there was not – ah! but that's long ago. Well – yes – I think I'll give him a chance – with a proviso. I hope he will succeed. Times are hard, I know, through this cursed Kaiserism. I feel it myself."

A clerk and notebook entered in response to a touch of the bell.

"Please take down as follows: 'Dear Mr. So-and-So, – I have your letter of the 22nd, and am disposed to give you a fair chance, reserving to myself the right of alteration or correction if necessary, and suggesting that you be wary of dealing with matters of a controversial nature. So send in a contribution when you like. Yours truly, &c.'"

"So. That's done. At this time of year we cannot afford to close the wells of kindness to any – let alone those that we know – for who can tell?"

Ding dong, ding dong, ding dong, ding dong.

"What ho! outside there – go round and brain those ringers, I can't think."

> The time is nigh when ye shall ring
> Your last glad Gospel story;
> And meet before the coming King
> In finished strains of glory.
> Alive with chimes, the Heavens shall reel
> In sudden maze of splendour,
> And burst in one last shivering peal
> To greet the saint's Defender.
> Sweet Christmas bells – 'twill not be long
> Ere Christ Himself appears.

"Well, it's quite certain that I cannot do any more work with that music so near to me. And it is near to me, somehow – more than usual. I'll go home. Let's see; what can I take with me for Sunshine in this snowstorm?"

Opening the communication door, the Editor said: "Good evening, every one. I wish you all the compliments of the season. Thanks. Mr. Erskine, a word with you; close the door, please. Do the usual thing, and don't keep open longer than necessary. I shall not be back until after New Year's Day. Farewell!" And, shaking hands cordially, he left the mill – the daily grind – for –

"Oh, Edward, how late you are! Where have you been? How did you come? I have been so terribly anxious."

"Why has my darling been terribly anxious?"

"Why, what a question! Look at the night – look at the weather! As dark as pitch; and the terrible snow, snow, snow. All sorts of evil possibilities have been crowding my mind and making me miserable. What if you had met with an accident? My dear Edward, how did you come from the City?"

"Well, I knew there would be no chance of getting a seat in the Underground, so I took a taxi; and we very nearly did meet with an accident. But I wanted to call at the 'Stores' on the way to get a little Christmas present for a charming lady of my acquaintance. There it is – a pair of winter gauntlets to keep your busy fingers warm."

"Oh, my dear Edward – how sinful of you to run risks at such a time for me! How did you nearly have an accident?"

"Why, another taxi, with a driver none too sober I fear, came rushing across out of Sloane Street without 'sounding,' and we couldn't see ten yards ahead of us. Our chauffeur slapped on the brake and pitched me nearly through the front window, and the handle of our starting crank caught the guard of the other fellow's hind wheel and was badly bent. Whether the guard was injured or not I don't know – he didn't stop, but went tearing along in the fog. I think it must have been what Sunshine would call a special Providence that intervened, for nothing less could have saved us I am sure. There, there, sweetheart, it's all over – and here I am, safe and sound, to be a lot more trouble to you yet."

"How dreadful! How awful! What about the driver?"

"I kept him to have something warm before he starts again."

"I'll go and see him, my husband – he is my preserver!"

"Well, don't spoil him over much, my dear."

Ding dong, ding dong.

Amen, so be it. What Christmas seasons have we spent at sea! It makes me smile, in spite of the tragedy of it, to think what tears may have diluted the sauce of the plum puddings at Home, as sad memories of an absent member arose who was far away upon the dark waters of the ever restless ocean. Poor absent member. Poor maligned sea.

Let me conjure up a special scene upon an extra special occasion.

A brilliant Christmas morning upon the bosom of a calmly azure bay (which as a rule is dreaded for its ruthless reputation), a whole ship's company, passengers and crew, gathered together on the quarter deck, with harmonium and hymn books. The British ensign streaming over the stern to greet the invisible choirs in harmony. "Eight bells" strikes, and led by our British monarch's brother – H.R.H. the Duke of Connaught, with his Duchess and their beautiful daughter the Princess Patricia – that motley throng, stirred to the very foundations of their being with thoughts of "Home, sweet Home" and loved ones far away, raise their united voices in the eternal song of praise; and all who compose that sacred gathering are "absent members!"

"Hark the Herald Angels Sing!" And they did sing! The tears that trickled down many faces started quavers that only enriched the melody; and who shall doubt but that every note was gathered up by attendant angels, along with all the worship for presentation to the Divine object of the assembly. It is scarcely necessary to go into all the details of that joyful day; as it began so it continued, as many another Christmas has done before and since, and will do again. Oh, for a look into the letters written for Home describing the scenes and the circumstances of the hour! Will the sweet memory of it ever be lost? Why should it?

One thing is most undoubtedly certain – though human nature, with its crowding and changeful environments, may, and in most cases does, surround events with a film of partial or permanent forgetfulness, all is recorded in imperishable type in the realms of Love and Eternal Christmas.

We have no peals of bells on board ship to stir the saddened hearts of those at sea on such occasions. It is only natural that all without exception, should feel the isolation – the separation from Home Sweet Home at Christmas time!

We had a pathetic illustration of this on the above occasion. A young woman, a second class passenger, broke down completely during the service, crying and sobbing as if her heart would break.

Some of the ladies present took her in hand until after the meeting, and then, sympathising with her, asked what the trouble was. She told them she had been brought up by her grandparents after the death of her father and mother – that the old man was a farmer in Kent, and that both were very devout Church members – that they had warned her to be constantly watchful, as "board ship" was such a wicked place, and sailors were all heathen. That our beautiful Christmas observance had awakened keen regrets that her dear old people were not with her to enjoy it, instead of worrying themselves to death at home about her, in her sinful and dangerous surroundings, &c., &c.

Hear, hear! Three good Christmas cheers for the Old Folks at Home, and for the disorderly surroundings at Sea! They, the old farmer and his wife, would no doubt receive another letter from Madeira that I would give something to look into myself.

I think there should be a post office regulation that all letters from on board ship at the end of a long voyage should be censored, and copies given to the captain to write stories about. What an "olla podrida" of useful and interesting knowledge there would be! The captain would have to live with his Sunday-go-to-meeting clothes and courtesy on continually, or he might catch cold.

Now, remembering that we are at sea and not on land, and that the manners and customs of Father Neptune are not to be despised simply because they differ from Johnnie Longshore's, we proceed first of all to inspect the traditional preparations for our carnival. Amongst the stewards on board all passenger steamers it is quite usual to find artists and orators as well as waiters and washers up.

In each passenger saloon there is keen competition amongst them to decorate their particular province according to the latest development of ancient custom, all glorified by the wand of one master hand in the chief steward himself. It is wonderful what a consignment of artificial flowers, shrubs, flags, streamers, and ornaments of every kind he indents for in prospect of the coming occasion. Some of the artists produce extraordinary effects by the aid of coloured soaps upon mirrors – pictures, many of them, that would turn professional passengers green with envy and astonishment. Appropriate greetings, texts, and compliments find expert portraiture, peeping out through holly and mistletoe in every direction; and in fact saloons look more like beautiful conservatories on Christmas Day rather than prosaic accommodation for the periodical consumption of beans and bacon.

But let it not be supposed for a moment that the beans and bacon are neglected in the general ministration. The chefs, as well as the stewards, lay themselves out for a supreme effort to glorify their particular and exceedingly important office. Healthy appetite is stimulated through the medium of enchanted vision; delectable viands nestling amongst sparkling glass, with glittering silver and steel, all mingled with flowers and fruit in wealthy profusion, whilst the band, audible but unseen, discourses quiet and appropriate music to complete the charming and poetical *tout ensemble.*

All this and more than the poverty of penmanship is equal to convey is the regular heritage of "absent members" upon their briny way from Home, Sweet Home to Golden South Africa on their Merry Christmas Day.

All this loving preparation for the occasion is carried out in dead silence overnight, while the unwitting travellers are wrapped in soft balmy slumber by the Berceuse movement of the ship, in order to exorcise the home-sick tendency as soon as they find themselves in Fairyland upon the beautiful, beautiful sea!

> Oh Sea, beautiful Sea!
> Restlessly throbbing through ages untold,
> Jealously guarding deep secrets of old.
> What were thy terrors whilst eras were young –
> When blackness of darkness surrounding thee hung
> Opaque in its palpable horror, e'er yet
> The sun's holy rays and thy waters had met?
> When "morning" first laid her warm hand on thy brow
> And crowned thee with gold, wert thou fair then, as now?
> E'er continents rose up dividing thy sway –
> E'er Life clave thy bosom, or toyed in thy spray;
> E'er Death pierced thy silent mysterious gloom –
> Its purity marring with stains of the tomb;
> Or man, all presuming, disdaining thy tide,
> Commanded thy service and launched in their pride
> His gossamer structures thy furrows to plow –
> Did fury convulse thee and rend thee as now?
>
> Oh Sea, beautiful Sea!
> Hoary, inscrutable, terrible Sea!
> Treacherous Sea – now smiling, now vexed –
> The mind that would read thee may well be perplexed.
> But courage, my brothers, there's love in its roar
> For trav'lers afloat and their dear ones ashore,
> With time it will cease as a barrier to men:
> 'Twill buffet, sustain us, enthral us till then –
> Only till then – Amen!

But hold – we are getting off the rails rather. Let's see – we discovered ourselves in Fairyland. Well, after breakfast came the usual short hearty hymnal Christmas service in the principal saloon with a crowded meeting, and the band leading the singing.

Then the round of visits between the various classes, with greetings and salutations; an exchange of friendly intercourse with those on board who had been total strangers to one another until the ice was broken by the unexpected amenities of the day. After this a well-served and richly deserved luncheon, followed by a full programme of pre-arranged deck sports and amusements until teatime. A welcome rest, even to the extent of a siesta, filled up the time until the "first bell" sounded the preparation for dinner.

We often hear reference made to the influence of mind over matter; but the influence of matter over mind is frequently quite as dominant. Without any collusion, but individually lured by the novel surroundings and circumstances, every one proceeds to dig out pretty things that had been packed at the bottom as not being required during the voyage, and the guests who collected at the Christmas dinner table were arrayed in admirable taste and in keeping with the splendour of the decorations.

When dessert came on, according to the invariable etiquette of the ocean, the Captain rose, and gave the toast of the evening in the words – "Ladies and Gentlemen – the King!" The band struck up, and all the company, British and foreign, joined in the National Anthem with one consent.

It is wonderful how this knocks the stuffing out of all remaining isolation and formality, and establishes cordial relations upon royal grounds.

In the particular case under consideration, imagine the feelings of the Captain and the whole company when H.R.H. the Duke of Connaught rose and proposed a second toast – "The Captain, Officers, and Crew of the Royal Mail Steamer *Armadale Castle!*"

"Pity the sorrows of a poor old man whose trembling feet had brought him to this pass!"[37]

After the toast was observed, the poor Captain, standing (not quite sure whether on his head or his heels) along with all his officers, and stewards, and chefs from the pantry, representing the entire crew, made his acknowledgments of the high honour done to them in very few words and in very doubtful oratory! I still live, however, which is more than I could have expected after such a severe shock.

During the dessert, also, programmes of a concert to be given on the main hatch at 8.30 were handed round all the saloons. These wonderful documents had been prepared before leaving

---

[37] From the poem "The Beggar" by the 18th-century minister Thomas Moss. The last words in the original are "your door".

Southampton by the Chief Steward's Department, who also were providing the entertainment. The heading of the cards, if I remember rightly, was as follows: R.M.S. *Armadale Castle* – Grand Christmas Concert in the Bay of Biscay – Father Neptune in the Chair. The events being excellent and varied. Amongst them I remember one in particular on account of its extremely ludicrous character, called "The Two Macs." It was really too funny for words, and is quite beyond my power to describe.

The attendance was an overflowing one, and our Royal Guests were quite unable to maintain any semblance of aristocratic gravity. I would not like to malign them, but I really believe they enjoyed the frolic as much as any of the rest; and it was a frolic – a most clever one. It broke the ice of all cosmopolitan reserve most completely, and made the chance companions of a day feel that they all had one interest in common.

Ding dong, ding dong.

If the chimes could have rung on board that evening, the ringers would have been the talented waiters, who, in addition to the ministry of tables and decorations, had given so much pleasure to the whole company on board, crew and passengers.

After the National Anthem had been sung, a little impromptu dance on the promenade deck was started, the weather being so mild, and the band eager to continue discoursing appropriate music; and when "Lights out" on deck was sounded, and all the revellers retired to rest, I expect there were very few sleepless pillows thinking over the events of the day.

On the following morning, all "absent members" who had been – only twenty-four hours before – saddened by the thought of distant "Home, Sweet Home," would feel ashamed to confess that they had scarcely given the subject a second thought, because of the whirl of kaleidoscopic enjoyment that they had passed through during their merry Christmas Day with Father Neptune.

Poor human nature! We are all slaves of the hour.

Ding dong, ding dong!

No. 24.
Midnight, December 31, 1919 – January 1, 1920.
Wishing all in the Homeland, in South Africa, and in transit
A Happy new era of Peace and Prosperity.

"PEACE! My conscience – what rumpus is that? Just as I was fast asleep and dreaming of angels. Oh dear, oh dear! I suppose there is no help for it."

Quarter Master! Here, sir. Go and tell the Chief Steward to let the men have a glass of grog all round, or no one will get any sleep tonight.

I quite forgot the ancient custom. At 8 bells, midnight, the whole crew, sailors and firemen, armed with penny whistles, accordions, tea trays, kettles, steel bars, cans, and in fact any and everything that can be pressed into the service of noise and discord, commence to march round and round the decks to their own villainous accompaniment, whilst one sinner continues ringing the firebell on the forecastle head, and another ruffian turns on the foghorn from a safe position on the funnel ladder where he can't be got at without a bow and arrow – until suddenly the boatswain's pipe is heard, and a raucous voice roars out "Grog oh!" Then all the "music" ceases like magic, and the lambs wish every one within hail "A Happy New Year," never forgetting to serenade the Captain with the same benevolence.

I have never attempted to ascertain the meaning of this most unmannerly mummery – but I have no doubt it has had its origin in some traditional exorcism that must make his Satanic altesse indulge in many a loud smile – if he is capable of such a relaxation of feature.

With the men, of course, it is neither more nor less than a jealous assertion of an ancient right.

I wonder what Mr. Pussyfoot Johnson[38] would have to say to it. Poor chap. If he were captain of the ship, I expect he would have to capitulate unconditionally, or be tossed overboard by the scandalised passengers – like Jonah.

It's very difficult to get to sleep again after such a concert. A mixture of vexation, musical degradation, compulsory submission, and interrupted enjoyment, keeps one's bottled-up feelings fermenting. It's not a bit of use trying to exercise a philosophic spirit. When one does get to sleep again, it is not angels that hover round – but disagreeable visions with spears, and clubs, and battle axes.

However, the clock ticks on, and the world continues to turn round, until the early steward comes along with the matutinal coffee,

---

[38] William E. Johnson, American Prohibition advocate

and you can afford to smile over the annual incident, and forgive the foolish paganism, until next time.

Beyond the above celebration common to most ships, nothing of importance in the way of ceremonial is considered essential to the occasion. The sailors rather expect a half holiday on New Year's Day and sometimes get it, but not always, and not in all ships. The firemen and stewards never get a holiday; the nature of their duties precludes it. The firemen never get a Sunday either; but all hands are expected to turn up smart and clean to muster at 10 o'clock on Sunday mornings in time for Church parade, which they can attend or not as they feel disposed.

Referring to firemen recalls a strange event that occurred on board the *Roslin Castle* a good many years ago. No doubt many people will remember the diabolical outrages of the so-called Jack the Ripper.

Well – we sailed from Blackwall at daylight on the voyage I am going to refer to, and one of the firemen, a new hand, was bundled on board very drunk, and soon developed delirium tremens. In his awful ravings he rehearsed the brutal murder of a woman outside the Victoria Dock entrance at 2 o'clock on the morning we sailed, giving substantial details of the crime, and comparing it with other similar abominations that he had committed. He laughed fiendishly and bragged that the police had never been able to catch Jack the Ripper, and that they never would.

He was, of course, locked up in a deck cabin under guard, and treated by the surgeon as a dangerous lunatic for the time being.

On the third day out he had tamed down, and ceased to incriminate himself. The second engineer paid him a visit at 6 a.m., and, finding the man apparently amenable to reason, and willing to "turn to," he – without consulting the surgeon or myself – let the man out and overboard he went with a frenzied yell that froze the blood of all within hearing.

The weather was fair, the ship was stopped, and boats were lowered, but no vestige of the suicide was seen.

I pitied the poor second engineer, and shall not mention his name.

On arrival at Madeira I posted a full account of the matter to Scotland Yard, in addition to my office report; and – coincidence or otherwise – on our return to England, I learned that the account of the murder at the Victoria Dock entrance was circumstantially correct, and it was the last of the hellish series.

Why the above should remind me of another mad incident – though of quite a different kind – I know not, but it is worth repeating.

I was third mate in a small sailing ship of Dunbar's called the *Lady McDonald* in the year 1861, on a cruising voyage in the East.

Returning from China, we reached the Straits of Sunda, between Java and Sumatra, and the wind and current being very baffling, the Captain anchored with a kedge in deep water awaiting a slant to get through. Early the following morning, appearances being propitious, we started to pick up our anchor for a fresh attempt. It was hard work. The Captain on deck aft kept asking what was the matter – "Why don't you get that anchor up," &c., and the mate on the forecastle head replied that it was most unaccountably heavy.

At last the anchor was sighted, and, lo! there was a strange tight rope over the fluke of the anchor. The ship was riding to the strain. The Captain, seeing the men gaping over the bows, bawled out: "What's the matter?" and the mate replied, "Foul anchor, Sir."

"Well, get it clear; we are losing our chance."

The mate sent a man down to lash the offending rope to the anchor, and then sent the carpenter down with an axe to divide it on each side of it, so that they could keep the piece and see what it was.

Having done this, and got the ship under way, we slipped through the Straits and proceeded on our voyage.

On examining the piece of "rope" attached to the anchor, it was found to be on an entirely new and unknown plan to all on board, having several copper wires running through it, and being covered with rubber and an outer sheathing.

Strangely enough, not a soul on board had the ghost of an idea of the scandalous thing that had been done. It was years afterwards that I saw a section of submarine cable for the first time and remembered our disgrace.

Now comes the strangest part of the story.

I think it was in the *Carisbrook Castle* in 1898, 37 years after event; we were homeward bound. Going into the smoking room one afternoon, which I scarcely ever entered, I was attracted by a discussion that was going on regarding submarine cables in general and their periodical examination and repair in particular. The speakers were officials of the Eastern Telegraph Company, one of them being a Director, if I remember rightly.

They were comparing notes, and relating most interesting experiences and enigmas. Amongst others, the elder of the two told about a puzzle they had never solved relating to the Java-Sumatra Cable, which had been under-run and picked up, to ascertain cause of failure, and to repair. They had found the two ends cleanly cut, but they did not fit together. Evidently a piece was missing, but there the investigation was permanently shelved!

These remarks blew away 37 years of fog and oblivion, and it is easy to imagine the surprise of all the listeners when I unveiled the mystery that had lain perdu all those years. N.B. – I should not have revealed this weighty secret, but that the old ship's bones had been buried long since in the sands of Algoa Bay, and the spirit of the dear old Captain was quite beyond the reach of communication even by such clever scientists as Sir Arthur Conan Doyle and Co. How strange, it seems to me, that I should have been led into the smoking-room at that particular time.

As soon as I had told my story, the Director quietly laid his cigar down on the table, wiped his spectacles and blew his nose, and then relieved his feelings by exclaiming: "The blamed fools are not all dead yet! If that idiot had cut his anchor adrift instead of the cable, and had sent in his claim for a new one, the E. T. Company would have given him a silver anchor instead of it, and a gold watch and chain as a souvenir of their appreciation. Steward – bring me a strong whiskey and tonic, please; I've had a shock."

I felt quite sorry for the old gentleman, and began to doubt my own wisdom in lifting the lid off the stew.

Again, I cannot explain why the relation of the above small item of history should "blaze" the trees of memory in quite a new direction, unless it be the unaccustomed "locality" of the incident that raises the spectre – the smoking room.

In the year 1883 the good ship *Warwick Castle* was lying at anchor in Algoa Bay on an unusually beautiful summer night. A slight undulation of the bay was just sufficient to awaken sound and movement in the slumbering steamer and to make the reflections of the brilliant stars dance and chase one another on the surface of the water. All Nature appeared to lie wrapped in peaceful sleep. No one appeared to be in a hurry to go to bed. Lazing on easy chairs on deck was too pleasant.

Six bells – eleven o'clock – struck, and, as if it had been a preconcerted signal, a cry went up, "Ship on fire!" and all was commotion. It was not our ship, I am thankful to say, but an American three-masted schooner that lay not very far from us – a vessel about 600 or 800 tons burden, called the *Gamecock*, laden with "notions" and petroleum for South Africa.

Fire bells began to ring all round us, boats were lowered and provided with force pumps and hoses, and the doomed ship was very soon surrounded with willing and sturdy volunteers for the work. Her crew was taken off, and the boats alongside pumped water into every opening, converting the whole vessel, in appearance, to an illuminated fountain.

It was magnificent, but it was awful. The fire gained rapidly in spite of all efforts, and seemed to lick up the water into steam. Flames mounted higher and higher, and at last the Harbour Master ordered the pin to be knocked out of a shackle and the ship to be cast adrift, lest she should sink in the anchorage. A jib was pulled up to allow her to fall off before a light southerly breeze that was springing up, and very slowly the deserted vessel was towed by boats clear of the other ships at anchor, and then left to drift ashore by herself on the northern beach of the bay, where she burned herself out in about twelve hours – a dreadful sight.

Her Captain had gone ashore the day before, intending to remain there until the vessel was ready for sea. Fortunately for him, he had taken his baggage with him. It must have been a nasty knock for him to hear next morning that he had no ship to go back to.

Gaily glanced the shimmering moonbeams on the waters of the Bay;
Undulations slowly moving helped the scintillations play,
Zephyrs, soft as maidens' whispers, soothed the weary seaman's rest;
Peace and beauty reigned co-equal: Porto Betsi looked her best,

Pillowed deep in shy reflections, half in light and half in shade,
Like great sentient creatures slumbering after toilsome journey made,
Safely folded – nothing fearing – bravely patient – far and nigh
Lay the gallant ships: their tracery faintly pencilled on the sky.

One sound only broke the stillness: 'twas the fretful, hollow roar
Of the restless southern billows quarrelling with the golden shore;
Never ceasing – never wearying in the lesson they would teach,
How that, turn by turn, men too must break upon the Eternal Beach.

Thought, on wings of inspiration, soared to realms of joy and love.
Judging by the calm, sweet present, what must be our home above –
Where no tears, no partings – Hark! What's that? What says that fearsome
 crier?
Gracious heavens! of wails most terrible – the cry of "Ship on fire!"

Dreams of heaven and peace, farewell! The savage flames of Hades rage –
Licking up their wooden bondage as wild creatures would their cage!
Boats away, there! Pumps and crews! Now bend your sturdy oars! Give
 way!
Salvage must be prompt, or futile! Let her go, lads – pull you may!

Hip, hurrah! Help here, a rope! Now drive the spluttering torrent in!
Pump boys, pump and burst the pipe! Let foe with foe strive which shall
 win!
Shouts and curses mingle hoarser, with the roaring flames pell mell –
A ship on fire at midnight is the carnival of hell!

Late – too late! Beware the mast – stand clear! No power on earth can
 save!
Slip the cable! Set the jib! The harbour must not be her grave!

Let her drive away to leeward lest amongst the rest she run –
Sink or swim – shove off! Now leave her. All is done that can be done!

Slowly turned the stricken ship, abandoned in her dreadful pain;
Driven from the haunts of vessels – never to return again!
In her anguish seeming still to watch the boat's retiring strife –
As the helpless patient dumbly pleads to surgeons for his life!

Doubly doomed! Diseased and desolate! A thing to fear and fly!
Every heave was like a sobbing prayer for mercy from on high –
Mercy not expecting! So she went to spend her latest breath,
Like a wretched, lep'rous outcast, in the wilderness of death!

Of all scenes to us the saddest, though through all the world we roam –
Sailors only feel as sailors can towards their floating home!
God, be gracious when Thou callest. When in bitter need oppressed,
Leave us not in death deserted. Lead us peacefully to rest.

My next voyage was in the *Roslin Castle*, which I took over
from poor Captain Jones. On leaving Cape Town, homeward
bound, we had amongst our passengers the captain and mate, as
well as two or three sailors belonging to the *Gamecock*. They had
been kept behind to attend the official inquiry regarding the loss of
their ship, and to make all business arrangements with consignees,
&c.

The mate was a moody, silent young fellow, who seemed to
prefer his pipe and his own company to mixing with others on
board. The captain, on the other hand, was a chatty and somewhat
assertive example of the proverbial Yankee type, not altogether the
kind of person to inspire feelings of affection for.

During the voyage home a canard got wind that there had
been some mystery about the burning of the ship in Algoa Bay, and
wherever it sprung from, it certainly lost nothing by flying. At last it
began to find expression in jokes and innuendo, and I feared that it
might lead to unpleasantness.

One evening in the smoking-room – there it is – the
"smoking-room" – it was the association with the smoking-room
that resurrected this reminiscence – well, one evening in the
smoking-room some hair-brained youth charged the captain directly
with having wilfully caused the ship to be burned! An ominous calm
settled down upon the little company in anticipation of "result";
but no one expected what followed.

The captain calmly said: "Waal, that's so. Mayn't a man burn
his own ship if he's a mind to? That schooner was insured for
20,000 dollars, and she was eating her head off. Something had to

be done to save the owners, so – waal, yes – we just chucked in a box o' matches and the job was done."

Conversation then became general, and they commenced to rag the captain, but he never lost his temper. He said: "Do none of your sailor chaps ever get rid of a hooker[39] that don't pay – eh?"

This was a poser. "But don't you think you are deliberately robbing the insurance company?"

"Not much," he replied. "I reckon to get 2000 dollars gratuity from them for the advertisement. The news will be printed in every rag in the States – that Messrs. So-and-So have planked the insurance on such and such a ship, and applications will flood them from all quarters. That's business – good business even on our side of the pond; don't your folks understand the benefit of advertising a good thing?"

Whether there was any foundation for the suspicions that had given rise to the above passage of arms, or whether the wily Captain was cleverly pulling all their legs for their persistent whisperings, I cannot tell; but there is no doubt that it cleared the air and improved the mutual relationship.

I would not recommend any of my brother Captains to assume that British insurance companies would feel disposed to agree to such methods of advertisement.

Once more, let me wish all readers in the Homeland, in South Africa, and in transit a Happy New Era of Peace and Prosperity.

[39] Old boat.

No. 25.

In the days of Auld Lang Syne, I think it must have been in the year 1880 or thereabouts, the labour question in Port Elizabeth was looking very serious. It was during the Basuto troubles if I am not mistaken, and the native locations were in a state of incipient rebellion, to say the very least of it.

It was almost impossible to get crews for the cargo boats in Algoa Bay, and delays in the shipment and discharge of cargo were hopeless and exasperating. White labour was not only scarce, it was unwilling. Such work had hitherto been a monopoly of the Black boys, and White men disdained to fill the gap. The ships had to put their own men into the lighters to do the work, whilst the coxswain and his companion lounged about and indulged in sarcasms and disparaging remarks.

We did the best we could for a time, against cross purposes and difficulties of every imaginable kind. It would almost appear that the tallymen and coxswains were in organised opposition to us – not through any sympathy with the revolted crews, perhaps – but because they, as White men, despised our men for doing "n—s'" work.

Things at the Bay became so tangled at last that the Chamber of Commerce in South Africa and the shipping companies at Home were compelled to take the matter up and come to some arrangement that would tide over existing difficulties until the clouds rolled by. Sir Donald (then plain Mister) Currie was elected the London representative of the combine, and he took up the business in hand with his usual energy.

Now, it happened to be a fact at that particular time that the fishing industry on the East Coast of Scotland was in very low water. Why, I cannot tell; if I ever knew, I have quite forgotten the cause of it.

At all events, arriving homeward in the *Warwick Castle*, Sir Donald sent for me to give him all the information I could regarding the difficulties of working in Algoa Bay, and the relative attitudes as between the White men and the coloured boys in the service of the ships and cargoes.

I was several times in consultation with him. He told me all about the fishery troubles in the neighbourhood of Dundee, and asked me whether fishermen would make good substitutes for the Kafir lightermen in the Bay. I quite endorsed his own opinion that their training and experience in the handling of boats in a sea way should undoubtedly qualify them for such work; and to my surprise he ordered me to prepare at once for a trip to Newhaven, where he was well known, and to select two hundred or two hundred and fifty of the ablest men I could find amongst the fisher folk, to go out under certain conditions of pay and provision, passage being provided for them free of cost, and lodging and food in Port Elizabeth supplied until they could settle down and pick for themselves; with a free passage also for their wives and children as soon as they should be permanently settled down in their new homes!

He, Sir Donald, was to let his brother James in Leith know all about the commission, and engage him to attend and help forward the work of selection and subsequent business arrangements in order to facilitate my errand.

I made one stipulation, however, before leaving him: That I should have two or three days wherein to move about as a casual visitor, so as to gather up all possible information, and watch the manners and customs of the natives from an entirely inconsequent point of view.

This proviso turned out to be extremely interesting as well as useful. I learned a great many things that I did not know before; at all events, in so far as the piscatorial fraternity of the little town of Newhaven was concerned.

Amongst other memorable items, the sea front is plentifully provided with posts – ostensibly mooring posts; and every post is provided with a man who sits upon it, all day long – probably to keep it down in its place – dressed in the regulation blue jumper, sou'wester, and sea boots ready for immediate service, which only occurs at well-known times and seasons. Those postmen are seldom seen without a pipe, and like the passing steamers, they smoke prodigiously.

Another interesting item is, that those Lords of Creation, who frequently spend whole nights of sleepless toil and danger upon the briny, consider it altogether *infra dig.* to do any kind of work after their boat is tied up. It becomes then the woman's turn – mothers, wives, sisters, sweethearts – all appear upon the scene dressed in skirts and aprons appropriate to the fishy nature of their occupation. Their lords and masters lounge around and watch them unload the fish and skilfully sort them into particular creels and baskets, and shoulder them away to the auction tables – sometimes staggering under dripping loads that would satisfy an ordinary Hercules – but not a man amongst them would lend a hand were his own mother in need of help. I won't answer for his dignified self-control were his *fiancée* in question.

This was forty years ago, remember. Manners and customs change a good deal in far less time than that. We have seen great examples of this during the last five years, without focussing the telescope for more distant reminiscences. I expect the women of to-day would pull those men off their posts and direct operations themselves from the vacated pedestals!

I found that a very mild and judicious exercise of hospitality tinctured with a little plug tobacco, or anti-Pussyfoot lotion,[40] unsealed the reservoirs of local conditions and aspirations in quite a marvellous way; and I began to understand that prevailing manners and customs were but the fruits of immemorial heredity and that latent hankerings after broader horizons might be pretty general were the rocks of fossilised antiquity once broken up.

On the third day of my visit Mr. James Currie arrived upon the scene, and we called upon the Provost and the Minister to explain our object. Both these gentlemen entered into the scheme with enthusiasm. We learned from them that the reports of poverty and discouraging outlook were quite correct, and that we should find no difficulty in enlisting as many men for emigration as we should require.

I did not anticipate what followed, however.

We put a short notice in the "Local," and called a public meeting for the afternoon following to hear a statement of the objects and prospects of the movement.

Mr. Currie was in the chair, supported by the above-named authorities; and although my memory is getting full of holes, I shall not easily forget his clever provincial advocacy of the cause. After enlarging upon the great advantages offered to those who were wise enough to seize the opportunity, as compared with the destitution and hardship of their present circumstances, he closed with what may well be an old Scottish proverb – though I have never heard it before or since – "Chiels, shall we mak chucky stanes o' fortune, or shall we keep oor ain fish guts for oor ain sea maws?" His hearers evidently understood and appreciated his meaning and let him know it with splendid unanimity!

I followed on with a description of Algoa Bay and the work that would be required of them there, giving full and unvarnished particulars from all points of view; along with the statement of wages and conditions of service. Then the Provost called for "questions" from anyone who might be wishing for further information, and I was heckled a good bit at first; but, having nothing to hide, it was easy to allay all doubts, and many began to ask when they could join, and where? The Provost closed the business of the meeting, by telling them to go home and talk the matter over with their wives and with one another, and to be at the Hall on the next afternoon at 2 o'clock, when I would enroll as many as were needed and who wished to join. The minister then commended the men and the matter to Divine guidance, and dismissed the assembly with a blessing.

---

[40] Alcohol: see No. 24.

The following day Newhaven was besieged! The news had got abroad and shoals of men from far and wide flocked in to offer themselves for emigration. It was most embarrassing. I stood at the door of the hall and picked out the physically fit one by one amidst a continual struggle for admittance; old men and mere boys amongst the crowd begging and praying for acceptance – poor fellows. Two hundred only were wanted, and two thousand more wanted to go!

After getting our number inside, and the doors closed, I addressed them once again, putting the plan very clearly before them, and begged any who were not quite decided in their minds to leave at once, in order that I might accept others in their places. About a dozen who had not been with us the day before did leave, and were replaced by anxious ones outside waiting for a chance.

Each volunteer was then supplied with a card which was to be filled up, giving his name and address, age, and conditions, married or single, which card was to be endorsed by the Provost and registered for emigration.

Many applications were sent in as substitutes for any withdrawals; and the remaining business having been landed over to Mr. Currie, I was really glad to get away from the disappointed majority, and make my report to Sir Donald, who was good enough to approve of what had been done, and to reward me very handsomely for my share in the transaction.

No time was lost in shipping the men out in batches. Generous arrangements were made for the families of married men until the husbands should be in a position to send for them. Barracks were organised at Port Elizabeth for the men themselves pending their independent provision of homes; and for a time everything worked very smoothly.

Most of the old coxswains took umbrage at the invasion of their ancient rights, and trekked away to the goldfields. Their absence led to no earthquakes either ashore or afloat. The fishermen had never enjoyed such good times before. To them, under present conditions, Algoa Bay was an Eldorado. Mostly members of the Auld Kirk, they were civil, obliging, and conscientious workers, and the embroidered language of the old *régime* was conspicuous by its absence.

A good many of the men got their families out in process of time and became citizens of Porta Betsi, made money, and set up "on their own."

It soon became evident that the muckle diel was not best pleased with this novel atmosphere of peace and prosperity in his erstwhile turbulent domain. So a few native boatmen commenced to drift back again to work, and united service begat race antipathy. Black and White could not work together, one or the other must go – and go up.

Naturally the White man could not put the Kafir over his head, so there was no alternative but to leave the native where he had been of old, and promote the new comers into coxswains and their mates.

This came about in due course without any wrench of principle; and the spirit of the new order pulled along smoothly with the re-establishment of the old custom. Failing the ancient posts of Newhaven, our friends the fisherfolk sat on modern bales of wool, and learned to harry the Fingoes at their work, but with good humoured banter instead of curses.

After a few years the links with the Emigration Committee commenced to grow weaker, and were ultimately dissolved; but the essence of the new continued for a long time to leaven the churlishness of the ancient class of cargo workers, to the great advantage of all the ships in the bay.

During bad times – I mean before the Scottish fishermen came out – we had to arrange as best we could in order to keep pace with cargoes and sailing dates. I speak, of course, only for myself and my own ship – though probably others sailed on similar lines. As we were deprived of coolie labour, and tally clerks were not to be had, our own men did all the cargo work in and from the lighters, whilst the officers kept the tally at all hatches, and I put in as much rest as possible in spite of the perpetual rattle of winches, and the shouting at the gangways, &c.

As soon as cargo was finished (and we generally worked right through), and the hatches were on and the boats away, I took complete charge of the navigation towards the next port, assisted by two quartermasters and a look-out man, whilst all the officers and crew turned in, dead beat, until our fresh arrival; and so on. It was the only way we could get along with any prospect of success and fair play. Of course, it depended greatly upon the weather.

It is a remarkable fact that, in spite of the old saying, "Misfortunes never come single," I have experienced quite the reverse. Our Lord's words appear to me always to emphasise the limitation expressed in the language, "Sufficient for the day is the evil (not 'are the evils') thereof." During all these labour troubles on the coast I remember no additional complications of either weather or circumstance, and I suppose my experience is no exception to the rule. Grace is universal, infinite, and eternal.

On one of the occasions referred to above, having a larger consignment of cargo than usual to take in at East London, I found my well-earned rest disturbed by a complete cessation of all noise and vibration. Becoming conscious of the delightful peace prevailing – it was a calm, hot summer evening in December – I strolled out, and, to my dismay, found that every living soul of the crew, officers and men, were fast asleep at their posts, winches stopped, and the cargo boats alongside as quiet as the ship! It was the queerest thing I ever remember. The ship appeared to be bewitched. It was about six o'clock in the evening, and there were still several loads of wool alongside to be taken in. What was to be done? I went to the galley, and the two cooks were sound asleep there. I went to the saloon and there were three of the stewards with their feet up on the settees in a similar state of repose. It was really too funny. I shook myself well in order to make sure that I was not in the same state also, and went along to the chief steward's cabin. There was no compromise about him; he was full length on his back on the sofa with his collar and tie on the table, reeling it off in perfect felicity.

I roused him up and asked him to set the cooks to work making a jorum[41] of strong tea for all hands, and then I went round and managed to awaken the officers, poor chaps, and got the work moving again until tea was brought round on deck, and in the holds, and lighters, and it was wonderful what an effect it had. I could not find fault with anyone, for I knew how willingly and loyally they had been toiling in Algoa Bay before we anchored in East London, and never a grumble amongst them. But we had grand men.

---

[41] A large bowl.

No. 26.

"CAPTAIN, I've brought my little girl to you to see if you can do anything with her, for I can't."

"What – Eva? Why, I thought she kept a pair of beautiful wings hidden beneath her pinafore like an angel in disguise."

"That so? Well I reckon they're not the right kind of angel if she has." (N.B. – Eva was four.)

"So; let's sit down here, and tell me all about it. Eva, come and sit on my knee and listen to a tale of woe. Now then."

"Well, you must know that we were in my cabin and I was doing some repairs of a sub-angelic nature, and Eva persisted in pulling things out of my basket and scattering them around; and I told her to stop bothering, and she wouldn't. At last I said I'd slap her if she didn't stop. An' she up and told me she was doing no harm – and why should she stop doing what she wanted to? 'Because,' I said, 'I tell you not to, and you are doing harm if you disobey.' 'Then I wouldn't be doing any harm if you didn't tell me not to, so I guess I'll have to slap you for making me do harm!' Waal, Captain, I was taken right aback, an' I looked at that infant for quite a time; and then I said, 'Very well, Miss Eva Joscelyn, as soon as we arrive at Cape Town I shall give you to somebody else.' An' you would never believe it, Captain – she said, 'Let it be somebody then that knows how to bring up children better than you do!' With that I was so vexed, I just laid her across my knee so's she could study the pattern on the carpet, whilst I appealed to her feelings with a slipper. An' I scarcely know how to tell you what followed, she actually took a sugar plum out of her mouth and said, 'Go on, if it does you any good; it doesn't hurt me!' Now what do you think of her, Captain – what am I to do with her?"

By this time the charming little delinquent was either fast asleep in my arms, or very cleverly simulating celestial repose. So we sat on chatting very quietly, and I could not help telling Mrs. Joscelyn that she evidently possessed a genius in embryo who would one of these days invest the family name with a halo that would be a credit to them all.

Just then the tea gong sounded, and unwillingly arousing the mighty atom to consciousness we filed off to refresh.

A day or two afterwards it appears that, being again rebuked by her mother for rebellious conduct, and warned that she would again be brought up "before the Captain," she replied, with magnificently comprehensive distortion, "Ya! Captain says I shall be a genuine umbrella to the whole family on wet days!"

Quite needless to say that this young lady was an American. Her mother was a very beautiful and charming member of Bostonian Society.

But oh! the sadness of it! How narrow the straits betwixt *meum* and *tuum* – between right and wrong.

These people, Mr. and Mrs. Joscelyn, had been particularly commended to me from high quarters, including my own honourable and greatly honoured Chief, as deserving of first rank and consideration on board the ship. He was, to all outward appearance, an American Gentleman *sans peur et sans reproche*; tall, handsome, courteous and kindly, he was beloved of all men. There was no pride about him. He was always ready to tell the children a story, or to join in a dance or a game of cards, and even the very cards appeared to favour him. It became quite a proverb in the smoking room that Dan Joscelyn had the run of all the luck.

In the meantime several of the less seasoned sportsmen were reputed to be losing large sums of money, and it was whispered that one young French plunger, a certain count, had hypothecated his credit to the tune of £1700. A feeling of doubt and uncertainty began to assert itself; and it led at last to a secret watch committee being formed by several of the colder-blooded businessmen frequenting the "Smoker"; but nothing was discovered beyond the usual fact that frequent private card parties were held in passengers' cabins, and that Dan was generally one of the number.

The night before we arrived in Cape Town, this Committee came to me in a rather excited state about 11 o'clock and said that they thought they had discovered the enemy in my friend Dan. It goes without saying that I pointed out the danger of thinking such thoughts without absolute proofs, and the sheer unreasonableness of suspecting such a man.

They told me they had found a neat leather case in the smoking room, containing two packs of cryptically marked cards, which had evidently been left behind; that this case had been seen in Dan's cabin; and that a watch was set to see who came to take it away from the smoking room.

We arrived at Cape Town at 7 the next morning, and had an early breakfast; after which I went to my cabin with our right welcome Company officials, and was joined there by the Watch Committee, who told me that the mysterious case had been removed at 4 o'clock that morning by the gentleman they had suspected.

"Well, what do you propose to do?" I asked. But nobody knew. We agreed that there appeared to be reasonable grounds for suspicion, but none for action. Foolish men and their money had been recklessly parted no doubt, and as long as men gamble over cards they must expect that the smarties will rule the roast.[42]

---

[42] The original version of "rule the roost".

After a while, Mr., Mrs., and Miss Eva Joscelyn came up in high spirits to say "Good bye." I let them go away a bit, and then called "him" back; and standing up face to face with him told him what he had been charged with. He turned livid, and I thought he would have fallen. I laid my hand on his arm and I said: "Is the game worth the candle to such a man as you? What must it end in?"

He said: "Captain, I thank you; I have been a fool. It ends here and now; believe me."

So finished a very unpleasant episode that was mingled with many pleasant memories. What a sadly mixed world it all is. Let us turn to something else.

I remember a funny thing that happened on board the *Roslin Castle* a good many years ago – also connected with American passengers.

We had a Mr. and Mrs. Head with us. They sat at my table three and four down; and one day at dinner conversation turned upon practical science, and drifted naturally into the groove of electricity. Some of our British enthusiasts were bragging about recent discoveries and adaptations, when Mr Head chipped in with a cold douche in perfect good humour, and said:

"O, you Britishers don't commence to use electricity as we do in the States."

"How's that?" asked one of the maligned nation. "We have electric telegraphs, and electric this, that, and the other – what have you got more?"

"Why, we put it to all kinds of uses that you never dream of your side of the pond. Amongst other things, we use it for all kinds of decorative purposes. Our ladies when they go to a dance often have their hair beautified with electricity."

"Come, come," replied the Islander, "how about the battery?"

"Oh, they carry that in their bustle!" Silence followed this remarkable statement, and some put their hands up before their faces in mock surprise, when Mr. Head rose with grave courtesy and said:

"Ladies and gentlemen, I'm sorry if I have said anything I didn't ought to say – I didn't intend to – I was only referring to the garment a lady stands in front of when she's well dressed – that's what we call it in the States, and we don't go behind a bush to say it."

It was rather a risky situation for the moment. Between an inclination to laugh and the fear of offending the dignified expression of regret on the speaker's part, conversation lapsed into generalities. The Heads were most lovable people, and frequently added piquancy to the table talk by their drolleries of diction so fascinating to plain matter-of-fact Englishmen.

We need not wander away as far as America to find fuel for fun in provincial dialects. On one of my earlier voyages, I think it was in the *Roslin Castle*, we started a daily lecture on the quarter deck during the run across the tropics. A certain number of gentlemen enrolled their names for one hour's reading in the afternoon, and the rest brought their chairs and their work, or their pipes, and sat in semi-circles round the reader. It was a great success – but I never saw it repeated, though I often suggested it. The reader for each day was to select what he liked; and it was held from 3 to 4 p.m. Amongst our passengers was a real braw Scotchman named Hunter, a leading member of the firm of Stuart MacDonald, in Glasgow, one of the very grandest and most lovable men from the Land o' the Liel; an old gentleman of the true Gaelic type with grey hair and full beard, and a brogue that was sublime poetry to those who understood it.

He enrolled himself, amongst others, for an hour's read on two occasions. The first was announced as Macaulay's "Lucretia"; and there was a large gathering in anticipation of some fun; and certainly such language couched in the very broadest of broad Scotch offered a promise of amusement. But they did not know their man. They came to jeer, but they stayed to pray. The rendering was certainly new, but it was beautiful and by his genius he unfolded the inwardness of the poem as few had ever grasped it before.

On the next occasion he announced his subject as "Rab[43] and His Friends" and the attendance was greater than ever. He hit the nail on the head this time. His foot was on his native heath, and his name might have been McGregor.[44] Work gradually subsided into mesmerised laps, pipes went out, and pocket-handkerchiefs were in fashionable requisition. I suppose that "Rab" was never more perfectly rendered. I met the old gentleman frequently afterwards in Glasgow.

A somewhat similar case occurred on a later voyage. A Mr. Black, a businessman of Fenchurch Street, was a passenger with us – a gloomy-looking person with black hair and whiskers, as well as being Black by name.

It was Christmas time, and some of the passengers were getting up a concert, and came to ask if I would do anything for the programme. I inquired what fixtures they had, and, finding that they still wanted several items, suggested one or two names as likely to contribute, when Mr. Black came along the deck towards us, and I pointed him out to them.

---

[43] Burns.

[44] "My foot is on my native heath, and my name is McGregor" –*Rob Roy* by Sir Walter Scott.

When he had passed I asked if they had secured him for an event. "Not much," replied one of them. "We are not organising a funeral." "Well, I don't know," I replied. "Coal makes a bright fire sometimes. Try him." They came back to me shortly afterwards, to say that Mr. Black had put his name down for a reading from Charles Dickens. So now they were in for it, and it would be my fault if there was an empty house. He had entered his turn on the first vacant line of their programme, which happened to be the last event in the first part.

There was a general anticipation of failure as the time approached for his recitation.

The saloon had been prepared for the evening, with the after centre table placed T fashion across the end. Mr. Black having been announced, he stepped quietly forward, and, bowing to the audience, said "Richard Doubledick. From Dickens's Christmas Stories." Walking slowly from side to side, with his hands clasped behind his back, he commenced to recite from memory the whole of that thrilling romance from beginning to end, having neither book nor notes of any kind, with grave and weighty pathos, standing still now and then to accentuate a particular passage with his hands, and then resuming his walk, and speaking all the time as if in soliloquy, seldom raising his eyes, and then only as not seeing anyone.

It was by far the most dramatic and impassioned illustration of sublime eloquence that I ever remember listening to at sea. So deep and general was the emotion that at the finish not a single expression of approval by word or act occurred, and the speaker bowed and resumed his seat in silent admiration. During the few seconds of interval, a fireman stepped forward behind my chair and whispered: "Would it not be well to put off the rest until tomorrow?" Evidently the speaker had clothed Charles Dickens's characters with actual presence, and led his audience into a visible scene of living reality. It was wonderful. I shall never forget it myself; and I hope, should Mr. Black be still living, that he may be led to read this recognition of his genius after all these years, and realise what a lasting impression he made upon his favoured audience, or one of them at all events.

The second part of the programme was not postponed. After the interval, the concert was resumed, but there were no more Mr. Blacks.

I think I must finish this scrappy paper with a tragic story at my own expense.

A rule was made by the Board of Trade, about 1885, I think, that all passenger steamers should be provided with a certain number of Holmes' patent lifebuoy flares. These were canisters about the size of a quart pot containing some inflammable ingredients that ignited when the tin was pierced and thrown overboard. Attached to a lifebuoy, these signals would, of course, be an important indication at night time of the neighbourhood of an accident, a man being overboard.

So far, so good. But by the time an inexperienced man got hold of the canister, found the pricker, and pierced the tin, the unfortunate object of general solicitude might be a considerable distance astern, or elsewhere.

I saw an opening for improvement by providing each lifebuoy and tin with an automatic frame for the instantaneous piercing and release of the buoy and flare by day or night, operative by any one simply striking the knob at the cry of "man overboard."

With the kind assistance of the Second Engineer I schemed out this frame and fixed it experimentally on the taffrail (aft). Then, to illustrate its utility, I gave the passengers and crew a little explanation and struck the knob – but – I had not allowed sufficient clearance for the tin at the angle of its release, and it stuck – to my mortification and the general amusement.

Of course the mistake was rectified at once, and it worked splendidly.

En passant, I may say that I offered the patent to the Holmes' Light Company on a royalty; but they refused the offer and altered the character of their tin to disqualify my arrangement, themselves pirating my idea by applying a principle of the same nature in a. different form. I let the matter slide.

The last paragraph is a parenthesis.

Some days later on – after my vainglorious illustration – we had a lecture in the saloon by one of our stewards, a very clever and droll caricaturist. His lecture was upon topical subjects, illustrated by burnt cork sketches on bed sheets, having an assistant with him provided with a common bull's eye lamp, which he facetiously referred to as the electric light.

After a number of really funny burlesques, a sheet was turned which made me instinctively grovel in my chair. The Lecturer announced that the Captain was a philanthropist as well as an inventor. He had patented a life-saving apparatus that only required a bang with the fist to bring a drowning man on board again; and if it did not act, it was not his fault! "Next please!" It was some time before "the next" could be heard for the howl of laughter that greeted his sally.

No. 27.

I HAD occasion to run over to Southampton on Friday to see my son[45] off for the Cape of Gold by the *Kenilworth Castle*. It was like old times to be moving about amongst brethren of the cloth as in the stirring days o' yore. There is such an Atlantic Ocean of fellowship amongst seafaring men – such a rough and tumble of bonhomie – that one forgets for the time being the rocks and shoals on the dry side of the world.

Of course the "Flag" has a meridian influence over every different section of the service, but that only accentuates the genial characteristics of the profession.

What a strange thing a bit of bunting is. Pray do not be shocked at what may sound like a vulgar expression, but amongst us sailors the Red Ensign that flies over all our ships is generally known as "the blood and guts of Old England," and as a matter of fact that is just what it is. It binds all seamen into one patriotic union – it carries, and has carried, the honour and credit of our race over every portion of the planet, in spite of shortsighted limitations, and the meagre support and encouragement so grudgingly conceded to our ships and sailors for the maintenance of discipline on board, and for their protection in foreign ports.

What the Red Ensign is to the Mercantile Marine as a whole, the Company "house flags" are to the crews who man the ships under their particular bit of bunting. They are the men; theirs are the ships; and theirs is the employ.

Dei gratia – and beyond all controversy, the "Union-Castle" Fleet, the South African Line, and the *personnel* in management and in charge, hold the royal standard of excellence over every other combine in the sun. This I maintain, and hereunto I affix my hand and seal. N.B. – I was, and still am, one of them.

Having fired off this sentiment, which has been fizzling for expression any time these last fifteen years, let us return to the simple fact of our visit to Southampton to see the last of my wounded soldier son, and perhaps for the last time, on his way out to the radiant shores of gold-veined and diamondiferous South Africa for health, on board the good ship *Kenilworth Castle* – my old friend and shipmate during the Boer war, Captain Gandy, being in command.

---

[45] Charles Douglas Robinson. He emigrated to South Africa in 1895 but joined the North Staffs Regiment for WWI and was wounded in France.

I had to run the gauntlet of a fair amount of good-humoured chaff for some mistakes in dates and data in these wonderful reminiscences of mine.

It appears, for instance, that I started a race home between the *Taymouth Castle* and the *Mexican* before the latter was built. Then I forget what ship it was.[46] And that I made one or two other mistakes in dates, &c., not involving any criminal consequences, fortunately, but rather reflecting upon the function that ought to regulate faithful reminiscences. I must sit up, and dot my I's and cross my T's with a little more regard for other folks' reminiscences.

I want to refer to an occasion when Sir Donald Currie made a voyage with me in the *Dunottar Castle*. To be safe as to the correct date, I shall confine myself to generalities. It was some time between November, '91, and March, '94. I forget what ship he went out to Cape Town in, but it was there that he joined the *Dunottar* for the coastwise voyage.

Sir Donald wished especially to see what kind of places Mossel Bay and the Knysna were. The weather was quite fine and the sea comparatively smooth. The *Melrose* had been instructed to meet us at Mossel Bay, and to take him into the Knysna, but she failed to appear. However, I took our ship into five fathoms water off the Pier End at Mossel Bay, where he could study the magnificent proportions of that enterprising port at his leisure. We started on our eastward journey after a few hours' detention.

About 3 p.m. we arrived off the Knysna and I turned the ship's head straight for the entrance, and paddled in as far as it was safe to go at our draught, whilst Sir Donald studied the beautiful view with his glasses; and it is a beautiful view. We signalled for the port boat to come out to us; but I expect the crew were away blackberrying or something else, for we received neither notice nor attention – so after waiting a bit, we turned out and proceeded.

We had scarcely cleared the land when we saw the *Melrose* hurrying along towards us, and much against my will, for fear of accident, Sir Donald insisted upon on my signalling her to stop and take him on board. So a boat was lowered, arid he left us to go into the Knysna, and we proceeded on our way to Port Elizabeth and eastward.

On our return coastwise Sir Donald rejoined us at Cape Town for the voyage Home. All the agents met on board to see him off, and we had a full ship and one over.

Our chief had reserved a cabin for himself at the foot of the companion way below.

---

46 Probably the *Danube*.

When we were well away the purser came to me with the disquieting information that there was one passenger on board, a lady, for whom no accommodation had been reserved – or, rather, whose ticket allotted her a "number" in a small three-berth cabin along with two gentlemen!

Every other berth in the ship was occupied, in all classes. Of course, it was an office mistake, but it was a very awkward one. We reviewed the lists and studied the situation from every point of view, but were hopelessly puzzled.

In the meantime, the lady in question continued to walk backwards and forwards on the lower deck in the passengers' alleyway, telling the purser that she proposed to persist in her promenade until he provided her with satisfactory accommodation.

Sir Donald heard of it after dinner, and came to my cabin to inquire what was to be done. I told him there were two alternatives only, and absolutely, and that the choice remained with himself: either he must give up his own cabin below and take mine, or we must toss the lady overboard.

"And what would you do?" said he.

"That is quite easily answered," I replied. "I shall sleep in the chart room."

He would have none of it, until all the lists had been submitted to himself by the purser; but facts were facts, and the lady was wearing out the alleyway carpet below; passengers, too, were becoming alarmed, thinking there was something uncanny about the queer pedestrian. So at last he submitted to the transfer of his goods and chattels, and "the lady," along with two other over-crowded females, found refuge in the vacated four berth cabin below.

I used the chart room, and slept in sections on a five-foot sofa. I began to get accustomed to it by the time we got Home, and might perhaps have come to prefer it if we had been a month or two longer on the voyage. So long as Sir Donald and "the lady" were comfortable what did it matter? – the world was still going round on its own axle-tree.

On the fourth day out from Cape Town a novel and unpleasant hitch of some kind was developed at the stern – evidently something wrong with the propeller. It was not regular, but at odd times and unexpectedly. Moreover, it was gradually growing worse, whatever it was.

Sir Donald began to get nervous about it. He was not the only one. The engineers claimed that all was well internally. The passengers were asking questions, too. I told Sir Donald that I feared a blade of the propeller was getting loose.

"Well," said he, "how do you account for it, and what might that entail?"

I explained my theory – for, of course, it was little more than a theory then, though I felt persuaded that it was correct; that the tip of a blade, which only cleared the keel by two or three inches at most when firmly screwed up at the base, would require very little play to touch the keel in revolution, since the base was about 3 ft. across. As to what it might entail, supposing the above to be correct, it was quite useless to expect anything but the unexpected. In any case we would have to go into Goree[47] and anchor in order to ascertain cause and cure.

We tried slowing down, but it was no better – in fact, the jars appeared to be still more pronounced as well as more frequent. At noon on the sixth day out from Cape Town the unexpected occurred. There was a rampageous shock aft, accompanied by a momentary stoppage, immediately followed by racing engines and a violently tortuous movement of the ship's stern. Steam was shut off, and excitement turned on, whilst examination was made; and then we proceeded on our way at half speed.

We had cast a blade; but we had three left. The wobbling action of the crippled propeller was very unpleasant, but we had lots of cause for thankfulness that nothing worse had occurred. I forget which of the Union steamers it was that threw a blade off, and through her own plating, and sank, just about where we ourselves were running the same risk. Was it the *Mexican*?[48]

Whether it was due to the uncanny motion or to the original cause, I cannot tell, but we soon began to realise that we were qualifying for a repetition of the accident, and anxiously hoped that we should reach Goree, Cape Verde, before it happened; and we did do so, I am thankful to say.

Before going in, I warned Sir Donald that the French authorities there were anything but friendly to the British flag – which was undoubtedly true at that time – and that he would have to be very diplomatic and *parlez-vous* with his best accent. He replied, "You will see how well I can speak their language."

We anchored under the guns of Goree about noon, and received a visit from the Governor and Port Captain almost immediately on arrival, wondering what had led to our coming in. Whilst Sir Donald was doing the correct thing with His Excellency, I explained our trouble to the nautical authority, and requisitioned a diver and outfit for work as

---

[47] Island off Dakar, Senegal.
[48] It was in fact the *American*, 1880.

153

soon as possible, handing him an envelope with two five-pound notes enclosed as a guarantee of good faith (by Sir Donald's instructions).

The diver, a stalwart negro, turned up smartly, but his diving dress was useless, having been holed by rats; so we had no option but to prepare for an undress rehearsal, he and I and the third engineer who was a bit of a water rat in his way, and took a keen interest in the propeller naturally.

We got to work at once. A boat was lashed securely alongside the stern post; the deep sea lead was suspended from the stern shackle alongside the propeller, by means of which we were to pull ourselves up and down at our work; the necessary tools also attached by lines at the convenient depth for service, &c. We extemporised diving suits out of flannel underwear. The weather was hot and beautiful, and the sea as clear as crystal. Everything was in our favour.

Fortunately for us, we found that the blade opposite to the lost one was the defaulter. It was not only loose, but was practically hanging by the nuts quite an inch from its base. By turning the propeller until the lame blade was perpendicular, it sat down firmly upon its own base, and we had nothing to do but screw up the ten great nuts by means of a four foot spanner. It required two of us each dive to attach and work this heavy tool bit by bit.

This may sound easy enough; but be it understood that thirty seconds is about the limit of a naked diver's endurance under water; and the pulling down and hauling up through twelve feet of sea water, as well as the effort applied, had to be performed within that limit of time each dip.

Another great difficulty was the maintaining of our position under water in order to bring any force to bear upon the spanner. The three of us carried on the work in triangular rotation for four solid hours, until our eyes were bloodshot and we were as deaf as posts; but the fact that that blade remained *in situ* for the rest of the voyage may be claimed as proof that we did not suffer for nothing.

Whilst we were in the thick of the work Sir Donald and the Port Captain came in the latter's boat to inspect. The former was horrified to find that the "Captain was running such risks," and ordered me at once to desist. It was my turn at the moment, so I desisted 12 ft. down and came up to blow like a whale at the end of my 30 secs. There was neither time nor excuse for stopping to argue the point; the work had to be done, and it was done; and as well as one negro and two Whites could do it. The pitch or angle of the blade was settled by itself. We had neither means nor power to make comparisons or alterations down there.

It may be of interest to some that a very simple means of watching work carried on under water is easily effected. All that is necessary is a watertight wooden tube, say, 2 ft. long and 12 ins. square, with a sheet of plate glass tightly bedded into one end so as to keep the water out. By immersing the glazed end ever so little and looking down through the tube marvels of visibility are revealed, distance being limited only by the greater or less transparency of the water. Added to this, as a medium sea water has an inherent magnifying power, the grains of sand at the bottom in 10 or 15 fathoms of water are quite clear and countable. The paint brush marks on a ship's keel are coarse and distinct.

Sir Donald and the Harbour Master sat in their boat under the stern with such a "lookometer" – as it is facetiously called – for over an hour watching operations; and they were quite able to judge when a nut was screwed hard down, much to the satisfaction of the former.

The virtue of the "lookometer" lies simply in the fact that the glass creates a "steady surface" to look through. 'Tis the ceaseless undulation of the palpitating sea that screens the treasures of the ocean from the prying eyes of man. Just so.

To make an end of our adventure and of this paper, which I fear has been losing a blade or two on the way and causing a good deal of wobbling, it was about 5 p.m, when we started on our way again; but before doing so, the black diver received a five pound gratuity, and the authorities gave us a most cordial invitation to make use of the port whenever any of our ships should require assistance of any kind again. Sir Donald was a good French scholar.

We continued to go half speed until we reached Finisterre, calling at Madeira in due course, and from there to Plymouth we put her on a little faster, but the movement was very unpleasant.

When the ship was dry-docked in London, the engineers would scarcely believe that the third blade had been doctored at Cape Verde, the job had been so firmly done, until they found that the angle or pitch was a bit finer than the others, which was in its favour.

Three cheers for three divers!

No. 28.

My last paper relating to the *Dunottar Castle* in Goree calls to mind a fateful voyage of the good old *Roslin.*

She was always a troublesome ship, partly because we did not understand her perverse disposition, and also because I am afraid we did not always go the right way to work for her reformation.

To begin with, she was a confirmed roller. Four hundred tons of iron Kentledge[49] was placed along the centre line of the holds. That made her worse than before. Her rolling period had been fifteen seconds; it was now thirteen, with a sudden jerk at each end. Some one suggested to Sir Donald that he should call in the Royal Naval expert on stability – Sir Something – I cannot be sure of my memory, so had better not venture a guess. He carefully examined the records, and recommended the "winging of the weights," by running 100 tons along each side of the 'tween decks, and ditto along each side of the lower main hold.

This was done. The rolling period was now 17 seconds, with a distinct hesitation at each end, that seemed, until we got accustomed to it, to indicate a doubt whether it was worth while to come back again at all.

It resulted in all but 100 tons of Kentledge for trimming purposes being removed from the ship altogether on her return, and thenceforth we took the rough with the smooth and rolled gaily along.

On the voyage I am about to refer to, we were fitted with a new propeller, of finer pitch than before, which, of course, greatly accelerated the revolutions, and shook the whole ship unpleasantly. This was bad enough, but worse was to follow. We called at Lisbon that voyage outward bound, instead of at Madeira.

After leaving there we got as far as the north end of Fuerta Ventura of the Madeira group, when a horrible shock occurred in the engine-room, followed by a grinding and grumbling of the machinery that sounded very dreadful, and the Chief Engineer came hastily up to the bridge and said he would have to stop for an overhaul.

I took upon myself to persuade him to let us struggle on as far as the south end of the North Island, where we could safely anchor, instead of drifting quite helplessly about with the risk of getting ashore. We were skirting the island at the time, within five miles or so.

It was very risky, of course, either way. The engines were evidently working against one another, and we were not making more than six or seven miles an hour with a fair wind and sail set. However,

---

[49] Weights used as permanent ballast.

in about four hours we reached the shelter of the south end of the island, and found a comfortable anchorage in ten fathoms of clear water, and not a sign of human habitation within sight.

It was beautifully fine and smooth, and some of our enterprising young bloods wanted me to let them have a boat that they might land and explore; but I considered this far too risky. Complications of many kinds might ensue, so I had to refuse. I was sorry, for I should like to have taken a run myself. The love of adventure is natural to our piratical derivation.

In the meantime the engines had cooled down and were being opened up. The trouble was found to be very serious. One of the "bridges" of the H.P. slide valve had been broken away, so that instead of shutting off the steam in action it was allowing the L.P. cylinder to work against a cushion of steam in the H.P. at the risk of blowing the top off or the bottom out, whilst the effective action was reduced to a very low percentage. The broken bridge was found in three pieces at the bottom of the cylinder between the ribs.

What was to be done? Well, I suppose the most forlorn hope does occasionally succeed. The broken bridge was a bar of steel, about 25 ins. long by 2½ ins. square. We could not afford to stop where we were for ever, so we set the carpenter to work, after a very anxious consultation, on a bit of tough old oak, to produce a "bridge" precisely similar in form to the broken steel one, and attached it in place by the original means, which happened to be very easily done.

I have not the remotest doubt that neither the Chief Engineer, nor the carpenter, nor I myself expected that the patch would pass one single "cut off" without being blown into the middle of eternity; but, nevertheless, at half steam pressure that patch took the ship to Cape Town! It was a mad thing to trust to such a device; and it was a mad-hatter who suggested the experiment, but what was to be done? We were anchored in a desolate corner of the earth with no prospect of early relief, and I am proud of the carpenter's skill and of the Chief Engineer's consent to test an utter impossibility – the chief responsibility being mine, and there is more to follow:

On arrival at Cape Town, very late, of course, examination was made, and we became quite popular; so many practical men wanted ocular proof of the truth of the report. The wooden "bridge" was carefully removed, and a brass casting made and fitted. The Chief Engineer insisted upon keeping the wooden substitute carefully for future sceptics to criticise and puzzle over. And so, in due course we galloped over our remaining work on the coast, and started for Home on our correct date. Our brass "bridge" was doing its duty to its own and our entire satisfaction so far, and we rolled and wriggled along gaily until we reached Finisterre; and then the trouble began.

We had a stiff northerly wind and high sea, attended by hazy weather as we passed the Cape about noon, and shaped across the Bay of Biscay for Ushant.

That same evening at 7 o'clock, the well-remembered shock with the subsequent groaning and fizzing of concentrated steam pressure occurred, and the Chief Engineer came rushing up to the bridge to report what had already reported itself most emphatically.

"We'll have to stop," said he. "I believe that brass bridge has gone."

I pointed out the high sea that was running, and told him that if we should stop now the ship would, of course, turn beam on to it, and almost certainly sweep the decks; and what could you do below with the ship rolling 40° or so each way? "You know what she is with 'way on her' – but we neither of us know what she would attain to with the 'way off.' Put her on half speed as we did before, and make up your mind that whilst the engines will work we must go. The risk of keeping her going is in my judgment far less than that entailed by stopping for problematical repairs, with the probability at best of having to be towed in somewhere at salvage charges. Encourage the machinery to the utmost of your power, but on no account let anyone do anything to risk stoppage. I feel persuaded that you would not get her started again."

"That is very likely," he replied; "but how about the responsibility in case of an explosion?"

"We'll have to divide it," I said; "but if you decline, then I must take it all. Carry on."

Pressure being reduced, we managed to struggle along about three knots an hour against wind and sea, taking it very kindly; and towards midnight both wind and sea had considerably abated and we were racing along at a breakneck speed of five knots a hour to the tune of groaning and fizzing sufficient for 15 (the good ship was not equal to much more than 13 at the best of times); but it was very anxious work; there was not much rest for any of us.

We passed Ushant about 3 a.m. on the third day after our breakdown, and reached the Eddystone at midnight of the day following, the weather having favoured us all the way from Finisterre.

The pilot hailed us off the Eddystone but there was no stopping. He got paid all the same. I arranged with the Chief Engineer to be ready on arrival at the anchorage to stop, and try the engines astern, and ahead.

As soon as I estimated that we had way enough to reach our objective, we did so. There was a kind of snort and splutter on each attempt, and that was all. The Lord had been very good to us!

We had signalled from Finisterre, so our authorities were anxious on account of our slow progress from there, and were awaiting us at Plymouth.

As soon as we were cool enough the H.P. was opened up again, and the brass bridge was found, as the steel one had been before it, at the bottom of the cylinder, between the frames.

It was proposed that we should remain at Plymouth until they could send for a new slide valve, but we said no. The carpenter and the Chief Engineer turned to and fitted the original "wooden impossibility," which had been carefully preserved as a curio, and we proceeded up Channel at small half speed and docked our ship safely and without undue detention or expense.

They were grand men, our Chief Engineer and carpenter. It only required our unprofessional goose to start the idea of a sheer impossibility (that they would never have dared even to think of), and they worked out the details with scientific ability and a wonderful measure of success. The old proverb, "Fools rush in where angels fear to tread," would apply to such a situation.

I was such a goose once. I was mate of a sailing ship[50] with a full general cargo for Christchurch, New Zealand. She was fitted with steam winches, the generating plant being practically the after-half of the ship's galley on deck; and we carried a "donkey-man" as a member of the crew, to do engineer's duty during the process of discharge, and to act as storekeeper and carpenter's mate between whiles. He was a fine, decent old Johnnie with one eye, and managed his "engine" stunt (how I hate that word! – where does it come from?) quite intelligently.

We had not got far on with our discharge when an explosion took place in the "engine-room" – the boiler had burst, and blown old Sykes out of one door and the cook out of the other, badly scalded with steam both of them. Pots and kettles performed marvels of agility, and for some minutes things were pretty lively.

The wounded having received first aid, the all-engrossing question was *que faire?* The captain was ashore and would not be back again until the next day at the earliest. The show, therefore, was mine.

On inquiry I found that there was a firm up-town – blacksmiths in a large way of business – who occasionally did smaller castings, and called themselves engineers. I went to them, and got their foreman to come on board at once with me. Sykes had been clearing things out in spite of his burns, and the boiler was cool enough for an examination to be made. It was a very simple

---

[50] *Star of India* from the date.

affair – an ordinary tubular boiler, about 8 ft. long and 6 in diameter – lying fore and aft, and opening into the after end of the galley.

By crawling into the firebox one could just sit in the combustion chamber at the far end. We found that the back plate of the boiler was cracked down one side of the firebox plating clear across two tubes, and the break was a quarter of an inch wide in some parts, the whole being about 10 ins. long.

My friend from "up-town" condemned the boiler – lock, stock, and barrel. I would none of it. Were we to discharge over 1000 tons of cargo by hand, and with a machine on board? Never! I got a piece of soft wood, and the carpenter with his tools, and from the inside gave measurements, &c., until we had fitted a patch that lay flat over the broken plate. The two tube holes were marked on our patch by means of a rocket stick and painted pad passed through. Then I returned to the shop with my man, and requisitioned a piece of ¾-in. plating cut to pattern, heated and hammered into shape of model, bored for two 1-in. steel bars the length of the firebox to pass through the tubes, with eight heavy nuts and washers, and a lot of red-lead putty.

I refused to leave the place until I was furnished with my indent, and they good-naturedly turned on all hands to complete the order; that is Colonial custom. With my beloved plunder I trekked for the ship about 6 p.m., and by 10 the same evening all was fixed to my satisfaction, and left to "set" until the following morning.

The captain was pleased, and wrote home to warn owners that the boiler would have to be repaired on our return. We discharged all our cargo, visited India and elsewhere for homeward freight, used our steam for the windlass and general purposes, and quite forgot all our troubles until the experts came on board in London, and, after investigation, pronounced the architect of our fortunes subsequent to the accident an ignorant and unutterable kind of durned idiot for daring to run an engine on such a repair. That wasn't much of an advertisement!

The expenses incurred for labour and material in New Zealand amounted, I think, to £3 10s. I suppose it would not be less than three times that to-day; but I am referring to the year 1871. I think I ought to have been a donkey-man myself instead of the donkey referred to above.

I used to be rather fond of mechanics as a young man. I think there can be no manner of doubt that I narrowly escaped being a motor-car nuisance by one patent of mine. Let me see if I can describe it. When ships grew too large for hand steering gear steam power was applied. The wheel in this case only actuated the valve that controlled the steam. There was no "feeling" in the wheel itself of any pressure, as of old, which was the soul of the steersman. The mechanical index in front of him was the only indication he had of the position of the helm. I corrected this by applying an artificial "feeling," which induced the wheel always to return to the central position on being released. A great friend of mine, Mr. Thomas Walker, of Birmingham, took out the patent for me, I being at sea, and an arrangement was made with Forresters, the steam steering firm at the time, to take over the patent on a royalty. When I returned, however, I found that Forresters had withdrawn, on the ground that a claim in my specification invalidated my monopoly, "on being released the wheel automatically returns to its own centre." It appears that this clause had been previously used in patenting a steam pump!

Now, every steam-steered ship in the world, naval and mercantile, is I believe fitted, in one way or another, with the principle of this invaluable adjunct to safe navigation.

What relation exists between steam pumps and steam steering gear I have never been able to ascertain. Anyhow, we lost our fees, and I have to be content with a wheelbarrow instead of a motor-car.

Roslin Castle – Tony Haslett Collection

No. 29.

On two, if not three, of my voyages we had the honour of Cecil the Great's company on board along with us, and it was indeed an honour. Genial and kindly to all, he still lived an entirely separate and magnanimous existence amongst the crowd.

What a rare and magnificent sample of the genus homo he was. A cosmopolitan Englishman in blood and soul, he was a Roman in appearance, and in Imperial instincts and nobility a startling resurrection of Julius Caesar in these superficial days of cramped worldliness.

Absolutely fearless of and superior to all public or private opinion, he was still reverenced and beloved for the very attributes that embraced him in solitary individuality. No man could be jealous of Cecil Rhodes. It would be about as reasonable to suppose anyone crossing Trafalgar Square to be envious of the figure of Nelson against the sky.

How sad it seems that so great a mind should have been removed upon the very threshold of his philanthropic projects; but He who controls the world makes no mistakes. We may grieve, but we must agree.

Rhodes used often to come to my cabin for a quiet smoke and a yarn, and many an interesting story he told me about his experiences in the land of his loving adoption! He was very true to Rhodesia especially, and a firm believer in the glory of its future.

It was rather remarkable that, so unmistakably Roman in appearance and character, he should have a strong bias towards Roman history and literature. His prayer-book, as he called it, was "Marcus Aurelius"; a copy of which always lay upon his dressing table, where he could dip into it during the process of dressing. He urged me to adopt the same plan, so that we might compare notes on our next voyage together. I followed his advice by procuring a copy, and he marked a lot of passages for me to ponder over. There can be little doubt, I think, that Marcus Aurelius may be classed as "Christianity without Christ;" and a very high standard at that.

Mr. Rhodes was, I think, the most complimentary man I ever met – not in speech, be it understood – for a straighter speaker it would be hard to find; but he was so essentially trusting, so sublimely free from all guile himself, that he could not believe in any lack of candour on the part of others. It would require absolute proof of *mala fides* to disabuse his trust in any man for whom he had conceived a friendly feeling; and the revelation of such failure would be attended with bitter sorrow to himself.

I should like to give an example of his transparent confidence. We were sitting in my cabin discussing various matters, and the subject of new docks at Cape Town bubbled up, and naturally led on to ships and sailors, their increase and accommodation, &c. I said: "By the bye, Mr. Rhodes, I have never seen your name on the lists of subscribers to the Seamen's Institute in Cape Town."

"H'm – no – I don't think I ever did send them anything. What are they doing?"

I told him what little I knew about the work out there; but after so many years I quite forget whether it was the old S.A.G. Mission, or the Missions to Seamen, or the Sailors' Home, so called, that was in question between us.

"Well, if you think I should give something, what would you recommend?"

"Upon my word," I replied, "I don't know what to say. You are reputed to be well off, and your name cannot be associated with a trifling sum; could you afford fifty, or hundred, or one hundred and fifty, say?"

"Take your pen and a slip of paper," he replied, "and write 'To the Manager, the Standard Bank of South Africa. Please pay the Secretary of the Seamen's Institute the sum of £150 on sight.' Now I will sign it."

"But hold," I said; "I must re-write this, I have only scribbled it."

"No, that will do," and without looking at the paper, he took the pen and signed it there and then.

N.B. – Let me explain. He had taken me by surprise in directing me in such a hurry, that I had picked up the first bit of paper I saw on the table, which turned out to be the back of a letter, and trusting to my memory until I could put it in proper form for signature, I simply scrawled along on the paper, mentioning merely the Bank and the sum, in an altogether imaginary series of hieroglyphics without any kind of sense whatever – and lo! Cecil Rhodes endorsed it! I put it in my drawer to think over.

He had not even cast his eye over what I was supposed to have written from his dictation.

I must, of course, explain what followed.

As regards the money order: I wrote a statement to the following effect, and pinned it to the cabalistic document above-mentioned: "I hereby certify that the attached scrawl bearing the signature of Cecil Rhodes is to be understood as conveying £150 to the Seamen's Institute of Cape Town. It was scribbled from dictation but not intended for signature at the time. I am responsible for the truth of this! Signed, J. C. Robinson – ship and date." The money was paid without any demur.

On anchoring in Table Bay at 5 a.m., the Harbour Master's boat came off to give us pratique, and arrange for our docking. Mr. Rhodes, dressed in his very unassuming brown suit and felt hat went ashore in the boat. An hour afterwards, the Mayor and Corporation came off in the steam tug to welcome the magnate – and found him flown. Just another glimpse into the individuality of the man; he hated show and ceremony of every kind so far as it referred to himself, and carefully avoided the suspected honour.

Mr. Rhodes asked me to dinner at Groote Schuur on one or two occasions, and in his curiously hospitable way said: "Come as often as you wish, and stay as long as you like, and don't let my presence or absence be any bar to your freedom of action." I never took advantage of his kindness, however.

Homeward bound one voyage – it was when the Union Company suspended their East Coast trade to Zanzibar – we were often upon the subject of the "open door to foreign intervention," as Mr. Rhodes called it, and he thought of stepping into the gap until better times veered round, being quite assured that a rich harvest of trade was ripening for the near future.

We discussed the kind of vessels that would be required; what ports should be encouraged as feeders to future railway communication, &c. He was evidently very keen upon the subject, and mentally linked up the whole country with his Cape-to-Cairo scheme and a trans-continental line from the West Coast.

We had not been many days in London when I received a letter asking me to come and see him at the Burlington Hotel. I went of course, and his greeting was somewhat of a surprise. He took me by the arm, and said: "I want you to buy me a steamer such as we have in our minds to run the East Coast work for the present. You shall have 10 per cent. on the purchase price, and all expenses. Will you do this for me?"

I told him that such a commission involved far too much for a hasty undertaking, but that I would make inquiries, and do my level best to meet his requirements, if I might submit offers and business to himself before closing,

"I leave the whole thing to you," he replied, "and I think you are going to get me a ship. Good-bye! l have to go."

When I got out into Piccadilly I took my hat off and fanned myself! What next? Automatically I walked westward, and brought up at Hyde Park Place, and pulled the bell of No. 5. "Is Sir Donald in?"

"He is." I sent in my card, and was admitted.

I told him all about it and of Rhodes's offer, and what had led up to it; and was surprised to find that he rather approved of the scheme than otherwise. He was evidently kept well posted in the history of all steamers in the market, and produced lists of them with full particulars. It was quite unnecessary to enter into requisitions; he knew all about the requirements of the proposed interregnum, but maintained that the work could not possibly be carried on with a single vessel: there must be at least two, and ought to be three. Moreover, the lists showed nothing that would really meet the case, and building would have to be resorted to to specification.

At last, he spotted one vessel laid up at Hull that might in some respects be suitable, but there was a doubt about bunker capacity, and we arranged that I should run up and make some quiet inquiries.

So far, I was more than satisfied with the result of my visit. To find my own Chief complacent and communicative, as well as sympathetic, was more than I had any right to expect.

I may mention that our little *Florence* had been doing a lot of cargo and passenger work between Cape Town and Delagoa Bay – occasionally still farther; and under Captain Hewatt, her exceedingly able and diplomatic commander, she had been cutting into the Union Company's mail subsidy, which may well have been a factor in the suspension or proposed suspension of the Union Company's separate monopoly.

The day after my strange interview with Mr. Rhodes and Sir Donald I went up to Hull, and put up at an hotel near the docks. I soon found my quarry, in a very awkward position to get at, but made friends with the mate, and, taking an interest in the ship's appearance, was asked to accompany him on board.

It didn't take long to ascertain all her "points" and, to my great disappointment, to find that she was not at all adapted to the proposed traffic. Bunker space quite insufficient; passenger accommodation only for third class – bad and very limited; and ship and engines in shockingly neglected condition. Bathos.

It seemed a pity, but there was no help for it. I had to go back to Sir Donald and give him my unsatisfactory report, and then to Mr. Rhodes. I am afraid he was disappointed in me as an agent, but he took the matter very quietly, simply saying that he did not think he should build a steamer.

Choosing a ship is very much like choosing a wife. If you make a mistake it is liable to be a big one and a lasting.

In this case all was well, I felt sure. Had I found a proper vessel Mr. Rhodes might have wanted me to take the whole matter in hand, and that would have been impossible. I was "D.C."[51] by love and long service.

It was a big commission and a very unexpected one; and is another illustration of the extraordinary confidence of the man. As a matter of fact, my past experience of shipbuilding and management may have justified his expectation from a business point of view; but it is surely not impossible to find an occasional blend of capacity and worldly wisdom that might be good for both, but would, at all events, not be to

---

[51] Donald Currie.

the disadvantage of one. His trust, therefore, was based upon a generous and complimentary estimate that sought for no guarantees and blew up his bridges behind him.

Requiescat in pace. Let no one ever breath a word against Cecil Rhodes to me.

Two of Mr. Rhodes's brothers and his sister travelled with me more than once. Colonel Rhodes used to say that he was one of the four or five who were judged too short in the neck on a certain occasion;[52] purely a matter of personal opinion. Miss Rhodes was a very cheery and charming personality, and a universal favourite on board.

If I am not mistaken, either she herself, or some one else for her, related a thrilling experience she once had on her brother's Groote Schuur estate, where he hospitably entertained a number of African residents in the shape of gnus, antelopes, gazelles, and other amiable creatures. Passing along one day, a lively young koodoo wishing either to make her better acquaintance, or to express resentment at her intrusion within his domains, charged out from cover across the open, and left her no option but to beat an undignified retreat towards the only gate to the enclosure, which she breathlessly vaulted over just in time to save the brute from being rude; and then she sat down and laughed aloud until her assailant slunk away quite ashamed of himself.

I am not inclined to believe the story altogether myself. I cannot help thinking that a gate Miss Rhodes could vault over would offer no insuperable obstacle to an antelope of any kind; but, of course, I may be mistaken. Calisthenics have worked such miracles amongst our womenkind of late years that one must not be too incredulous of well-authenticated feats of arms and hands, &c.

Doctor Jim has also many times favoured us with his company on board during voyages backwards and forwards between the Land of Fogs and the Sunny South, He also was a man of mark amongst us all. Ever ready to lend a willing and able hand in promoting the amusements or welfare of the body politic. On more than one occasion, in cases of accident or serious illness on board, he has promptly responded to a call for special surgical or medical aid on the part of the ship's doctor.

On one notable occasion an "obstacle race" resulted in two serious injuries to the head. One young fellow dived off the house into a canvas contained pond, and nearly broke his neck on the deck. It was a considerable time before he could be persuaded to "come back."

In the other case, the same race, bounding up the awning deck ladder, one of the athletes cracked the top of his skull against the

---

[52] Frank Rhodes was one of the Transvaal Reform Committee nearly hanged for High Treason under Kruger.

coaming, and was laid up for the remainder of the voyage. Doctor Jim and the ship's medico were in continual attendance upon the poor chaps.

l never liked those dangerous competitions on board ship, where everything is as hard as the pavement in front of the Royal Exchange; but my fears and warnings were for ever laughed out of Court. It was all very well so long as it *was* well, and it was unusual to have two calamities at one "Sports"; but even one was too many for me whilst they were under my care. There were many proposals that I felt called upon to put under an absolute ban, and it used always to result in disappointed zeal.

I myself very unwisely tried once to promote my chief officer, our present Captain Gandy. General Walker (?) gave me a fine old Boer flint-lock gun at Cape Town Castle. I took it on board, and we were examining it amongst us. I was doing my best to blow down the barrel in order to clear the touch hole, whilst Gandy was clicking the lock for all he was worth in the endeavour to make a spark. Failing in my part of the attempt, I put the ramrod down, and feeling "obstruction," applied the screw, and found four inches of a buck-shot charge in position!

I don't blow down barrels now.

No. 30.

IN June, 1895, we started in the *Tantallon Castle* to open the Kiel Canal for the German Emperor. The history of that epoch-marking cruise has been so fully treated by the late Sir Henry Lucy, who was Mr. Punch's representative on board, that I shall not presume to give any details, except in so far as they may relate to unrecorded incidents of the voyage.

It rarely falls to the good fortune of a common or garden mercantile marine Commander to go to sea with such a notable company of grandees, and to receive, as we did, so many and such important Royal visitors on board in a foreign port. I am inclined to think that the memory of it all was years old before I realised the British and International honour that fell to my share on this wonderful voyage.

In fact, I think I may go one better still, and say that I do not think I have attained to the eminence of my privileges yet, and fear that I am incapable of appreciating so great a responsibility.

Is there not an old tradition, historical or classical, or both, that a vessel once put to sea which carried Caesar and his fortunes? This might well head the present paper, but I have forgotten the quotation and the circumstances. It would be like carrying coals to Newcastle were I to repeat the list given by Sir Henry Lucy in his book, "Log of the *Tantallon Castle,*" but I may mention a handful of those who have helped to make history before and since our cruise.

The "Grand Old Man,"[53] Sir John Buchanan, E. P. Mathers,[54] Moberly Bell, W. W. Ouless, R.A., W. L. Wyllie, A.R.A., Melton Prior, W. Garland Soper, Montague White, several of our own commanders, as well as Company's representatives at home and abroad, heads of departments, &c., some hundreds in all, guests of Sir Donald Currie and his family circle, most of whom were present with him in his beautiful mail steamer.

There were twelve ladies also amongst the guests, who played the role of sugar in the tea with great success.

This cruise was not the first on which Sir Donald took the G.O.M. for a sea trip. There was one in the *Dublin Castle,* another in the *Grantully Castle* round Great Britain, a third in the *Pembroke Castle,* when Tennyson accompanied them, and they received on board to luncheon in Copenhagen the King and Queen of Denmark, the Princess of Wales, the Emperor and Empress of Russia, the King and Queen of Greece, and other members of Royal Families.

---

[53] Gladstone.
[54] Editor of *South Africa.*

Before returning to our muttons, I think I must repeat a story I once heard of this last-mentioned Royal visit; but I do not vouch for the truth of it, though my knowledge of the man and his quizzical manner of speech seem to harmonise to a certain extent with the account. Captain Harrison was in command.

He was an exceedingly shy man; but he had a breezy, off-hand manner when upon level ground.

At Copenhagen, when the Royal visitors were expected to arrive, Sir Donald told Harrison to come to the gangway and do the honours of the ship along with himself. But Harrison excused himself, on the score that he was not accustomed to hob-nob with "court cards," and he proposed to keep out of sight. Sir Donald knew his man, and with a laugh let him go and shut himself up in his cabin.

After the luncheon party had returned from below to enjoy their coffee and burn incense on deck, Harrison had occasion to leave his room to attend to some duty below; and, passing along the alleyway, he came across a very charming lady and little girl, looking down into the engine room, who turned to him with a sweet smile as greeting an officer of the ship in full dress uniform. Harrison, of course, "dowsed his royals" – in other words, raised his cap, and offered to show them round; he could do no less.

"An zis?" she said, pointing to the engines.

"Oh, that's where they boil the eggs," said Harrison.

"Oh, zat is curious," replied the lady; and, pointing to the next door in the passage, which led into the galley, she asked: "An zis?"

"Oh, that's where they turn the screw."

"Ah, zat is intairesting! An you are ze – ?"

"Oh, I'm nobody – I'm Sir Donald Currie's lob lolly boy.[55] They call me the 'Captain' for short."

"Ah! zo! I vas sure I did speak to to ze Chief of ze beautiful steamship."

With a laugh Harrison, who had begun to feel the subtle influence of refined female magnetism, said "I suppose you know all these folks here?"

(By this time they had stepped up the after ladder to the promenade deck, and saw the Royal party at the further end.)

"Oh, yes – I know zem all."

"Well, tell me who they are. – Who is that Pirate in the white waistcoat leaning against the rail?"

"Oh, zat is ze King of Greece."

"H'm; and the gentle lady in the red feathers?"

---

[55] A lowly position, historically the ship's surgeon's non-professional assistant who did the cleaning up.

"Zat is the Queen of Denmark."

"Dainty little party! And who is the mild buccaneer talking to Sir Donald?"

"Ah, zat is ze Emperor of Russia."

"And the dignified old boy sitting beside Princess Alexandra?"

"Zat iz her farder, ze King of Denmark."

"Well, I don't know. Seems to me they are a very ordinary looking crowd for Royalties. The Princess Alexandra is by long chalks the best of the bunch. I love her. We all do over our side of the water."

"Ah, yes! Ve also. Ve luf her ver much. She is zo beautivul an' zo good."

"Right you are," agreed Harrison. "Now, I suppose you belong to them, don't you? May I ask your name?"

"Oh zertainly, wis pleasure. I am ze Queen of Greece; ze pirate is my husband; an' I am zo please for zis charming converzation I have enjoy so much."

And she held out her hand to Harrison, who was standing dumbfounded and speechless before his amiable Nemesis, unable to do anything but blurt out a garbled apology as he bent over and touched her fingers with his lips, cap in hand, and backed away down the ladder to look for an open coal bunker to jump down.

Supposing the above to be even partially true – and it is quite possible – I feel sure the Queen did enjoy the joke; and, after all, Harrison came out of it right royally; but woe betide anyone who should have the temerity to refer to the matter before him afterwards. Though shy with ladies, he could be very prompt with masculine criticism. He was a fine, handsome, manly fellow, and for two years was Governor of the convict station at Cape Town.

We must get back to our own bit of history. Sir Donald's programme was to call first at Hamburg, where princely courtesies were exchanged between ship and shore. We remained there about four days, and it was one gigantic picnic.

We received quite a large number of unwelcome as well as welcome German visitors on board; the former consisting of cockroaches of a somewhat different type to our English speaking ones. These evidently approved of their new quarters, and bred and multiplied at such an astonishing rate that it became necessary later on to enlist the services of French specialists to discourage them.

Sir Donald told me to engage a pilot for Kiel at Hamburg; but the demand had exceeded the supply, and there was none to be had. So he wired to Kiel for one to be sent over, and a man arrived just before we left the Elbe; but he turned out to be no pilot, but the skipper of a fishing trawler. He had no certificate, and had never been on board of a big steamer before. It was quite wonderful the way he tucked into the good things of the *Tantallon*, and what a thirst he had for Bass's ale. His capacity seemed to be unlimited.

We proceeded gaily along around Denmark to Copenhagen, where we docked; and Sir Donald again entertained Royalty on board. Of course the G.O.M. was the prime attraction. The whole of Denmark seemed to be converging towards his centre of influence. The crowds were wonderful.

The King and Queen, the Crown Prince and Princess, and five other members of the Royal house, as well as the Prime Minister of Denmark, all graciously accepted Sir Donald's invitation to lunch on board.

In the meantime the whole region round about was becoming packed with a quiet, orderly, silent, and observant multitude. It was almost uncanny from our upper deck to survey such an ocean of calm humanity.

I was going round on a tour of inspection with Prince Waldemar, and calling his attention to the motionless masses, I asked if it were always thus with them, that Members of the Royal Family received no special expression of welcome from their subjects on such occasions. He replied that the King and Queen were round and about amongst the people too frequently to attract anything beyond ordinary attention and civility; but that they could be moved when they felt so disposed.

I protested that they ought to be moved now, considering that the Prime Minister of Great Britain was making his bow to the family of our own beloved Princess of Wales. And I asked him to drill me into the Danish ovation corresponding to our own "God Save the King." This he did after some trouble and amusement.

When the time came for the Royal party to land, I watched my opportunity, and as the King and Queen stepped upon the gangway, I jumped up onto the rail alongside, and waving my cap on high, gave tongue to my lesson with no uncertain voice and started a storm ashore that lasted for some minutes.

I can fancy the Prince relating the circumstances of my education at their own table at the Rosenborg that evening. His coaching had evidently been very successful and bore good fruit at the time; though the only word I seem to remember now is "Koenig," or something very like it.

After the Royal party had disappeared, Sir Donald ordered the ship to be thrown open to the patient crowd in waiting, and we were very soon overrun like an ant heap. Sentries were placed here and there, directing the floods all in one direction, and though all were keenly alive to take advantage of their opportunities there was no trouble. They were as quiet and orderly on board as they had been ashore, and as amenable to discipline and guidance as a well-drilled army.

171

Of course, everyone had one particular object in view – to see the G.O.M.

He had a deck cabin on the promenade deck aft, and sat there with his door open, reading. It was impossible to hurry the visitors past this point too arrogantly. Many had no doubt come from considerable distances for the sake of feasting their eyes upon this world idol. Poor dear old man. He was well aware of the popular interest he evoked, and sat patiently there, probably with his book upside down, for three solid hours, the canonisation of all democracy up to date. Well would it have been for our nation had the balance of public opinion crystallised at that point. The devil has been very busy since then. Two extra heart letters, O.N., have been introduced into the word, which have not only changed the spelling, but have degraded the meaning for the remainder of time.

After leaving Copenhagen we made for Kiel; not a very long voyage. We had a strong westerly wind and beautiful weather throughout. Sir Donald came on to the bridge when we were drawing towards the entrance of the port, and asked where the pilot was. I had quite forgotten that we had anyone on board answering to that description, and told him so. He was angry with me, and ordered me to have him up and hand over charge to him, because he did not wish to offend the authorities by not taking a local pilot. I explained to him what I had already found out about this "navigator," but he insisted, and I – though Captain of his ship, and solely responsible to the Board of Trade – took upon myself the extra responsibility, and sent for the trawler man.

He was found, as usual, discussing "Bass" pale ale with the Hamburg pilot. When he came up I asked him if he knew where the ship was. Looking round, he pointed out the lightship, and called it by its right name. "Very well," I said, " can you pilot the ship into Kiel safely?" He reckoned that he could. "Then take charge, and remember that the occasion will probably call for particular attention to particular plans, which will, no doubt, disclose themselves as we advance." I pointed out the telegraphs to the engine room, and the ends of the ship, and showed him the chart on the table.

Sir Donald was standing by, nibbling his beard, as he always did when he was vexed. I took my station beside the man at the wheel. We had not turned round the lightship very long when a steam whistle on our quarter drew my attention to a steam launch racing after us, with an officer waving a flag on a stick. I called the pilot's attention to it, but he only grunted that it was nodinks.

"Hadn't we better stop and find out?" I asked.

"Oh, ver well – stop!" And we did.

We had only been steaming half speed, but it took the launch some time to get up to us; and the strong westerly wind and choppy sea had fairly soused all on board her. Consequently the German harbour master climbed on board in a decidedly effervescent state of mind. He came on to the bridge with Mr. Cassidy, my smart and most excellent chief officer, and asked who was our pilot? I saluted and pointed him out. A brisk altercation in German followed, and he shrugged his shoulders, and said in good German-English: "This is no pilot," and pointing out, in the distance, a white flag with blue cross, told me we were to anchor a ship's length to the right of it.

Mr. Pritchard, our purser, another dear old friend and shipmate of mine, having, with his usual tact, completed our official business to the entire satisfaction of the offended authority, and dried his outer man by means of a bottle of champagne applied inwardly, we once more proceeded slowly towards our allotted position.

Sir Donald was all this time on the bridge, and I was really in a quandary. Between my duty to the ship, and his evident desire to show confidence to the Germans by trusting the vessel to a German pilot, I was between Scylla and Charybdis. The poor trawler evidently didn't know what to do; between the helm, the engines, the tide, and the weather, he was at his wits' end, and the result was deplorable. I was afraid to interfere lest I should offend my chief; and I determined to abstain so long as the ship was not in danger of some fiasco.

At last, between going ahead, stopping, and reversing, twisting the helm about in all directions, the wind and tide were taking the ship into their own hands, and we were practically "in irons." Then I stepped forward, and, knowing my ship, made a bold venture as a forlorn hope, and, contrary even to my own expectation, she responded, and backed round into our correct position. Down went the anchor, and down I went, to thank God for help that I knew I didn't deserve, because I was so jealous and mortified.

This sounds very like egotism. Perhaps it is so. No one is able to judge himself.

A little seagull flew over my head as the anchor went down, and cried, "You have offended Sir Donald by your success." I know that meant the reduction in value of a "scrap of paper " in prospect.

The next morning, however, without any explanation, he said, "Pay that man off."

(To be continued.)

173

No. 31.

I QUITE forget how long we were at Kiel, but I do not think it was more than two days – closely packed days they were. The whole place, afloat and ashore, was in a frenzy of excitement and bunting and bands. The Royal yacht *Hohenzollern* was cruising about in and out with stately dignity and great effect, greeted by acclamations from all the Fleet.

Sir Donald was notified that the "All Highest" might pay a visit to the G.O.M. on board the *Tantallon Castle*, but it did not materialise. Preparations on a grand scale were made for his reception, and I am bound to say that we were all excitement in anticipation of the honour.

What strange beings we are! One man is elevated to the skies to-day, and to-morrow is esteemed less than human; the manifestation of dignity and honour to-day; a creature beneath contempt to-morrow. And yet, even in his degradation, most men in his actual presence would instinctively rise and pay him the outward respect due to no ordinary person; no doubt on account of the unsuspected sympathy with what had and might still have been.

Kiel is a splendid harbour; and adorned as it was on the particular occasion with the united fleets of most countries, it was indeed magnificent. It was the middle of June, 1895, and the weather was glorious on the opening day. The Imperial yacht with the Kaiser on board was to steam through the new canal from the Elbe, and arrive at Kiel about noon.

The programme was carried out, like all German arrangements, to the letter; and the guns blazed away in grand style. Amongst so many ships saluting, it was a constant roar for some time as the *Hohenzollern* steamed slowly round inspecting and signalling. The Kaiser occupied an elevated structure over the navigation bridge, whence he could see and be seen by all round.

Not a dog might wag his caudal appendage during the progress of that Imperial pageant. Quite right. It was the Kaiser's little show, and may have led to the later claim of "Deutschland über Alles."

After the official opening was completed, a share, a very limited share, of liberty was accorded to the foreign ships. Woe betide any one, or anything, that took advantage of such liberty for any undignified behaviour or display.

On the occasion of our beloved Queen Victoria's jubilee celebration at Spithead, when all the naval power of the Empire was stretched out in three imposing lines of peaceful warning, I was scandalised to see a cutter of the fishing boat class tacking backwards and forwards amongst the mighty ships of war, under white mainsail and jib, the former marked with great black lettering "Beecham's Pills," and the latter "Worth a Guinea a Box"! Good gracious! Such a national act of insubordination at Kiel, and the delinquent would have been sunk by a shot from the nearest man-of-war without a funeral service, and, in my humble opinion, the verdict would have been serve him or them right. To allow such a display of contemptuous insolence to pass without condign punishment only encourages ignorance and disloyalty.

After lunch at Kiel the G.O.M. and some friends went on board an English yacht to visit other friends, and they had a very narrow escape from being run down by an Italian steam launch. The old gentleman stuck to his own ship after that.

The display of bunting in Kiel Harbour was quite a sight. Ashore as well as afloat, flags, flags everywhere. All the fleets were dressed in rainbow style, and in the beautiful sunshine the general effect was Fairyland. We only wanted Oberon and Titania to complete the picture.

After dinner in the evening, these were to give place to illuminations, prepared in the most wonderful way; but we had an unrehearsed illustration of magnificence that knocked the bottom out of all human skill and preparation. About eight o'clock in the evening, just as the ships were turning into wedding cakes, a most awful thunderstorm broke over the town and bay. The lightning was extraordinary, and was precursor to a deluge of rain through which the illuminated ships in the distance looked like ghostly blurs mixed up with blinding flashes, and serenaded with rolling peals of thunder.

It certainly was a strange combination of the human and the Divine – and the human went under in the competition. It seemed almost like a judgment upon the circumstances and the ceremony; but I do not pretend to advance any theory or cause for such a thought,

The storm continued until near midnight, and most surely gave rise to great disappointment amongst the authorities afloat as well as ashore. The expenses of such a day must have been no small tax upon the Nation itself.

The following day Sir Donald took his guests about, and entertained other guests on board, and it was a case of junketing from morning till night. The G.O.M. remained on board. I don't think he cared about risking a second collision.

I must mention a small matter of amused memory. As Mr. Gladstone would not leave the ship, and Sir Donald could not very well leave his other guests entirely to their own excursions, he tackled me to go and keep the old gentleman company during his absence; telling me that he, the Great Mogul, particularly wished to have a yarn with me – I fear that my chief was, on this particular occasion, indulging in taradiddles. However, I told him that I had a character to maintain; that I was a good old-fashioned Tory, and had no wish to tamper with edged tools to the whittling away of my political rectitude. He said, "Nonsense," and pressed me to go. I still objected, on the ground that I had no wish to incur national indignation by wrecking the professed principles of the people's William.

He told me not to be silly, but "do as I tell you," and turned away huffy. Of course, I had to obey orders. I went, and did what I could; but it was no use He was evidently afraid to unmask his batteries and risk a broadside; but we got along all right on principles of total abstinence from exciting topics until Sir Donald returned. For the sake of Liberal posterity, perhaps it is as well that our voyage didn't last longer than it did.

Sir Donald decided to leave Kiel that evening, and gave me sailing orders to proceed to Gottenberg; so, while all the guests were at dinner, we got under way.

Amongst our own Company guests on board was Captain Ritchie, Marine Superintendent of the Leith and Hamburg line of steamers belonging to Sir Donald's brother, James Currie. He (Captain Ritchie) had been with the firm for many years, and, like the Irish pilot of tradition, he knew every shoal and rock around our saucy little islands and the North Sea. He was a splendid man as well as an accomplished navigator.

From Kiel to Gottenberg is about 200 miles. The nearest way, and the most direct, is *via* the "Great Belt," that runs through the heart of Denmark. *Via* Copenhagen is further round, and the water is also shallower in the narrows. I elected to take "Belt" route. It is very tortuous, but well lighted and I inspanned[56] my friend, Captain Ritchie, to stop up with me and give me the benefit of his expert knowledge. We had a beautiful starlight night and no wind. Shore lights and lighthouses were reflected in the smooth lake-like surface of the sea, and such a panorama of various coloured illuminations all around was quite a novel experience to me. Captain Ritchie's knowledge was invaluable, arid we wound along, in here and out there, in a marvellous way for a big steamer. It was a relief to get into the Cattegat and plain sailing.

At daybreak it began to get hazy, and by 7 o'clock I reckoned that we ought to be in pilotage waters, but nothing was visible.

Still creeping along dead slow, with the lead going, I picked up a big boulder through the haze with a tiny cottage on top of it, and stopped. Again I sent for my friend Captain Ritchie, and asked him what kind of lighthouse we were to look for, and whether he could locate the dimly-defined boulder and wee housie. He took a look through the glasses, and, to my great surprise, said: "That is the

---

[56] Harnessed.

lighthouse! Most of them round here are like that – just a cottage with a dome roof in which the light is."

It was still very hazy, but no pilot boats were in sight, and I knew that Sir Donald wanted to waste no time, because our ship had to take up the mail sailing. On consulting the local chart along with my Chief Officer Cassidy, I put her on and made for the port. Had it been clear I should certainly not have done so. By the time we had passed our boulder, and there was no room to turn, it cleared a bit, and we found ourselves surrounded with boulders and weird rocks on every hand; with here and there an index of one kind and another – all clearly charted fortunately – through a very serpentine channel of some considerable length. The view reminded me of a great cemetery of tomb stones. I had the chart open on a table in front of me, but it failed to convey any idea to the uninitiated of the remarkable features of the port and its approaches. Pilots and small craft under local skippers would find no difficulty, of course, but we could claim no such immunity.

When we were about half-way through, Sir Donald came up on to the bridge, and, looking around, with a tremor in his voice, said, "Where is the pilot?"

"Haven't got one, sir – thick outside" –

"Steady, starboard – steady. Stop her. Half speed ahead. Port. Slow ahead both. As you go. Port. Hard a-port. Stop both. Steady starboard. Half speed ahead starboard. Slow ahead both. As you go. Stop her. Half astern both. Stop her. What water have you?"

"Seven fathoms."

"Let go the anchor." Brrrrrr!!

During this little *séance* my dear old chief held on to the bridge rail, pale as a ghost and trembling visibly. When the cable finished rattling, he turned to me with a queer look, and said, "You have done it well, but don't do it again."

When it was all over I commenced to tremble myself. I had no time to do so before. Sir Donald's injunction was timely but unnecessary. Captain Ritchie, dear old man, when Sir Donald brought the matter up before him later on, said, "Oh, it's easy enough when you know your ship, and have good men at the wheel and the engines."

The fact is that Sir Donald had wired his agents in Gottenberg to have a pilot on the look out for us before we left Kiel; and we had missed him in the haze, I suppose. At all events, another pilot was sent off as soon as the party landed; and when the "animal" came alongside he refused to embark unless he was to receive his fees and gratuity at once! It is to be hoped that all Gottenberg pilots are not tarred with the same brush.

We remained there the one day only, and started for England, Home, and Beauty the same evening.

On the way back Mrs. Gladstone was good enough to nail me for a "little chat" as she called it. It amounted to an amiable request that I would let her know "whether there was anything in the wide world that her husband could do for me, and that it would give him great pleasure to do it."

I jokingly said that if he would offer me an Admiral's Commission I should feel disposed to accept it.

"No, no, no, I'm not joking," she said. "Tell me what you would like."

"Well, really," I replied, "I understand that Mr. Gladstone has translated and published Homer's Iliad. I should love to have a copy if he has one to spare."

"I'll tell him so," she replied.

To finish this little episode – after our arrival in London, I received a small shilling book entitled "Land Marks of Homeric History," with the initials "W E. G." on the fly-leaf. This may seem rather a small token from the great man of our realm – but I was not aware at the time that the work I had asked for ran through twenty-four volumes, and doubtless the G.O.M. punished my unintentional audacity by sending this little booklet. The great author is dead and gone, but I apologise to him still in thought for my stupid mistake. I had an idea that the Iliad was about equal in length to one of Tennyson's Idyls. This will illustrate the profundity of my classical attainments.

I cannot rake up any more actual reminiscences of this twelve days' trip to Hamburg and Kiel, with the Royal interlude at Copenhagen. But I think, rightly or wrongly, that all the junketing and speechifying and hob-nobbing in Hamburg had much to do with the establishment of so-called friendly relations between German and English shipping firms on the East Coast of Africa. All the concessions made were made to the wily Teuton. All the professions made were made to the credulous Britisher. The former have continually augmented, whilst the latter have as continually been diluted.

From infinitesimally small beginnings our friends, the recent enemy, have skilfully acquired power and influence over natives and native industries, whilst we have, in exact ratio, been losing ground, and in some cases have been warned off and deliberately kept out. The war has, of course, corrected a good deal of this anti-British and therefore anti-native welfare – I might indeed, from my own point of view and conviction, say anti-mundane welfare.

But all the fools are not dead yet. A good many are already listening to the blandishments of the wily Boche. Apathy is at the bottom of all our national failures. There is a distinct want of adhesion in our character – a lack of the Imperial instinct of a permanent nature. This disposition can be roused into active unity under the stress of great misfortune; but it falls asleep again as soon as the crisis is past. What a pity!

The Japanese teach us a great lesson under this head. Loyalty and patriotism are the first principles of their school training, and they unite the whole Empire as one unit. We have a lot to learn from them. In compassion towards so-called native tribes all over the earth, the German element should be kept out, until he can appreciate the claims of others, and knows how to govern dependent peoples.

No. 32.

WE carry singular passengers occasionally between England and the Sunny South, and *vice-versa*. I don't mean humans, though strange samples of the Genus Homo are not uncommon. "O wad the gods the giftie gie us to see oursels as ithers see us." We are all strange folk to one another, if not to ourselves. Some lunatic once gave it as his opinion that all men are mad, and that the differences are only in degree. Whether he meant to include women in his sweeping summary I cannot tell. His verdict may be wise, but it is scarcely complimentary.

Away back in days of hoary antiquity, before the amalgamation of the Union and Castle Companies, our mail steamers used to call at Ascension and St. Helena alternately. It was before the former was reduced from the registered dignity of tender to *H.M.S. Flora*, with a naval captain and crew as governor and guard, to the rank of a bos'n's watch. Ascension in those days was a cinder heap, with a conical hill crowned with a plantation called Green Mountain, the proud result of untiring industry and gardener's skill. The island was peopled with seagulls, land crabs, turtles, and grubs. The latter found healthy subsistence amongst the wide-awakes and other marine birds, and attained to giant proportions, many being as large as one's finger. They infested the shore regions in millions, boring into the volcanic formation, and were a perfect nuisance. They made their way everywhere, and defied the authorities to dislodge them.

At last a happy idea was started, and immediately acted upon. The Admiralty at Home was requisitioned to send out a consignment of crows and starlings, and the shipment was made with us, I cannot tell how many there were of each brigade; but comparatively few died in transit. It was hoped that the grubs would make a wholesome provision for them.

There was one important item that had been overlooked, I believe. Ascension has no water supply of its own, or had not at that time. Inhabitants were limited to a certain ration of water per day, which was condensed at considerable cost. How about rationing the corbies? Water exposed in troughs would quickly evaporate in the solar heat of Ascension. I don't know how they met the difficulty; but we landed the birds. In addition to the crows and starlings we had a consignment of blackbirds and thrushes to give a poetical touch to Green Mountain. But the liquor question would affect them, too.

If I remember rightly, Captain Parsons was Governor in those days. An interesting story is told of him. A certain number of civilians – mostly tradesmen and small shopkeepers – were permitted to reside and trade on the island. In addition to the naval contingent and a batch of

Kroomen,[57] the total census might run into about 150 or 200 souls of both sexes.

Though limited in numbers, there was a good deal of competition amongst the lady element. Jealousy and ill feeling waxed so acute that unseemly disputes used to occur even at the church doors, concerning the rules, or lack of rules, governing official and civilian precedence. There was quite a nice little stone church of Gothic architecture in the settlement, capable of accommodating sixty or thereabouts. The controversy became so keen that Mrs. So-and-so would not enter the doors if she saw that Mrs. Some-one-else was there before her, and so on. At last they concluded that something had to be done. They called a committee of all the ladies in the island, and agreed to lay the whole matter before the Governor, and to abide by his decision, the church question to be the test, and to decide all else. Having arrived at this amiable concurrence, they went in a body to Captain Parsons – who was not a married man – and laid their matters before him, asking for his verdict. With all gravity he weighed the pros and cons, and said: "All things being equal, let it be the rule henceforth that the eldest shall enter first, followed by the rest according to age."

This obviously fair judgment was a poser. The grey-haired grocer's wife, unable to disguise her own seniority, accepted the situation and appropriated the front seat for herself and family. The rest remained outside. History does not record the final issue.

We took out a charming young lady, along with the birds, to marry the paymaster of Ascension. We could not wait to see the ceremony performed, but I walked up with them on arrival to see their pretty little future home, and to drink the bride's good health.

On our return from South Africa a year afterwards we called at the islands again, arriving at Ascension about 9 p.m.; and as it was dead calm and quite smooth I took a run ashore with the governor's boat to greet Mrs. Paymaster. I went to the little home and found doors and windows open and a tiny pink lamp burning in the hall, but no one seemed to be about, and I was afraid to make a noise for fear of frightening the inmates at that hour – about 10 p.m. On returning to the jetty – only a stone's throw away – I found the paymaster and told him where I had been.

"My word," he said, "it's lucky that you didn't wake the baby, or he would have awakened the blooming island."

I congratulated myself upon my lucky escape from starting a mutiny.

Ascension is a great place for turtles. A long stretch of sandy shore on the north side of the island is called Turtle Beach. It appears

---

[57] Africans from the Liberian Kru tribe, sometimes recruited as sailors.

that the creatures come there to lay their eggs. These parent amphibia vary in bulk from two to four hundredweight, and their eggs hatch out into beautiful little jet black johnnies about the size of a 5s. piece. Strangely enough, turtles of no intermediate size are known in that region. What becomes of the young ones during the interval of growth? I believe they live prodigiously long lives, probably hundreds of years. Four of these giant marine reptiles were put on board of us – three to London addresses, and one a present to myself. In addition to these, I purchased quite a number of the newly hatched ones from a boatman. It appears that they have a sea water pond close by the beach, and the men go out with lanterns and in the moonlight during the hatching season, and collect them on their way to the sea; then into the pond they go, and are quite satisfied to remain there feeding upon seaweed or anything else that is tossed to them, but they never seem to grow any bigger.

I put my squad into my bath, having arranged for the water to be kept at a certain depth – the tap continually running – and they arrived at home quite safely and went to the Zoo. During the voyage they had many fascinated visitors, but public interest was centred in the big ones on deck.

By means of an awning and some spars we arranged quite a roomy pond before the bridge, and put the three London ones into it, where they afforded endless amusement to all and sundry.

The one they gave to me, I dropped overboard as soon as we were clear of the Island. I have a great horror of turtle killing; they take twelve hours to die! I shall not harrow my readers' feelings by describing the dreadful process.

Turtles are quarrelsome beggars amongst themselves – but their movements are so slow and deliberate that their pugilism is too ludicrous for words. It takes them about five minutes to make up their minds that they have been insulted, and another five to consider whether it would be advisable to conduct a policy of attack or defence. If either belligerent decides to take active steps, she very deliberately turns round and eyes her opponent, and commences to open her mouth; whereupon the defendant takes advantage of the time to move slowly round with her armour plating towards the aggressor.

During these preliminaries the onlookers become far more excited than the gladiators, and with their watches in their hands cry "Time" and plank their finances on the issue. As a rule the impetuous fire-eater forgets what she was contemplating and goes to sleep.

I myself went to sleep one night in my bunk, which was over a double line of drawers, so that the bunk board was quite 4 ft. above the floor. It was a calm night in the tropics, and I was wrapped in soft dreamy slumbers mixed with odours of Cologne; said odours becoming more and more pronounced, and accompanied by a grunting and scratching at my bunk board that seemed to materialise my dream in a remarkable way, until an extra whiff and struggle led my hand automatically to the electric switch at my head – and I found myself face to face at a distance of 12 ins. from a huge 4 ft. porcupine that was on his hind legs, trying to climb into my bed, staring at the sudden blaze of light! Being arrayed in a light pyjama suit I had no desire for such affectionate advances, and tried to get out.

This I at last effected by throwing a sheet over his head, which gave me time to jump out, arm myself with a camp stool, and call for a quartermaster. The brute showed fight, but together we managed to edge him out through the open door, and he stampeded along the boat deck and fell ten feet over the end and broke his neck.

We had three of them on board in one large cage, and they had eaten their way out. A search discovered a second beast behind the line of boats, and he saved all trouble by jumping overboard. We never found out what became of the third.

We had two young lions with us one voyage not long ago, and they were in iron dens on the boat deck, too. They were splendid specimens and fairly well behaved, except when a passenger was taking his dog for a run or any babies or little children were about; then the band played! The beasts were a dangerous source of amusement to young people as well as to older ones, and we had to erect an enclosure round the cages to prevent any one from getting too close to their claws.

The butcher, who had charge of them, managed to gain their amiable approval until they would accept a trifle in the way of a beef steak or even a mutton chop out of his hand. I took their photographs on several occasions. One was particularly successful, taken with the lens between the bars of the cage, so that the lion seemed to be in the open. That butcher of ours was no doubt endowed with some sylvan characteristics; everything in the way of birds and animals took to him almost at once. He could handle them with impunity whilst others could not come near them. I think it was on this same voyage that he brought home some young seals and penguins from Mossel Bay, and it was fascinating to see those creatures swarming and fondling around him as if he were one of themselves. We kept the seals in a canvas pond on the boat deck, like the one the turtles were in. I think seals in confinement are inclined to become domesticated as it were. They appear to delight in showing off when they have an appreciative audience. At other times they will lie quiet for hours.

Passenger fares ought to be raised when the ship carries wild animals. They are a daily picnic to most people.

Years ago there was a man in Cape Town, Dr. Something, who was I fancy connected with the Zoo in Regent's Park. He used to ship

Home serpents. That is a kind of thing I don't love. As Artemus Ward[58] or Ally Sloper[59] once said – they're too long for their width and they're damp. I was afraid of such passengers. They were carried in cases with glass lids, and these had to be removed in order to place their food and milk inside; and I was always anxious for fear of an accident.

A box of snakes came on board one voyage without a bill of lading, which turned out to have been smuggled in by the second officer for some serpentine friend in London. This particular box got on my nerves, and one night in the S.E. trades I had a vivid and horrible dream – that one of the wretches had escaped and bitten a lady passenger. I got up in a state of cold perspiration, and told the "Second," who was on watch, to go at once and launch the whole thing overboard, and he did. Dreams may be of small account in these practical days, but I could not have kept those things on board after that nightmare.

When I went to sea I was always on the look-out for some new thing myself, and was never without a living companion. On one voyage in a sailing ship, when in the China Seas I observed a large bird flying high one afternoon, and I lay low. We were not very far from Sumatra, and I knew by its flight that it was not a sea bird, and that it would probably settle upon us somewhere for the night. It was calm and smooth. As I expected, after sundown it drew nearer, and just as darkness set in I saw it alight on the extreme end of the fore to'gallant yard on the port side.

I waited patiently until about 10 o'clock, and then made my way up very cautiously on the opposite side until I also reached the yard, and could distinguish my quarry faintly outlined against the clear sky, but looming rather larger than I had expected. However, I slid quietly, slowly, and cautiously along the yard, flattening myself as much as possible until I was within a yard or so. Then I stopped to study the situation, scarcely breathing. The bird was as big as a large turkey, and was balancing itself with slight elevations of wing and neck as the ship moved gently upon the undulations of the sea. Should I attack or desist? If was evident to me that he had a suspicion I was an enemy of some kind, because now and then he lowered his head and stretched his neck at full length towards me to reconnoitre.

The temptation was too strong. I just waited for the next "inquiry," and grabbed the neck close to the head with my left hand, holding on to the yard with my right for all I was worth. My prize instantly doubled under, and seized my upper arm in its talons with the grip of a vice. In this relative position, with two enormously long wings extended, I had to get in to the mast the best way I could. My guardian

---

[58] 19th-century American humorous writer.
[59] Comic strip character.

angels were very good to me. I was inextricably mixed up with a full-grown golden eagle, with only one arm to work with, 80 to 90 ft. above the ship's deck. At last, getting my leg and arm round the rigging, I managed to pull claw by claw away till they were all doubled together like two fists, and then, tying his legs together with a rope yarn, I tied his head also to them and clambered down with him upon my arm like a huge basket.

I kept him for a few days tied up, but he would eat nothing, so let him go in sight of land, and he said "Good-bye" with mutual regret.

Fortunately for me, my arm was thin; the talons overlapped and only the points pricked into the flesh. That was quite enough for me where I was.

No. 33.

I have been pleased to receive several kindly letters of appreciation from old-time passengers referring to these rigmarole sailor's yarns of mine that the sporting Editor of *South Africa* has been bold enough to publish.

Amongst these, one was from a gentleman who made more than one voyage with me, being accompanied by his brother on one occasion. We were excellent friends – birds of a feather, in fact – and I trust he will not be offended with me for mentioning his name.

Mr. John Newberry and his brother had considerable business interests in Basutoland, and I am going to record a little history that I received from him at first hand – subject to lapses of memory – which will not be to his disadvantage, though he may say I ought not to have given him away.

To me the story was extremely fascinating; it cannot be less than interesting to my readers.

Subsequent to the Basuto trouble, when driving across country in his Cape cart past a native settlement and farmstead, he became aware of distant singing, evidently a hymn tune. Pulling up, he stopped to locate the direction of the sound, and drove towards it.

He was led to what would be called a shack in Canada. I don't know what the native name is for a hut where outdoor farm rubbish is kept. Getting down quietly and looking in, he saw a grey-haired old Basuto standing at the further end with a book in his hand, holding forth to some dozen or so of other natives squatting in a most uncomfortable way, there being scarcely room enough to stand in, let alone to sit down; and the old man at the end had to keep his head down, and his body bent, beneath the sheet of corrugated iron that formed the covering of this novel place of worship.

My friend remained until the conclusion of the meeting, and then got hold of the old man for information. Finding that on the outbreak of trouble, their missionary had been warned off at a moment's notice, a little band had been endeavouring to keep a light burning as best they might until the dawn of better times; he, the old herdsman, having been elected leader.

Mr. Newberry, finding that the present company was only a part of the results of missionary labours in the district, pointed out that the shack was scarcely appropriate for such service, and offered to supply them with timber, bricks, glass, and material generally, as well as a plan clearly drawn out, if the old man and his friends would undertake the building. This they joyfully promised to do.

A site was selected, and purchased from the Chief for a very small sum, and in process of time the extraordinarily generous provision of all the necessary material was dumped down to the care of the old man; the plan, extremely simple, and calculated to accommodate 100, being carefully explained to a number of "the Church" before my friend left the country.

It was during our homeward voyage that he told me this interesting story, and smilingly remarked that he would be much interested on his return to see the result of their labours.

He did return with me about a year afterwards; and on the following voyage he was again a passenger homewards. Remembering the story he told me, I particularly asked him on the way out to ascertain and let me know the result of his munificent provision; and the following is his report.

On reaching the spot, he found that the brickwork of the walls, with the spaces for the two windows each side, and the doorway, had reached a height of six to seven feet, and there had stopped. Naturally the poor congregation were once more holding their meetings in the old shack!

It was with feelings of bitter disappointment and sorrow that the old man explained to their benefactor that they had altogether failed to understand from the plan the method of roofing the little chapel, and it was over a year since they had suspended work upon it.

Mr. Newberry consoled the church by sending for a builder to come and direct operations; and before he left the country again he had the supreme satisfaction of attending a meeting in a little cathedral conducted by the same grey haired old Basuto. He was so deeply impressed by the transparent earnestness and reverence of the man, that he endowed him with a living wage in order that he might be free for mission duty and service so long as he should remain in charge of "The Church," or until a missionary should arrive to relieve him.

I know not what this matter cost my generous friend from first to last. No doubt he was well able to bear the expense; but that is neither here nor there. Many men in South Africa and elsewhere might be able, but how many would be willing to do likewise? I consider that it was wonderful; just the kind of thing Cecil Rhodes would have rejoiced to do without giving it a second thought; and no doubt just the kind of thing he was constantly doing without ringing a bell – for no man knows the length of the list of his unpublished and unsuspected benefactions.

I must write Mr. Newberry and ask him for a sequel to his story – there must be a sequel[60] – but we must let this go through first of all or he might issue a writ of injunction against me!

---

[60] Mr Newberry wrote to the journal in March 1920, saying that the little church had been much enlarged, but that it was actually in the Free State, though near Basutoland, and inhabited by Basuto people.

It is quite refreshing to meet with instances of this kind occasionally. It gilds and glorifies our human nature, and lifts it out of the mire of universal egotism.

I have vivid recollection of another charming instance of liberal hearted charity that occurred on board the old *Roslin Castle*. We sailed from Dartmouth on Saturday as usual. It was summer time and we had a goodly number of passengers with us.

On the following morning, Sunday, I was round about amongst them on deck trying to find some one to act as organist for the service at 10.30. One after another declined on the score of inability, and at last I gave it up and said: "I suppose we shall have to be satisfied without any singing."

A tall hand-some man leaning against the rail on the quarter deck heard me speak, and asked what the trouble was; and I told him that amongst all those passengers I could not find a single one able or willing to play at the morning meeting.

JC on Armadale Castle, Dec. 1905

"If that is all, Captain, I shall be glad to play for you if you will allow me to do so."

"Allow you! Indeed, I shall be only too glad of your help. May I ask your name?"

"My name is Joseph Levi, at your service, Captain."

"Mr. Levi, you are a Jew. This is exceedingly kind of you; but pardon me for asking – are you one of us?"

"Not in the sense you mean; but your scriptures are our scriptures; your psalms and chants are ours also. In so far as I am able, I will unite with you in worship, and where we differ, we can do so without disagreement. I know your Church Service perfectly, and shall be only too glad if I may be of any assistance in so good a cause!"

We shook hands on that, and Mr. Levi, who was an accomplished musician, continued to play for us during the voyage. What a lesson for some of us narrow sectarians! We never travelled together again, I am sorry to say. He was a younger man than I; and if he should still be a member of Jo-burg society, I hope he may stumble across this poor reminiscence, and know that his kindness and Jewish charity have never been forgotten, and will be remembered through all eternity.

I feel tempted to stray from diamonds and gold to a prosy little village called Bongate, in Westmorland, a suburb of Appleby on the River Eden, one of the most beautiful trout streams in the country. My clan all belonged there and thereabout. My father was a clergyman, and he spent three or four years[61] of ministry in Jamaica.

On his return to Bongate, the old Vicar, Mr. Bellus,[62] tackled him, and after the usual greetings and welcomes, said: "Look here Robinson, you have been at sea enjoying yourself, and I want a holiday badly. I wish you would relieve me for a few weeks whilst I go and fish."

"Certainly, with pleasure; go right away at once."

"Thank you with all my heart, and look here, Robinson, we are trying to raise funds for a new organ in the Church; do what you can to keep it before the congregation."

"All right, Bellus."

Exit B.

A few days afterwards my father met another old friend, Mr. Thompson, the banker at Appleby. The usual salutations passed and as they parted my father said: "By the way, Thompson, I am taking old Bellus' duty for him for a week or two, and he asked me to try my hand at raising a fund for a new organ in his church: would you be disposed to help?"

"Do you think they require an organ there?"

"I do. It's a wheezy old 'Kist o' whustles' they have there now."

Mr. Thompson tore a bit of paper out of his notebook, and scribbled some cabalistic signs upon it, saying, "Put that in to the cashier as you pass the bank any time."

"Thanks. Good-bye."

A week or so afterwards, passing the bank, he remembered the scrap of paper, and digging it out of his waistcoat pocket he went in and presented it to the cashier, saying, "Can you make anything of that?"

"Oh, yes. How will you take it?"

"Take it – take it in my hand," said he, extending that member.

---

[61] Ten years, 1839-1849.

[62] Rev. Thomas Bellas was vicar at Bongate church from 1823 to 1880, when he died aged 91. The *Westmorland Gazette* reported in August 1849 that Rev. Robert Robinson's younger brother Joseph had collected funds for a new organ at Bongate – presumably the brothers collaborated.

"But would you prefer notes or gold?"

"What is it?"

"It's an order to pay you fifty pounds on demand."

"Fifty pounds! Is Thompson in?"

"Yes."

"I'd like to see him."

"Certainly; show him in."

"Good morning, Thompson. I asked you for a subscription for Bellus' new organ the other day."

"Right; have you put in the order?"

"Yes; and your cashier tells me it is fifty pounds. I didn't ask you to buy a new organ, Thompson. And, by the bye, it didn't occur to me before that you are a Quaker!"

"What has that to do with the matter? You say you want a new organ; very well; as it appears to be your custom to praise God by machinery, by all means get as good a machine as you can. I'm only too glad to help!"

My father left the bank, as I have heard him say, a richer, a wiser, and a sadder man.

I should like to close this episode by quoting some old-fashioned proverb appropriate to the occasion; but unfortunately I cannot think of one, though there must be such. I am no hand at inventing clever sayings.

To return to Mr. Rhodes. I think it was in the *Dunvegan Castle* one Sunday evening, after our service in the second saloon as usual, that he came up to my cabin.

After fitting himself comfortably into the lounge chair and lighting a cigar, he said in his dreamy, soliloquising voice: "I think you are going to convert South Africa!"

I am afraid I smiled a mixture of deprecation and guilt – for no man can be held responsible for "visions," even presumptuous visions – provided that they do no one any harm.

Mr. Rhodes continued in the same far-away manner: "I, too, have had my ambitions, but there are many opponents. I want to build and endow a university under the shadow of Table Mountain, but they won't have it. The cry goes up that it would ruin all existing collegiate establishments. But what a mistake it is. A first-rate 'Oriel' at Cape Town, with the pick of the professors, combined with the matchless salubrity of the South African climate, and the glittering prospects of the probable future, would be a continual invitation to the vital forces of the Empire abroad and at Home, who in their best days would flock in to profit by education and opportunity, bringing *the best traditions of our race and religion along with them* to consolidate Colonies and Mother Country upon the rock of unassailable loyalty and mutual interest."

A tremor in his voice betrayed the brightness of *his* vision, as he switched his handkerchief across his face whilst reaching over for the matches to relight his cigar. I said nothing; I was afraid to break the charm.

He smoked away in silence for a bit with half-closed eyes, and then, in a scarcely audible voice, murmured, "The Church is always at the bottom of such failures. I went Home this last time hoping to find some central National Church organisation to which I could hand over a fairly considerable endowment – for the Church of England is my Church, as it has always been. I love the old establishment, but I was quite unprepared to find in it a soul without a system. The Thirty-nine Articles, which I committed to memory years ago, are proof of the soundness of the former; but the so-called 'body' consists of so many members at variance one with another that I found no representative organisation to whom I could entrust, say, a million with any certainty that it would be wisely used!"

Just then there was a knock at the door, and Dr. Jim walked in.

"Hello!" he said. "What's up, Rhodes? I want a walk; come along."

And so the spell was broken that might have led on to other fascinating heart-searchings and disclosures. Have we no more Cecil Rhodes, or must he remain a sole representative of a separate genus – a *rara avis in terris nigroque similima Cygno,*[63] as the old Latin proverb has it? I suppose that no one who ever knew him failed to love him, and to treasure his memory as a rich dowry. I am one of them.

---

[63] Juvenal: "a rare bird in the lands, and very like a black swan".

No. 34.

TO the uninitiated, journalism is a profound mystery. Many times I have made attempts to enlighten the British public through the Press upon issues that seemed to affect the country, the kingdom, the Empire, and the world, and have met with the most perfect want of success; and yet on one notable occasion a simple, natural, and professional act of kindness on my part was got hold of by some omnivorous reporter and magnified into a miracle. To my surprise, on my return I found that it had not only been published locally, but copied from paper to paper from John o' Groat's to Land's End!

This marvel took place in September, 1899 – twenty-one years ago – and in case *South Africa* escaped the original infliction, I am going to repeat the story myself, with embellishments that did not appear at the time because they were not known; the matter appearing to be too unimportant for details. I will keep to the title under which it originally appeared – "Ocean Mails."

We arrived in Cape Town in the *Carisbrook Castle,* homeward bound, on a Monday morning, and found the *Lismore Castle,* Captain le Soeur, in dock, just arrived from England. Instead of sailing coastwise as usual, he was under orders to return Home at once, and was to start at noon the following day – Tuesday.

The outward bound mail steamer should arrive at Cape Town on Tuesday, and generally did so. Captain le Soeur came on board of us after breakfast, bitterly lamenting that unless the mail arrived in decent time the following day there would be grievous disappointment on board at missing their Home letters, and could I do anything to help them; would I bring the letters back with me, and if the two ships met at sea would I stop whilst he sent a boat for them?

After a minute's consideration, I told him I would rather not stop with the South African mails on board for the sake of a handful of ship's letters. "But," I said, "I think we can do better than that. Come up into the chart room. What is your speed?"

"11½."

"Very well, ours is 16. You will have twenty-four hours' start of us, and will therefore be 276 miles to the good when we leave. In four days you will have covered about 1100 miles, roughly speaking. We, in three days, should make somewhere about 1150. Isn't that so? Consequently, we should pass you, say, about noon on Saturday next. Now here is the chart with my regular course laid down. Lay that line down on your chart also, crossing the meridians in these same latitudes, and look out astern for our ship on Saturday morning and get into our wake.

"Then, we will pull up our big holiday ensign; and after we have passed you about half a mile or so we will drop your mails overboard marked with a red flag, blow our steam whistle, and dip our ensign at the same moment. The rest is your business, to lower a boat and pick them up."

Agreed with thanks. Nothing to make a fuss about.

The *Lismore* passed the "Mail" the following day whilst still within sight of Table Mountain.

On our part, I collected her letters and parcels, &c., and enclosed them in a small barrel, properly ballasted to ensure its keeping "this side up with care," and covered all over with an envelope of canvas painted with two coats to keep it water tight; upon it was also painted the legend: "Ocean Mails"; and a three-foot staff, with a two-foot red flag attached, completed the outfit.

According to our calculations, on the Saturday morning early we sighted the *Lismore Castle* ahead, and passed her about noon. All our passengers were in a ferment of excitement over the affair as if the safety of the *Lismore* depended upon her success in retrieving this precious parcel. Telescopes and binoculars were in great demand; and when the steam whistle sounded, and the flag was dipped to indicate the launch of the momentous barrel of loves, of hopes, and disappointments with which we could have no kind of concern, the agitation was surprising. Several sympathetic natures were in tears as the little red flag danced away upon the waves towards the approaching *Lismore*. One fine young fellow grasped a lady round the waist for fear she should faint, and, thankful for the temporary support during the excess of anxiety, she quite unwittingly surrendered, until the cry of the watchers went up like a gasp, "They've got it." Then realising, for the first time, that somebody might be looking, I suppose, she indignantly turned upon the presumptuous octopus, and damaged her fan across his ears. That was the only accident that happened at our launch of the letters for the *Lismore*.

But there is a little sequel to the story, which gave rise to the newspaper reports I have referred to above. The whole subject disappeared from my memory like a dissolving view.

About a fortnight after our arrival in London, a parcel was handed to me at the office as I was on the point of rejoining my ship for another voyage, on opening which I found a framed document produced by the artists on board the *Lismore,* thanking me for the "Ocean Mails," and illustrated with barrels, and mermaids, and flags, and sea monsters in a marvellously clever and gratifying manner.

A gentleman who was standing beside me when I opened the package made some remark and asked for particulars, which I gave him roughly and started for the docks. That gentleman turned out to be the "omnivorous reporter" fishing for "copy" at the office, and it was I who inadvertently gave away the show. Had I sent the full account along with the artistic testimonial (which I still have amongst my treasures) to some – or to the special paper in which it appeared, it would no doubt have been returned to me with a polite note of thanks and regrets that space was limited. I hope the Editor of *South Africa* will not take this as a hint.

In the last paragraph I used the word "inadvertently." I recalled to memory a curious mistake, as we believed afterwards, that was made on board the *Dunottar Castle*, I think, about the year 1892.

We had the honour on that particular voyage of having on our passenger list Dr. Alexander, Archbishop of Armagh, who was taking his daughter out to Cape Town to be married. She had all her wedding presents with her in two heavy dressing bags. She had them put upon the sofa in her room, and went up on deck to say good-bye to friends and to see the ship start. We were lying at anchor off Netley, and passengers had come on board by the tender.

All being finished, the whistle sounded, and visitors scurried off on board the tender again, and just as she was moving off, one of our officers spied a large handbag under the ladder at the gangway, which he saw a man place there as he climbed on board the tender; and he called out, "Here – you've left your bag behind you."

The mate of the tender, who was superintending, said, "All right, hand it up – he'll find it," and up it went.

Now this was decidedly "inadvertent." We had started and got into the Solent, when the purser came up to me to report that a big robbery had been committed, that Miss Alexander had lost all her wedding presents. The two dressing bags had been cut open at the back of each, and all contents had disappeared; hundreds of pounds' worth of jewellery and ornaments, &c.

We sent telegrams ashore by the pilot at the Needles, to the dock authorities, and to our Company at Southampton, and a list and description from Madeira by mail, but nothing more could be done. I heard afterwards, on our return Home, that a pile of jewel boxes, &c., had been found in a latrine in Southampton Docks, and a hand bag! How about that hand bag? I can only suppose that the man who was seen to place that hand bag under the ladder as he climbed on board the tender had got a scare somehow that he was detected and had wilfully deserted his plunder, which, through our inadvertence, he would probably regain on board the tender when his scare was over. Of course, this is only a surmise. Poor Miss Alexander, It's hard lines upon a young lady just starting off upon her own to do so under such a cloud.

The reference to a marriage recalls an interesting instance of multiple matrimony that I played a rather insignificant part in myself once in India. I was in command of the *Carnarvon Castle* sailing ship, in Calcutta. It was practically the universal custom in those days – 1874 – for the captain of each ship to engage the services of a "Dubash," generally one of the Hindoo business men, who acted as legal adviser and agent for the ship during her stay in port.

Some of these Dubashes were great swells in their way, and they were undoubtedly extremely useful and necessary. It would be practically impossible for any master of a ship to carry on his work alone, even though he could speak the language like a native. The Indian mind is a sealed book to the European, and it requires an Indian to cope with it. A good Dubash was a veritable treasure and, fortunately for me, I was led to adopt one of the very best.

He was like one of the Ginns of the Arabian Nights. He knew everything and everybody, and withal was very dignified, quiet, and retiring. If I remember rightly his name was Muttee Lall.

We became great friends, and in fact he conceived quite an affection for me, which he displayed in many little acts of disinterested kindness. Before leaving Calcutta, on our second voyage, he asked me to dinner at his house, saying that he wished to introduce me to some of the Indian manners and customs. Of course I accepted, and went in uniform.

Before dinner was served he asked me if I would consent to be introduced to his wives. I was surprised at the plural, and also at prospect of seeing Hindoo ladies. Accepting his invitation, he led me to the back of the house, to a verandah that formed one side of a quadrangle, with windows and green venetian blinds all round. After standing there chatting for a few minutes, he said:

"Now, will you kindly turn and look in that direction, and please bow."

I did as requested, and could not help smiling as I saluted, cap in hand, in correct naval fashion.

"Thank you," he said, "that is all. They have seen you and appreciate your courtesy, but you do not see them!"

I made some obvious allusion to my disappointment, and we adjourned to dinner, which was served up quite in the best English manner, only that some of the good things were no doubt creations for the occasion.

After a very pretty dessert and excellent coffee, we took our cigars to the reception hall and were divanned and cushioned for a luxurious smoke. Very soon a party of native musicians came in with novel kinds of instruments, who, after salaaming to mine host and then to me, seated themselves in a semi-circle and began to shame the silence of the hall.

I had not time to grasp the meaning of the orchestra, when a bespangled and glittering figure in tights and a floating gossamer shawl, looking like a scaly mermaid in all the colours of the kaleidoscope, sidled in, and made a musically conducted reverence to Mr. Muttee Lall, and then turned to pay me the same compliment, to my exceeding dismay, as another similarly arrayed – or unarrayed – sylph entered and went through the same evolution, followed by a third, and then a fourth; the only difference between them being in tone and colour of the fish-like close-fitting dress and floating drapery, if such it might be called.

All joined in a weird calisthenic kind of sinuosity, called a Nautch Dance as I understood afterwards – to the surprising strains of tom-toms, cymbals, and Indian fiddles, accompanied now and then by a kind of dirge or chant that was not unpleasing. The orchestra warmed up at times to a mild crescendo, but it was mostly soft and sensuous, as the quartette dance also was dreamy and voluptuous.

It was quite evident that the exhibition – so dear to Eastern eyes and ears – was arranged for my particular delectation, as the dancers wove their webs of winning wiles in rhythmic action round the English Sailor Sahib, who knew not what to do or where to look in order to disguise his scandalised discomfiture!

Still, I am glad I saw it once. I never wish to see it again, I couldn't help saying to myself at the time: "J. C., this is no place for you; better go home to your good ship."

I don't think a Nautch dance amongst the native girls of South Africa would be a great success. So far as my personal experience goes, I am surprised that the men of the radiant Colony so signally excel in stature and beauty of figure, whilst their women are so pigmy and ungraceful. No doubt my experience has been both local and limited. Still, Robbie Burns' lines would scarcely apply in the sunny land of gems and gold –

"Her prentice han' she tried on Man,
And then she made the Lasses oh!"

No. 35.

In the year 1880 – indelibly recorded in my memory – we left Dartmouth, outward bound, in the *Warwick Castle*, with a long passenger list and a full cargo. The weather was nasty, and the prospect uninviting. On deck we had six valuable horses and the usual pair of milch cows of those pre-historic days, besides a lot of sheep and other foodstuffs. The wind was south-westerly, fresh; and it was not over clear, the atmosphere being laden with moisture, relieved occasionally by spells of very cold driving showers: an insidious kind of fine rain that investigated every buttonhole and overlap of one's oilskin armour.

We ploughed along against a lumpy head sea, keeping well to the westward in order to avoid too neighbourly an acquaintance with Ushant, which we knew we should not be likely to see at a reasonably safe distance in such murky weather.

Towards evening, however, there was a distinct change for the better, though we were still pretty busy scattering the splinters around, and the barometer was steadily going down.

About 5 o'clock, in spite of the weather, I heard some singing on the main hatch. It turned out to be a small band of five members of the Salvation Army, the first contingent for South Africa, who had determined to bombard the ship, as they expressed it, and concluded that the sooner they opened the campaign the better for everybody. They commenced singing hymns to various rolicking and inappropriate secular tunes, as was the custom in those early days.

Being rather scandalised at this irreverent combination of things mundane and divine, I went down to them off the bridge, and warned them that they might bring a gale of wind upon us if they persisted in such improper psalmody.

They looked at me to see if I were serious or joking, and then at one another, and laughed. I just shook my finger at them, looking very grieved, and returned to the bridge. There was no more bombardment that evening. I could see that they were not feeling very happy in their middle distances. Anyhow, it was getting damp and murky again, and there was a general exodus of the non-executive.

The meteorological conditions next day were no better, and a long N.W. swell added liveliness to the ship, to the great discomfort of our passengers, amongst whom was Rider Haggard, who had a cabin on deck aft.

Towards evening it became evident that we were in for trouble, The swell abeam from the N.W. began to assume growing importance, causing us to roll most unpleasantly, and the wind was increasing to a gale, and hauling more to the westward.

By ten o'clock we were at the end of our tether. In the darkness, the advancing foam-crested rollers loomed like hills of ocean threatening to submerge us; and the *Warwick* was indulging in a regular corkscrew performance between the head sea and the swell abeam. It was blowing a full gale from the westward, with the promise of more to follow, and it became necessary to "heave to."

A little careful management carried this manoeuvre through without complications, and we lay with the wind and sea a little on the port bow, and the increasingly vicious N. W. swell on the starboard bow; but we were in comfort as compared with the previous situation.

Nursing a ship under such circumstances is pretty much like nursing a baby at any time, only more so; it is a case of continual watchfulness and expectation of the unexpected.

By midnight the wind had hauled round into the nor'west and increased rapidly, the Atlantic rollers becoming tremendous. In harbour the *Warwick Castle* was an important-looking steamer as seen through the spectacles of those days; but at daybreak on the following morning she was a veritable cockle shell in the majesty of that ocean panorama.

It would require a larger pencil than I am using to do justice to the scene. As the sunrise made its influence felt, "the heavens declared the glory of God!" The sky was wonderful in colouring where a glimpse of it could be seen through the piled-up wool-sacks of gold and silver thunder clouds. The lower reaches towards the horizon were indigo and green, except where blotted out by the hurricane hail squalls that drove the spume over ship and sea in blinding sheets. It was magnificent, but it was dreadful.

The good ship behaved wonderfully well. Up, bravely up to beard the charging swell, and dive through the foaming crest into the yawning gulf beneath, burying herself forward in the lap of each succeeding sea, and shooting the inundation over from both sides against the bridge.

One horse was killed, and more than one box was smashed up; both bridge ladders were demolished, and all things movable at the fore end disappeared; but, strange to say, both the poor cows, in boxes lashed against the break of the forecastle, escaped entirely owing to their protected position, the green seas washing right over them. What their feelings must have been during that awful twelve hours, poor things, no one knows – because their moans could not be heard during that howling tempest.

The climax was reached about 8 a.m. in one universal and terrible cyclonic squall and deluge of hail that brought the wind round two points more towards the north, and lasted for about twenty minutes.

That having passed, like a great curtain of disappointed fury, astern of us, the glorious sun shone out upon a picture of marine magnificence that Charles Dixon[64] would have revelled in. Even we ourselves rejoiced in it, but that was, perhaps, by contrast with what we had just passed through.

I felt at liberty then to leave the bridge and make a tour of the decks to see what was to be seen, and specially to inquire into our passengers' welfare. I looked into Mr. Rider Haggard's room, amongst others, expecting to find that he had gone below. Not so, however. He was in the upper bunk smoking a cigarette, watching his cabin baggage floating about in as much water as the sill of the closed door would admit of. Evidently he is a philosopher as well as an author. He was quite cheery, and like the "chiel amang us takin' notes".[65]

The rest of the deckers were pretty much in the same condition – none had gone below. One poor dear fellow, a Frenchman travelling for his health, was equally cheerful, and also consoling himself with a cigarette. I cannot tell whether his night's experience increased his lung trouble, but he died before we reached Cape Town.

The gale was fast abating and the swell was losing its vicious crests. Squalls were less frequent, and not so violent; but, alas! the good ship *Warwick Castle* was heading N.N.W. for Greenland, instead of S.S.W. for the fair land of feathers and fortunes. If we could only get her round with her head in the right direction, we should have a fair wind and favouring sea: but, alas! we were still under the yoke of past fury, and must patiently "bide a wee." We lay there breasting the ridges until I began to think I was unduly cautious, the conditions having so greatly improved by 11 o'clock.

Let me explain in few words that after a hard gale and heavy sea, the waves, subsiding, are periodically stirred into fresh mischief by "three seas," which can be observed approaching in the distance by their towering crests of foam. Several minutes may elapse between "threes" and "threes," the intervals becoming longer as conditions improve. It is these trios that we have to reckon with in manoeuvres such as I was contemplating.

At 11 o'clock therefore we prepared to take action at noon. Reefs were taken in topsails and trysails ready for instant use; all passengers were sent below, doors and windows being "storm blinded"; "all hands" were at stations; engineers were raising steam to full pressure (we had been only moving the engines sufficiently for steerage purposes before); and, I was watching the distant horizon from the upper bridge for indications of the fateful trios.

---

[64] British maritime painter.
[65] Robert Burns, "A chield's amang you takin' notes,/And, faith, he'll prent it."

At 8 bells, noon, up went the fore trysail and staysail! and all was ready for the fore topsail, so soon as the ship should be round far enough for it to draw. A few minutes more, during which all hands were no doubt wondering what I was waiting for, and lo! the silver crests ahead gave warning of the "charging three." Down they came and she took them bravely, scattering the heavy spray over the fore part of the ship.

Full speed ahead! Hard a starboard! Sheet home fore topsail! And then the great anxiety! Will she answer in time, or will the next trio overtake the manoeuvre?

The good ship pulsated to the sudden pressure, and commenced to veer round on her helm, until she was gathering speed and paying off handsomely. Up fore topsail! Wind and sea this time nearly abeam – when the foaming crowns of another trio showed up in the distance, apparently resolved upon asserting their authority in protest against our attempt to evade.

Will she do it? By this time sails and steam and helm had done wonders. Wind abeam! One point abaft! Two points abaft! If we can only get it four points abaft all will be well! But no; the influence of the "first" presses her over to leeward – and again she comes rolling to windward under the second foaming mountain, that throws her back at a serious angle (but all the time she is racing away from the wind and has it now four points abaft), and as it breaks in blinding spray over the ship fore and aft, we catch an instantaneous glimpse from the wicked summit into the awful lap that we tumble into almost on our beam ends to windward with a rush that seems like perdition!

Away goes the fore topsail out of the bolt ropes, and the trysail keeps it company, the great sheets of canvas fluttering away to leeward in the wind like wild creatures of an unknown genus. For two eternal moments the ship appears to have exceeded her righting lever, as the crest seems ready to engulf her. But the speed she has attained by this time is her salvation; the wave thrown off from the bow is sufficient to knock the feet from under the threatening sea, and it falls over itself and alongside, filling the decks fore and aft, and washing away everything movable!

Praise God from whom all blessings flow! My second officer, who was at the engine telegraph on the bridge with me, was at that last climax sick as a dog, and had to go below in a state bordering upon collapse. Otherwise, not a soul was hurt on deck or below, I am more than thankful to say. The ship was now on her proper course, heading for the Sunny South, and speeding gaily along regardless of "trios."

What a revulsion of feeling! What a transformation of circumstance! Surely no two associated events could be more diametrically opposed. Doors were unsealed, storm blinds were stowed away. Children were running about on deck glorying in the beautiful trios racing after us. My friends of the Salvation Army were assisted on deck wrapped up and quite unwarlike. I couldn't resist the temptation to go down and cheer them up with a little chaff about the result of their bombardment, and invited them all to join our choir in church and scatter the brigades that way.

It was quite interesting later on to hear the stories of the passengers of all classes during the last twelve hours. Surely their experiences had been cause enough for grievous anxiety, and a sound excuse for downright alarm. Many of the women folks had crowded into cabins together, finding comfort and hope only in community of fear, encouraging themselves and one another in some cases by starting a hymn with somewhat weak voices.

One middle-aged gentleman named Bruce, from over the Border, tickled his hearers at dinner time by telling them, in all soberness, about three o'clock in the morning he just put his trousers and slippers on, so that he might be ready for a call at any moment, and then wedged himself safely into his bed and read the 119th Psalm through. Good man! He couldn't do better.

En passant. After the big squall at 8 o'clock in the morning, referred to above, I made rough notes and sketches of sea and sky, and subsequently produced a chalk drawing of the ship and surroundings at that time, which was afterwards photographed at Port Elizabeth, and sold in large numbers for the Seamen's Poor Box. The drawing, framed, I gave to Sir Donald for his office. He demurred at first, saying it was a poor advertisement for passengers. I differed with him, and said he could show them what ships could stand at sea without starting a rivet. He looked at me with a whimsical twinkle in his eye, as much as to say, You don't know much about shore tactics. However, the picture was hung up in his private room at 3, Fenchurch Street, and was there for a number of years, until one Easter spring cleaning it was taken down, along with other mural decorations, and vanished. I heard afterwards that Mr. Ernest Martin, our erstwhile agent at Port Elizabeth, annexed it – or, in plain, unvarnished English, took it without leave.

I have always regretted the loss of that drawing of the great *Warwick* gale of 1880. We were signally preserved through it as compared with many other less favoured vessels. There was one of the big Orient steamers that sailed outward bound at the same time as ourselves – I quite forget her name for the moment, though I knew the ship so well; she got badly mauled in the gale and had to put back for repairs.[66]

---

[66] Probably the *Chimbarazo*, severely damaged Feb. 1880 with four deaths and numerous injuries.

We saw many others "hove to," and making more or less heavy weather of it. One unfortunate ship was rolling so frightfully that she dipped the two ends of her navigation bridge under water every now and then. She was not far from us, and the sight of it was most distressing. She must have been laden with badly-stowed railway iron or other heavy cargo.

When we came to count up our own costs, they were really very trifling. The horse was the most valuable item. Two bridge ladders, two horse-boxes, half-a-dozen sheep pens, and some loose deck gear; it was really nothing. Before heaving to we had taken all the sheep out of the pens, and put them into some empty deck cabins in the alley way. The result of this was curious; the emanation from their wool, I suppose, peeled all the paint and polish off the walls and furniture, and left the cabins looking like rag shops, and smelling much worse. But we saved our muttons, and they were very comfortable as compared with the two pathetic cows. Poor things, they did try hard to tell us afterwards what a horrible twelve hours they had spent.

With Sir Donald Currie a tradition had sprung up in the Company that strength and good work at all costs must be the ruling principle in shipbuilding and outfit. And we profited by it – an accident to the steering gear, or anything else, in fact, and this memory might never have been recorded.

****
- - AMENDE HONORABLE.—
(By gracious permission of the Editor of "South Africa.")
At the end of my last article, No. 35, I indulged in a little badinage at the expense of my earliest acquaintance in the "Castle Company," Mr. Ernest Martin. I confess I was scribbling against time to catch the issue of *South Africa*, and on reading the article over in cold print yesterday I was grieved to find that my clumsy smartness was capable of anything but a friendly interpretation. Besides, I have recalled the fact that it was Mr. Martin himself who told me that he had found the drawing referred to in a storeroom, and that he had, with complimentary appreciation of my poor work, saved it for more honourable service by removing it to his own house.

N.B.-This note is entirely spontaneous and uninspired – at all events by any human intervention.

J. C. ROBINSON.
March 21, 1920.

No. 36.

AND last of the present series; and crape 4s. 11d. a yard!

From the commencement of these sailor's yarns, or reminiscences, I have been perpetually haunted by the mighty atom, or ego. The I, I, I continually has been an eyesore to me; but I could find no escape from it. At first I made up my mind to try, as far as possible, to write in the third person, and consign "ego" to the limbo of oblivion. And indeed, I made the endeavour to do so in paper No. 2; but the result appeared to be more stilted and egotistical than the vain unvarnished pronoun. It seems evident that personal experiences admit of no qualifying evasion. Let this be my excuse for the limelight which I cordially dislike.

There is another matter that I must mention. I was warned before launching upon the ocean of Public Opinion to abstain as much as possible from "walking on the grass," for fear of hurting the susceptibilities of any critical friends. But I must ask indulgence from all in this final effort – for "dance upon the lawn" I must. This may sound cryptic perhaps but to indulge in mixed metaphors, it will unravel itself.

There are many of my dear old friends and acquaintances who will most likely be wondering that my written memoirs appear to lack a certain spontaneous acknowledgment of God's guidance and continual help, which, at sea, and at the time, I seldom failed to express. May I therefore remove all doubts at once as to any apparent forgetfulness on shore of that which was the secret alone of all my success during 48 years upon the beautiful ocean, by clearly stating that in my own humble opinion, nothing less than Personal Providence could have safely steered so weak a vessel for so long a period through such turbulent waters. It admits of no qualification.

Let me give one instance which exemplifies what I mean. I was succeeded in one of my commands by a grand old-fashioned seaman, greatly superior to me in every way as such – Captain Duncan. A great friend of his, and of mine, one of our own head men, went on board to greet him.

"Hello Robert, got another ship, eh?"

"Yes-s-s – bigger than the last."

"I see you have a text over your head there; did you put that up?"

"No-o-o. Robinson left it there."

"Are you going to take it down?"

"No-o-o, I daren't; the ship might sink!"

"Come, Robert – you're not superstitious, are you?"

"No-o; but I am not going to touch that text."

"Right you are, old chap, I congratulate you."

The text was: Proverbs iii.6.[67] My motto, carved out with gold lettering on a polished teak batten.

I have the greatest admiration for my brother seamen of the mercantile marine, and am always proud to read accounts of their prowess in times of crisis and difficulty; our own lists of captains and officers was remarkable for its individual and collective excellence; I am not fit to wear the sea boots of most of them. I can only suppose that the uncommon charm and proverbial regularity of the South African service attracted such numbers of youthful aspirants that the managers could afford to be particular in their selection of the most eligible. Be that as it may, I loved and esteemed them all, with one or two exceptions; and reckon that these only required a little more personal acquaintance to remove superficial misunderstanding.

No doubt I was one of the exceptions to others for the same reason. What conundrums men often are to other men. Women are much cleverer in such matters. They take one another's measure right away, and "go nap"[68] on their estimate.

In the *Dunottar Castle*, homeward bound, about the year 1891, amongst our passengers we had a black clergyman named Dwané, from Bomvanaland,[69] one of the firstfruits of missionary zeal in that district, who had been educated and ordained in the Presbyterian Church in Scotland – if my memory does not deceive me. He was a very remarkable man, and I took a great fancy to him. It was difficult to detect any flaw in his English or his enunciation; and in fact, to hear him without seeing him one would scarcely doubt that he was listening to a Britisher. He came Home with us on Church business, and returned with us about a year afterwards, having successfully negotiated his commission.

I suggested to him one day that he might give us an address at one of our Church services in the saloon. He said: "I should be happy to do so, captain, but what would the White folks say?"

"We can easily dispel all doubts upon that score," I replied. "I will announce at morning service that you are going to give us an address on 'missions to the natives from a native point of view' at the evening meeting, and those who object need not come. In fact, quite a number never do come of an evening."

"Very well, I am in your hands."

I told one or two people about the arrangement beforehand, and it got around generally, so that on Sunday the announcement was stale

---

[67] "In all thy ways acknowledge him, and he shall direct thy paths."
[68] Stake all.
[69] Coastal area of Eastern Cape.

news to the congregation. There were no comments, however, and our friend said he was afraid I had scared away all the worshippers.

To my great delight and his no small surprise, however, the saloon was not big enough for the people. We were crowded and squeezed out into the passages. It was quite a unique occasion. Mr. Dwané preached a missionary sermon, beginning with his own personal experiences before his conversion; the fear of the White missionary, "who rose from the sea" to bring the good news; "who could do no wrong."

I must give one or two of his leading points, because they gave rise to a good deal of discussion afterwards.

First: "How is it that I come as a delegate to your country seeking help for the extension of church accommodation in mine, because our converts, the fruits of your Scriptures and missions, have become so numerous that our churches no longer have room for them, whilst your own Home churches, in the midst of crowded populations, are for the most part very thinly attended, especially by men? Have you, White folks, who sent us the glad tidings, discovered any better way, or are you destroying the faith that once you preached?"

Second: "It is a common saying amongst the White races of South Africa that a Christianised native is a native spoiled, because he adopts all the vices of the White man! Think for a moment; the native still believes that the White man from the sea 'can do no wrong.' The native is told by the missionary that work is the common lot of Christian men, and he goes down to the seaports to find it. Is it surprising that he should seek to imitate his masters, still believing the first tradition? and is it not surprising that his masters should expect that the raw native who has only just been lifted out of darkness into light should attain to an exalted standard, that they themselves have failed to reach after eighteen hundred years of Christian civilisation?"

Third: "Your missionary teaches the native that your Bible is the living word of the living God, and enjoins the regular study of it as the privilege and duty of every Christian man. Does the missionary speak for the White man as well as the Black? How many of you White folks follow this precept? Probably all have Bibles, and possibly all Bibles will be witnesses against their possessors; and how can you expect the raw native to follow the teaching of that which he never sees in your hands, and often not in your actions?"

There were other points that I have forgotten, but I think these are sufficient to show that Mr. Dwané was a brave man, as well as an enlightened one. After the meeting, our smoking room became a debating club, and poor Dwané's ears must have burned.

"Black n—! What business had he to talk like that to us?" &c., &c. The natural reply would be – Why did you all come crowding in to be talked to. Well, well, "a man's a man for a' that."

I was sorry to hear some years afterwards that Mr. Dwané had seceded from the Presbyterian communion, and organised, or at least joined, an independent body calling themselves, if I was rightly informed, the Ethiopian Episcopal Church; and later on, that he had severed his connection with that also, and had joined the Church of England. I don't like so many changes, but have no doubt that he will settle down right side up eventually. He is not the only man who has turned his official coat inside out; that is, if the reports about Dwané are true.

This story about Dwané recalls a particularly interesting and impressive rendering of a remarkable sermon preached by a negro minister in Barbados (?) celebrated for his graphic illustrations. Author unknown. It was given to me many years ago by a friend long gone, and will bear repeating.

Wen de trumpets am a'tootin,' an' de stars dey am a'shootin,'
An' de owls dey am a'hootin' in de trees;
Wen de earf' it am a'quakin', an' de dead dey am a'wakin',
An' de rebels am a'shakin' in de knees;
Wen yo' heah de rollin' tundah, an' de rocks am rent asundah,
An' de hosts am in deir wondah standin' awed:
An' yo' find yo'self a tremblin', wile de Nations am assemblin' –
Oh! sinnah! Wot yo gwine to tell de Lord?

Wen de planets am a'knockin' at each oder, an a'rockin',
An' de tempes' seems a' mockin' at yo' woe;
Wen de darkness am a'fallin', an' de buzzads am a'squallin,'
An' de angels am a'callin' yo to go;
Wen de sun hab quit his shinin', an' de brak wolves am a'whinin,
An' de mo'nahs lie repinin' on de sod;
An yo's ast to tell de story, w'ot yo doin' up in glory –
Oh! sinnah! wot yo gwine to tell de Lord?

Wen yo' see de rightious swingin' up de golden stairs, a'singin'
Till de earf it am a 'ringin' wid de Psalm;
Wen dey fol' deir wings an' rally in de crystal ribbah valley
Singin' Halleluia, Hally, to de Lam'!
When de hills dey am a'crashin', and de sulpha fires a'flashin',
An' yo feel de cuttin' lashin' ob de rod;
Wen de sheep am' bein' chosen from de goats – wot yo
       supposin',
Wicked sinnah, yo be gwine to tell de Lord?

Oh! befoh de vial's broken, and de wrathful fiery token
Wid its awful flames is chokin' up de sky;
Fo' de Dragon gets a'barkin', and de earf begins to darken
Ask de massa for to harken to yo' cry;
Stop yo' sinnin' an' transgressin', listen to de wahnin' lesson,
Get yo' wicked knees to pressin' on de sod;
Wen yo's at de Bar, an' Satan am a eyein' yo', an waitin' –
Tremblin' sinnah! Wot yo' gwine to tell de Lord?![70]

I don't know much about the characteristics of the coloured races in South Africa. My only personal experience of them has been limited to the "boys" we used to carry round the coast with the ships to do the cargo work in the different ports; we generally carried 40. I always found them like a lot of children in those days, hard working and obedient; full of willing energy, and extraordinary staying power; singing and dancing during every interval of labour, and good natured and loyal to excess. Their amiability was equal to the severest tests; and in our coastwise work these were pretty frequent, but never a grumble nor a demur. One couldn't help loving them, and too frequently taking advantage of their untiring service.

But there was nothing of the smartness of repartee, or the incisive wit that are so conspicuous amongst the coloured races of America and the West Indies. Probably the stock from which these were originally derived – inhabitants of the tropical regions Central Africa – may be more caloric by nature and by the instincts of self-preservation.

I am afraid that the uncoloured races are responsible for the differences and developments in both cases.

I remember my father telling us a story once that was quite typical of the negro servants of Jamaica. He was Rector of Kingston, and on a certain occasion had to divide his ministry between three parishes, Kingston, Vere, and Spanish Town. So he took them seriatim, morning, afternoon, and evening on Sundays. On a certain week day, paying his parochial visits, which he had to do on horseback, on passing through one of the estates he found the coloured women folks at their weekly wash tubs in the open.

After halting for a few words of "benefit of clergy," he asked the one who was nearest the gate to open it for him. "Iss massa!" As he was walking his mount through, she laid her hand on the bridle, and said; "Dat was fine sarmon you preach las' Sunday, sah!"

"Oh! I'm glad to hear it, Nana. Which church were you at?"

"Vere, sah."

---

[70] Written by Robert J Laurence and published in the first issue of the NAACP's journal *Crisis*, November 1910.

"Oh, yes; in the evening?"

"No, sir, in the. afternoon."

"That's right. So you liked the sermon?"

"Yes, massa; did this ole woman lot o' good, sah."

"Well, I'm glad. What was the text?"

"Oh, de text – was – de tex' was dat – I forget de tex', sah."

"Now, Nana, you say the sermon did you a lot of good, and you have forgotten the text. What was the sermon about?"

"Oh, de sarmon – de sarmon was butiful sarmon. It just fit de tex' sah, and did dis ole woman's heart a lot o' good, sah."

"Now, I'm afraid you are deceiving yourself and me. How do you account for it, that you have quite forgotten sermon and text, yet claim that they have done you good?"

The old woman put the corner of her apron into her mouth, and having tasted the dressing, she quietly led the horse round to the fence on which the linen was hanging, and handed the edge of a sheet up to her tormentor, who took hold of it expectantly, and said, "Well?"

"Any water dere, sah?"

"No; quite dry."

"Any soap dere, sah?"

"No; it's well rinsed."

"All de better for dem, massa."

"Thank you, Nana; massa has learned a useful lesson. Farewell!"

YES – FAREWELL –!

****

J. C. ROBINSON.
March 21, 1920.

Armadale Castle – Tony Haslett Collection

Carisbrook Castle – Tony Haslett Collection

Conway Castle – Tony Haslett Collection

Captain J. C. Robinson, probably on the Armadale Castle

MORE YARNS FROM JC

These are from a series of captains' yarns collected by Alfred T. Story
and published in *Strand Magazine*, Jan-June 1896 (pp. 205-210)

... The next yarns I shall give are from the private log of Captain J. C.
Robinson, commander of the *Tantallon Castle*, whose experience at sea
has been long and varied. Captain Robinson is a man of striking
presence, but of still more striking
character.

In speaking of himself, he said,
"I am a Westmorland man, my
ancestors having been squires of
Bongate, and holders of very
considerable property in the beautiful
vale of Eden for many generations —
until a better and more wholesome
state of things came in, and their
successors, despising the lap of luxury,
scattered their enervating influence to
the four winds, and joined the ranks of
that noble army of soldiers who are
employed in the manly struggle for liberty and daily bread.

My father was the first to drift away from the old patrimonial
scenes, and having passed through Oxford with credit to himself and
family and taken holy orders, he joined Bishop Lipscombe in Jamaica for
some years, and then, having been driven from the West Indies by
repeated attacks of yellow fever, he returned to England and settled
down as rector of St Mary's, Newmarket, where he did good work for six
years, when he died, a young man still, from a chill contracted in the
performance of the duties of his office.

I myself was educated at Appleby, and still look upon and love
that place as my particular corner in our beloved country.

I first went to sea in the year '68, in the employ of the Blackwall
Line, and after making a number of voyages to Australia, New Zealand,
India, China, America, and elsewhere, I entered the P. and O. service,
finally joining the Castle Line, and taking command of the sailing vessel,
the *Carnarvon Castle*, in '74. I remained in command of the *Carnarvon
Castle* two years, and was then transferred to the steam service. I have
had the honour of commanding in nine of the company's ships, finishing
with the *Tantallon Castle*, in which Sir Donald Currie recently carried Mr.
Gladstone and a large party of friends to witness the opening of the
Emperor William Canal.

My early days at sea, like those of most other sailors, were
chequered with the usual round of amusement and privation, hard work

and danger. When I look back upon those days it always seems to me a miracle of Divine Providence how so many boys who go to sea, and remain there to become experienced seamen, get through scatheless, seeing the many perils that surround them. I could give you numberless instances from my own experience, and as you doubtless wish to make your yarns as varied as possible, a few instances of the way in which Providence preserves youths in the midst of perils will be interesting.

Narrow escapes[1]

When a midshipman in the *La Hogue*, while lying in Sydney Harbour, I was cast away in a dinghey, alone, during what is called by sailors a 'southerly buster' — that is, a squall —and having escaped to the signal ship at anchor, was given up as lost. Early the next morning I frightened all my companions by turning up in the cabin, they thinking it was my ghost.[2] On another occasion, while sailing a ship's boat during a regatta, also in Sydney Harbour, we were run down and smashed up by a brig, and I, along with another, went right under the brig's bottom, and came up astern, much to the surprise of those who witnessed the accident.

Food

On another occasion we were starved at sea until we were really reduced to skeletons.[3] For three weeks we had no meat of any kind, for a fortnight we had nothing but biscuit and water, and for one week the biscuit was reduced to a pound per man at work, and half a pound to those who were laid up with scurvy – the latter being twenty-five out of thirty-two; and the water was reduced, for that last week, to a teacupful per day. We were all going about watching for showers, and when the showers did come, we would tie our handkerchiefs round anything that would afford an opportunity for the water to trickle down it, for the sake of having something wet in our mouths. When we got into Falmouth, the captain went on shore and sent off provisions and the men fell to on the raw meat as it came over the side and gnawed it like hungry dogs. We who belonged to the cuddy set a better example by cutting off a hunk of beef and sending it to the cook to fry, with the intimation that he need not take too long over it, as we did not wish it to be overdone. On my arrival at home they had my portrait taken, and they keep it to this day as the best possible visible definition of a line – length without breadth.

---

[1] Subheadings added.

[2] See No. 18 of his memoirs

[3] See No. 12. Probably the *Orient*, 1862.

I can give you an instance of the opposite danger of a boy going to sea – though it did not happen to myself. A little gutter-snipe stowed himself away on board a ship I was in, sailing from London, and having been brought to light after we had got to sea, he was carried before the captain. He was a rosy-cheeked, smart-looking little fellow; but his cheek paled and his eye dimmed before the harsh looks and threatening words of the captain. 'Which shall it be,' at length said the skipper – 'four dozen with a rope's end, or go up the mast for four hours? Which do you prefer?' The little fellow looked up at the swaying masts and from them into the captain's face; then in a tremulous voice he said he would rather have the four dozen. He got nothing, of course, but was set to work, and became one of the ship's boys. Harry soon developed into a prime favourite with everybody on board; he was smart and active, and as the life agreed with him he became quite fat.

It is the custom on board ship to have plum duff – that is, plum-pudding – on Sundays and Thursdays. One Sunday a pudding was placed before the captain. It weighed at least a pound, and as everybody declined to be served with any, he said, 'Somebody has got to eat it' and told the steward to fetch the boy Harry. He came up, and the captain asked him if he would like some plum-pudding. 'Yes, sir,' said the boy. The skipper told the steward to seat him on the beam in the skylight – over the top of the table. This was done, and the plum-duff and a spoon handed up to him. 'You are not coming down out of that until you have finished the pudding,' said the captain. The dinner went on, and had been nearly completed when, glancing up at the lad in the skylight, the captain asked him if he had finished the pudding. Harry said he had. The steward was ordered to lift him down. When this was done the captain said, 'Come here, sir! Did you enjoy that pudding?' 'Yes, sir, please, sir,' said the boy. 'But I should have enjoyed it much better if I had not already had a good dinner' – a reply which elicited a hearty laugh from all present.

Cooking

While on the subject of food on board ship, I may as well give you a yarn or two in which I acted as cook. It is a good thing for a lad who intends trying his luck at sea to learn a little about cookery. My education was not attended to in this direction, and on the few occasions when I have turned my hand to the culinary art it has been for the most part with indifferent success. But on one occasion I may pride myself on the result of my labours. We had been wrecked and were living for the time on a desert island on the coast of South America.[4] There were a hundred and

---

[4] *Duncan Dunbar*, 1865

ten of us in all, crew and passengers; and amongst the latter was a young lady who was very delicate and, likewise, very pretty, who could not touch the food prepared in the rough way we had at our command. On noticing this, being naturally moved by beauty and suffering, I took a line and hastened to the rocks, and, after a deal of trouble, caught a decent-looking fish, which I prepared in the usual way. I scraped the scales off the skin, took out the entrails, toasted it on a ramrod over the fire, browned it nicely, and then, putting it on a biscuit with a little pepper and salt, I took it to the young lady, telling her that I had got it on purpose for her, and she must eat a little. She did so, and I believe it was the means of so tickling her palate, that from that day she took quite naturally to her food.

My second experience in the culinary art had a different sort of ending. Having arrived in the Port of London from Australia, the captain sent for his wife from the north of England to live with him while in dock. The next morning after her arrival, having come on board the vessel from my lodgings, the captain heard me moving about, and called out to know if there was no breakfast. I said no, there was no breakfast and no cook. He then begged me to go and buy some meat and cook them something for breakfast. I replied that I was no cook, but that I would get something and see if I could make a stew. Having procured some steak and onions and potatoes, I proceeded to make what I thought was a very nice Irish stew. The smell of it was very appetizing, and when placed in the cuddy, the captain and his wife did not need much pressing to set-to upon it. When he had had a plate of it the skipper hurried away to dress, in order to go and enter the ship at the Customs, leaving his wife still at table. After he had left, Mrs. Skipper devoured two or three more platefuls of the stew. Indeed, I thought she would never finish, and was not a little disgusted, although she did praise my cooking. After a while, however, she became violently sick, and remained so for several hours, all the while blaming me for having put some deleterious compound in the stew. I could not think what had happened at the time but have since learned that copper pans should always be carefully cleaned before being used – which I, only a first mate, and no cook, had not done.

JC meets his future wife

"Talking about wives" said Captain Robinson, "reminds me of my own wife, whom I first met at sea." He then proceeded to narrate the following yarn:

"We had set out from Plymouth, where we took up passengers for New Zealand,[5] and were bowling along in fine breezy weather across the Bay of Biscay. I being the chief officer, the captain and I were walking up and down the deck yarning, when the steward struggled up the ladder with a bundle, and deposited it on the deck, put a pillow under one end of it, and disappeared. Shortly afterwards he appeared with a second, and deposited it in the same manner, and then with a third. The captain and I, standing at a respectful distance, concluded that he was handling human beings, and from the way in which they were bundled up that they were feminine. Drawing up towards them stealthily, the old man pointed his finger at them, and whispered: 'Ladies – champagne!' I went down below, and got a bottle of champagne; and, as the ship was rolling about, I took a teacup, fearing a glass would come to grief. Having opened the bottle, I handed it to the captain. He approached the first of the bundles, funked it, and came back. He then told me to take the champagne to the ladies. I made an attempt to do so but being at that time as bashful as the captain, I also shirked the job, and told him it was his business and not mine. Whereupon he ordered me to go and give it them at once. Having approached the first bundle, I knelt down to summon up courage to lift up the rug that covered her, when the old man brought matters to a crisis by giving her a kick. Instantly a pair of black eyes, looking startled and indignant, showed themselves from under the wrappings, and I explained as well as I could that it was not I who had thus called her attention, but the captain, who wished her to have a little champagne, as he thought it would do her good. Having taken a little with the blandest smile, she asked if she might give a little to the other ladies, and sick as she was, she crawled on her hands and knees, and quietly gave a little to the two other girls who were lying on the deck. Then returning to her place, she thanked me for the champagne, and tumbled once more into a heap, covering her head with a shawl.

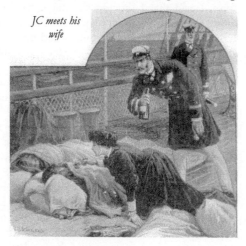

JC meets his wife

---

[5] This was on the *Star of India*, between 1871 and 1874.

"The captain and I retired to a distance to discuss the situation, and after a bit he suggested that they might require a little more champagne. I said: 'Very well, sir, you need not bother, I will go and give it to them.' Upon which he replied, very curtly, 'I can do it myself. You go forward and haul down the jib.'

"This," continued Captain Robinson, "was my first introduction to my wife. Being struck not only by her personal appearance, but also by her consideration for her sisters in adversity, I thought probably she might be equally good to me some day. At all events, one thing led to another, until, at the end of the voyage, we were on speaking terms, and before I left the port we were taking the passengers to, I had given her an engagement ring.

"We sailed to India with horses, and then proceeded to England. I was to write to her from India, and she was to answer my letter to England. I duly wrote, but on my arrival in England I found no reply. I waited for a mail – still no letter. I then concluded that our brief acquaintance had proved like many others of the same nature – too fragile to last, and so I wrote to her to the effect that as I supposed she had repented our engagement, and that that was the reason of her not replying to my letter from India, according to arrangement, I took leave to release her.

"I then sailed for China. In China I received a brief note from her, informing me that, 'having received no letter from India, no reply was possible.' At the same time she returned me the engagement ring and two or three other little mementos. Acknowledging these in due form, I said that I thought she might have dismissed me with a little more ceremony, without the necessity of denying the receipt of the Indian letter. In process of time – and this correspondence occupied in all something like four years – I received a still more curt reply: ' Dear Sir, – I repeat that there was no Indian letter. – Yours truly.' I was now indignant, and replied, 'Dear Madam, – Let it be sufficient, once for all, that, whether you received the letter from India or not, I wrote from India. – Yours truly.'

"Now it appears that on receipt of this note, the lady for the first time began to think that I was telling the truth, and went to the provincial post-office, where she was living with her brother and sister, and made inquiries that resulted in nothing. Not satisfied with this, however, she wrote to the Postmaster-General in Melbourne; but still failing to get any satisfaction, she persuaded her brother to take her to Melbourne – a distance of 130 miles, most of it being done by horse and trap. There she saw the Postmaster-General in person, and succeeded in so interesting him by the story of the lost letter and her concern about it, that he had the post-office turned inside out to try to find it. Still, however, without effect. Then the Postmaster-General asked to know all the dates and circumstances touching this important letter. The young lady told her story – the date I should have arrived in India, the date of my sailing for England, etc. Naturally he came to the conclusion that the letter must have been posted between the dates of my arriving in India and my departure for England. Then the records were looked up, and the Postmaster-General, putting his finger upon a line in the ledger, said: 'On such a date the mail steamer Rangoon, carrying the mails from India, sank in Galle Harbour, in the Island of Ceylon. The mails were recovered after being a fortnight at the bottom of the Bay. Having been dried, those letters that were decipherable were sent to their respective addresses; but the major part of the correspondence, being pulped up and illegible, was packed in bales and sent to their destinations. Those that came here,' said the Postmaster-General, 'were put down in the cellar, and there they have remained ever since.'

"The strangest part of this strange yarn," said Captain Robinson, "is still to be told. More and more anxious to help to unravel the young lady's romantic story, the Postmaster-General had these bales brought out of the cellar and opened, and the dried-up paper pulp gone over piece by piece, and everything decipherable laid on one side. The whole of the staff of the post-office was drawn into the work, so interested was everyone in finding the missing letter. The name sought was 'Sayer,' and all bales marked 'S' were ransacked without success. But still the work was not given up yet. They began again at 'A' and worked right through the alphabet until they came to the bale marked 'T' and as the letters were passed from one to another the lady finally put her hand on one and said, 'That is the letter.' The Postmaster-General and all the rest gathered round said, 'That is not "S" – that is "T" and the name is Taylor.' The lady said, 'You do not know how badly he writes; that is an "S" and the name is "Sayer."'

Well, to cut a long story short, this proved to be the missing letter, and Captain Robinson subsequently received a formal note stating how it had been recovered. He replied in the same strain; but before dispatching the letter, memory carrying him back to the time when the dark-eyed beauty was lying sick on the deck of the *Star of India* bound for New Zealand, and the champagne that was a means of introduction to her, he inclosed a second letter in which he allowed his feelings to flow in the old groove. This was marked not to be opened until twenty-four hours after receipt, but the sender afterwards learned that of the two missives this one was opened first – a woman's instinct telling the recipient which letter contained that which would be the most pleasing to her.

"I need not tell you that we were married not long after that," concluded Captain Robinson.

THE WRECK OF THE DUNCAN DUNBAR

"Wreck of the Duncan Dunbar, Australian passenger ship, on the coast of Brazil" – Illustrated London News, 2 Dec. 1865

It was when JC, aged 22, was 2nd mate on the *Duncan Dunbar* in 1865, taking passengers and cargo to Sydney, that the shipwreck occurred which apparently confirmed him in the deep religious beliefs he held for the rest of his life. His application for his 1st Mate's certificate in 1866 lists "Duncan Dunbar – wrecked" in his service record, and the following account is taken from *The Times*.

On 6th November 1865, *The Times* reported that the passengers and crew who had set out for Sydney on 2nd September and been wrecked on the reef Las Roccas off Brazil on 7th October, had just reached Southampton, having been brought home on the mail steamer *Oneida*.

The Board of Trade enquiry held at Greenwich Police Court in December began by questioning the first officer who stated that a seaman had been sent up to the foretopsail-yard, looking out for breakers ahead (though they thought they had passed Las Roccas already). "About dusk the second officer [J. C. Robinson] was sent aloft. At 8 o'clock [the first officer's] watch commenced, and the captain then ordered him, after stationing the seamen, to go aloft and relieve the second officer. He met the second officer on the main deck, and he [JC] told him [1st officer] there was 'curious water ahead,' and he was going to tell the captain. Witness then went aloft, and when on the lower topsail yard he called out 'Breakers ahead.' The ship ... almost immediately struck." He seems to blame JC: "His opinion was that had the second

218

officer sung out when he first saw danger, and the helm of the ship been put up or down, the vessel might have cleared the reef."

The next day 2nd officer J. C. Robinson (misnamed J. C. Robertson in *The Times*) said "that from 7 till 8 o'clock on the evening ... he was on the lookout on the foretopsail yard with a man named Andrews. At 8 o'clock he observed something curious in the water ahead, and he told Andrews to keep a sharp look out while he went below to inform the captain of what he saw. When he reached the main deck, he met the chief mate, who was about to relieve him aloft, and he told him he had seen something curious in the water. He then went to the captain, and told him. Captain Swanson asked, 'Where?' and on witness looking over the port bow he observed breakers. At the moment the chief mate called out 'Breakers ahead!' but the vessel struck."

The passengers now take up the story, which was reprinted in local papers up and down the country, and indeed worldwide:

"... She struck on the reef at about half-past 8 in the evening. As soon as the alarm of 'breakers ahead' was given the helm was instantly put to port with a view of clearing the danger. The vessel, however, struck upon an outlying portion of the reef as she was answering her helm. Every effort was made to get the ship off, but in vain, as she she went on at high tide, and on its falling became firmly fixed on a bed of rock. Cargo was thrown overboard with a view of lightening the vessel. The foretopgallant mast was cut away for the purpose of easing the vessel, which was rolling heavily from side to side as the tide fell and the sea struck her. The pumps were diligently worked, and kept the water under until the rudder was lifted and the sternpost broken away, when the water poured heavily into the hold and pumping became useless.

"Soon after the vessel struck the captain went in one of the boats to take soundings around her, and see if there was any part thereof on which a landing might be effected. He fancied, but could not be at all sure, that there was some part on which we might land. As the boats could not carry all on the wreck, the captain determined to await daylight, and then land us if there was any available spot; and, if there was not one, to take all from the wreck in the boats and on a raft.

"Most anxiously did we look for the first streaks of dawn. It is impossible to describe the state of mind in which we passed the hours of that most awful and trying night. The vessel was rolling from side to side and striking most violently at each roll in a way which seemed to threaten her instant destruction. There were the unceasing roar and the white expanse of the remorseless breakers; above the din resounded the shrill and mocking cries of myriads of birds, and around us rolled the dark waters, in which it seemed that we must soon be engulfed.

"It is impossible to speak too highly of the conduct of the ladies at the time the vessel struck, and during the whole of that most fearful night. Not a scream was heard, and with perfect resignation and quietness they awaited the termination of that trying state of things, whether it should result in their preservation or their being swept into the dark and horrid waters around us.

"As day dawned every glass was used, in the hope of discovering some place uncovered by water on which shelter, if only temporarily, might be taken. The captain again went in a boat, and succeeded in getting through the breakers to a landing-place on one of the two banks or islets of sand which rise about seven feet above ordinary high-water mark. Preparations were at once made for landing. The passengers were lowered in a chair over the stern into lifeboats, it being impossible to get the boats alongside the rolling vessel. By 7 we were all landed. On landing we found that the little islet or bank of sand was covered with pig-weed, but there were no signs of water. During this day the captain directed the landing of water and provisions. Unfortunately, four out of the five water puncheons got at were lost, being stove in by wreck, or having drifted away, and our anxiety was lest we should fail in procuring a supply of water for the party on the reef, consisting in all of 117 souls. For the first two days we had only half a pint of water apiece, although toiling in a severe and unaccustomed manner under a broiling sun, the thermometer being at 112. On the day of our landing a tent was erected near some heavy pieces of wood, which were evidently part of what is given in the chart as the Syron Beacon which appears to have fallen some time since. The island seemed quite covered with birds, which, from their very wildness, took no more notice of us than to move a few feet out of our way as we walked among them. The ground swarmed with a large species of earwig, and was in many places honeycombed by the holes of land crabs. Our meal on that first day consisted of a small piece of nearly raw meat and a morsel of ship's biscuit. The ladies slept that night under the tent, and the men in the open air – at least slept so far as it was possible to sleep in the unceasing din of the screeching birds and under the attacks of the crabs and vermin.

"On Sunday afternoon the foremast and mizzen mast were cut away, and on Monday the mainmast was also cut away. Again we worked hard at getting water and provisions ashore. On Tuesday an empty 400-gallon tank was landed, and in it we put our water, as soon as it was landed, in small vessels.

"On the morning of Wednesday, the 11th, Captain Swanson, with one of the passengers, Mr. Galloway, and six seamen, started in one of the lifeboats, for which mast, sails, and rigging had been made and fitted on the reef, intending to try and reach Pernambuco, and there procure aid for us. Every day we worked at getting ashore as much provisions and water as possible, as we knew that at the first high or heavy sea the vessel must go to pieces. Most mercifully, the weather was throughout fine. We ultimately succeeded in getting four iron tanks ashore and a more encouraging supply of water. All the water and provisions landed were placed in a separate tent, which was denominated our 'store' and most strict watch and guard was kept over them, as on their preservation depended our sustenance until we should be rescued. We managed to get ashore some wine and barrels of beer, which were most acceptable to keep up our strength.

"Five vessels were seen by us passing the island; but our signals failed to attract them. At midday on Tuesday, the 17th, a steamer was seen approaching the island. It was distinguished to be one of the Royal Mail Steam Packet Company's vessels, and proved to be the *Oneida*, Captain Woolcott. Our hearts swelled with thanksgiving and joy as we observed the vessel making for the reef.

"It turned out that Captain Swanson had, after having encountered heavy weather, been taken into Pernambuco by a vessel which he fell in with [the *Hayara*, an American ship], and had, under the advice of Captain Doyle, Her Britannic Majesty's consul at that port, sought aid for us of Captain Woolcott, the *Oneida* being then on her homeward voyage to Southampton, with the Brazil mails. Captain Woolcott, with the consent and approbation of Lieutenant Rainer, R.N., the naval agent in charge of the mails, readily agreed to go to our aid.

"By 2 o'clock the *Oneida* was off our landing-place on the reef, and at once we started for her. Most of us had lost all our baggage, having very little beyond the suit of clothes in which we landed on the reef. The *Oneida* had arrived at Las Roccas in 21 hours after leaving Pernambuco, a distance of 259 miles direct. By 6 o'clock the *Oneida* was again under way on her homeward voyage."

The report states that no one died, and no bones were broken, and the rescue came just in the nick of time as sickness was beginning to break out: it was all seen as providential and a "special mercy".

The enquiry found no one to blame, except the Brazilian authorities for not maintaining the beacon on the reef, and Captain Swanson was especially commended. There followed a vitriolic discussion in the *Times* letters columns about tides and leeway, with the Admiralty Hydrographer laying the blame on the captain and others fiercely defending him.

Artist Thomas G. Dutton subsequently painted a picture of the passengers being rowed away from the stricken ship, based on a sketch made by 2nd officer J. C. Robinson; a copy of this was presented to the New South Wales Library by the daughter of one of the passengers. The illustration in the *Illustration London News* (shown at start) is similar to this, so I assume that was also taken from JC's sketch.

The only reference to this event by JC that I have found is amongst the *Strand Magazine* yarns, where he prides himself on catching and cooking a fish for a young lady passenger while shipwrecked off South America.

J. C. Robinson got his First Mate's Certificate in January 1866 at the age of twenty-three.

"Wreck of the 'Duncan Dunbar' on Las Roccas, coast of Brazil.
Disembarkation of passengers, on Sunday morning, October 8th, 1865"
by Thomas G. Dutton
"from a sketch taken of the spot by J. C. Robinson, 2nd Officer"

CAPTAIN J. C. ROBINSON
(Captain of *Armadale Castle*, 5 Dec. 1903)
.... He comes of an old Westmorland and Cumberland family, and his progenitors were millers for several generations. His father, however, forsook the family profession for the Church, served in the West Indies, and subsequently became Rector of St Mary's, Newmarket, where it is recorded of him that, after a lengthy and bitter war with the jockeys, he finally converted the whole fraternity by extracting one of the then Duke of Bedford's racehorses from a ditch into which it had fallen, just as the horsey men, despairing of getting it out again, were about to shoot it.

CAPT. ROBINSON'S NEW APPOINTMENT
(Marine Superintendent, 18 Aug. 1906)
... In the olden days, when the steamers running between South Africa and Great Britain used occasionally to carry a somewhat rowdy element, Captain Robinson gained the reputation of being a bit of a martinet. As a matter of fact his claim to that title was based upon the fact that he studied the comfort of his passengers, and insisted upon maintaining the discipline of his ship, with the result that the noisy people, whose ideas of enjoyment prompted them to sit up until the "wee sma' 'oors" singing or playing cards, found their pleasures considerably restricted – and other passengers slept in peace and blessed the skipper who had made their slumbers possible.

EARLY RETIREMENT OF CAPTAIN ROBINSON AND CAPTAIN MORETON (20th Jan. 1913)
... Their careers have been full of usefulness and kindliness and they will both leave the busy world better than they found it. It has often been my pleasure to refer to the religious exercises observed by Captain Robinson on his voyages and to break a gentle lance with those who sometimes cavilled at them. 'Onward, Christian soldiers' was ever the invitation of the Captain, and if everyone did not respond that never daunted Robinson. Plenty did, and he was happy and grateful. And even amongst those who did not turn up to the morning service on deck the bulk were mindful that 'an atheist's laugh is a poor exchange for Deity offended.' Before we parted at Southampton ... I had tea and talk with Captain Robinson, and if I were to sum up what he said it would be in such wise as this: 'For a long life, abounding in good things, in a capacity for enjoying everything worthy of enjoyment, in reciprocal attachments and contributions with multitudes of men and women, in more than my share of health and happiness, I reverently thank God both that I am alive and that I have lived.'

JC aged 63, 1906

II: The Life of J. C. Robinson, 1843-1925

JC was the eldest son of an Anglican missionary, who in his turn was the eldest son of a Westmorland miller and farmer. The family had been successful millers for generations, but the business finally failed under JC's uncle Joseph (his father's younger brother). JC's father Robert went to Oxford University (where he rowed in one of the earliest boat races), and travelled out to Jamaica in 1839, the year after slavery was finally abolished there.[1] He served under the energetic reforming Bishops Lipscomb and Spencer.

John Charles Robinson was born on 8 July 1843[2] in Kingston, Jamaica. He was the first child and was named after his grandfathers, John Robinson of Bongate Mill, Appleby, Westmorland, and Charles Wright, a London attorney. He spent time as a child living with his grandfather in Appleby, at The Terrace, Bongate,[3] along with his younger brother George Lipscomb[4] and was educated in Appleby.[5]

JC's father, the Rev. Robert Robinson, weakened by repeated bouts of yellow fever in Jamaica, returned to England in 1849 with the rest of the family and lived in Appleby until he resigned his Jamaican position for the Rectorship of St Mary's in Newmarket, Suffolk. The family moved to Heath House, Newmarket in 1851. "The open and fearless manner in which [Robert] reminded his flock of their duty to their Maker" made him less than popular at the start of his ministry. [6]

Apart from his bad health and abandoned career as a missionary, the Rev. Robert had lent a large sum in Jamaica, which he lost, and he was forced to borrow from his successful uncle Matthew Robinson (also a miller).[7] His wife Sarah Ann died in 1854, and Robert died of pneumonia in February 1856, leaving six orphans and barely enough funds to pay his creditors.

The plight of Robert's orphans caught the attention of the press, led by the *Bury and Norwich Post*, and a vigorous campaign was raised to keep the children from the workhouse. (No relations were able or willing to take them.)[8] **"CASE OF DESTITUTION – ORPHANS OF A CLERGYMAN, a graduate of Oxford"** announced *The Times* on 17th April 1856. The public responded generously and three of the boys were sent to the Clergy Orphan School, Canterbury.[9] JC, at 12 rising 13, was however too old. He may have been sent to a navigation school.

We next hear of him sailing on the *La Hogue* (Captain John Williams) to Australia from July 1858 as a midshipman.[10] The *La Hogue* was a large frigate-style three-masted ship, popular with passengers. JC recalls experiences at Sydney in his reminiscences Nos. 17 and 18.

La Hogue

He made the same voyage July 1859-April 1860, and then in August 1860 sailed as midshipman and Ordinary Seaman on the emigrant ship *Lady McDonald*, London to Plymouth to Port Adelaide (Master Henry Biles). They returned June 1861, and he set out again on the same voyage as 3rd Mate in November 1861, returning Feb. 1863 (see No. 24).

In June 1863, JC sailed as 3rd Mate on the *Vimeira* to Australia returning July 1864 (the *Vimeira* transported passengers, cargo and sometimes convicts, for Devitt and Moore; Captain J. Green). On 26th August 1864 he applied for a 2nd Mate's certificate; he was 21, and gave 8 Holland House, Kensington as his address – this was the home of his mother's sister, Maria Wright.[11] He achieved his certificate on 31st August (31972).

The following month he sailed as 2nd Mate on the *Vimeira*, returning July 1865.

On 28th August 1865 he sailed as 2nd Mate on the *Duncan Dunbar* from London, and on 2nd September from Plymouth with passengers and cargo for Sydney (ship owned by Dunbar, captain J. B. Swanson – who had also captained the *Vimeira* and *La Hogue*). As described separately, the ship was wrecked on a reef off Brazil, but by great good fortune, all passengers and crew were finally rescued and taken back to Southampton. The family story is that his great Christian devotion dated from this event. As 2nd officer just coming off watch when the ship struck, JC was questioned at the enquiry, and the 1st officer suggested JC should have sung out sooner. However, he was not found to be at fault.

Soon after the enquiry, on 6th January 1866, JC applied for his 1st Mate's certificate, and got it four days later. On his application, he gave the address of 15 Harrap Street, Poplar, London E1 (right on the Thames, by the present Blackwall Tunnel)[12] – but an address c/o William Pine, The Willows, Bridgwater, Somerset on his certificate.

He gives the *Orient* out of Liverpool for his next two voyages; he was 2nd Mate and the first return voyage took just over a year, the next just over 14 months. The *Orient* was carrying railroad material to Calcutta, and there is a dramatic account of the first voyage in his fourth piece.

There was then a change of pattern from late 1868: after a gap of six months, he sailed as 4th mate on a short voyage from London on the P&O's steam vessel *Poonah*[13] to the Mediterranean, and repeated this three more times, on voyages lasting only one or two months. These short voyages finished on 21 July 1869, and on 31 August 1869 he commenced a voyage as First Mate on the *Excelsior* from London., returning 8 October 1870.[14] From the dates, it seems likely that this was the ship of that name, possibly a steamship, travelling to "Kurrachee" and returning from Bassein in Burma in October the following year. The Suez Canal only opened to navigation on 17 November 1869, so although voyages to Indian ports "by steam via the Suez Canal" were widely advertised the following year, this one looks too early to have taken the shortcut. He does not mention this trip in his memoirs.

On 16th November 1870 JC took an examination for his Master's Certificate of Competency, which he achieved on 19th November. Again, he gave his address as The Willows, Bridgwater, Somerset. He was now 27.

For the next four years, 1871, 1872, 1873 and 1874, JC was Mate on the *Star of India* to Australia and New Zealand. The Surgeon Superintendent Dr Cumming wrote in his report on arrival in Australia in December 1873: "Captain Holloway kindly placed the Ship's Library at the service of the Emigrants and I am glad to say that a great many of them availed themselves of the privilege of using the books which were issued by Mr Robinson the mate who has been most zealous in his endeavours to make all persons on board comfortable."[15] As JC said in his "yarns" in *Strand Magazine*, it was on this ship that he met his future wife, Mary Ann Bell from Armagh, and they married some time before 1877. After the *Star of India,* JC began his long service as a captain on the Castle Line's Cape Town run.

In 1881 JC's family were living at Birkbeck Road in Acton. The oldest son, Charles Douglas, was born in 1877 and daughter Maribel Ellen in 1880. On the 1881 census, JC's youngest brother Arthur Sextus is there,[16] and there are a couple of servants. JC's and Mary Ann's remaining children, Harold Percy (1882), Annaliese Mary (1884), Launcelot Alec ("Lannie", 1886) and Kathleen Elise (1888) were also born in Acton.[17]

By 1891, the family had moved to Blenheim House, Manor Road, Chipping Barnet, Herts. and the census shows a family called Gray from Jamaica staying with them, as well as a live-in nursemaid, housemaid and cook. Some time before 1901 the family moved to Manchester Road, Shirley, Southampton.[18] Sons Charles Douglas and Harold Percy had gone by then, Douglas to South Africa and Harold Percy to sea.[19]

Meanwhile Scottish shipping magnate Donald Currie had, in 1862, established a regular sailing ship service to India, known as "Currie's Calcutta Castles". The first steamships entered service on the India route in 1872 and the same year, Currie started a passenger and private mail service from the UK to South Africa. In 1876 the company became the Castle Mail Packet Co. Ltd. and shared a mail contract with the Union SS Co. They got a contract to carry Dutch mails to South Africa and in 1900 the Castle Line merged with the Union SS Co. to form the Union-Castle Mail SS Co.[20]

J. C. Robinson was to become "one of Currie's best-known commanders", [21] beginning as captain on the sailing ship *Carnarvon Castle* from 1874-1877 (Nos. 1-3). Mareschal Murray goes on to say: "J. C. Robinson was one of many Currie men who, having trained in the East India *Castles,* formed a nucleus of efficient officers for the coming venture into steam. The change to steam caused much regret to Captain Robinson, as it did to many others" – as JC recounts in his third piece.

From 1877 JC began on the steamships *Balmoral Castle* and *Conway Castle* as Mate, and then through the 1880s, 1890s and 1900s to 1906 he captained the Castle Line Mail Packet ships *Taymouth Castle, Warwick Castle, Dunrobin Castle, Roslin Castle, Norham Castle, Pembroke Castle, Dunottar Castle, Tantallon Castle, Dunvegan Castle, Carisbrook Castle, Kildonan Castle, Walmer Castle* and *Armadale Castle* to the Cape in South Africa.

It was a time of turmoil in South Africa, and 1877-9 saw the 9th Xhosa or Kaffir War between a branch of the Xhosas and the Fengus, in which the British and Cape Colonists became involved. In 1879 occurred the Zulu War, with the battle of Isandhlwana (and Rorke's Drift) and the defeat of Ketshwayo/Cetewayo at Ulundi. JC was involved in carrying British and colonial VIPs to and from South Africa; he was also asked to help in solving the resulting labour shortage on the docks at Port Elizabeth.

More peacefully, on 1st May 1882, a paper on "Madeira Meteorologic" read to the Royal Society in Edinburgh, thanked Captain Harrison on the *Dunrobin Castle* and Captain J. C. Robinson on the *Warwick Castle* for "carrying out the obliging intentions of Sir Donald Currie to facilitate our voyage and transport, either way, of large astronomical instrument boxes."[22]

The journal *Nature* in 1883, 1886 and 1887 noted that Captain J. C. Robinson had presented the Zoological Society's Gardens with various creatures: two Madagascar Porphyrios from Mozambique (aka

Purple Swamphens), a dwarf chameleon from South Africa, and a ring-tailed coati from South America.[23]

In 1890 on the *Roslin Castle* JC set a new record speed from Cape Town to Plymouth despite strong northerly winds, quarantine problems and the Governor being late with his despatches.[24]

In 1893 the *Dunottar Castle* was narrowly missed by shells of the Royal Artillery practising on the heavy guns of Picklecombe Fort in Plymouth Sound. JC was furious and wrote a strong letter to the press about this "inexcusable outrage." "The passengers were very much alarmed. ... women and children screamed, and there was great confusion on board." Two more shells were fired astern of the ship even after she was at anchor. This incident was reported in a number of papers.[25]

In 1895 JC, with Sir Donald Currie aboard, captained the *Tantallon Castle* across the North Sea to take VIPs including Mr & Mrs Gladstone to witness Kaiser Wilhelm II opening the Kiel Canal.[26] [27] JC talks about this in pieces 30 and 31.

Around 1895 JC also found time to visit Appleby and have his grandparents' gravestone at St Michael's Church, Bongate (now in private hands) refurbished.[28]

In 1900 when the Union and Castle lines, previously bitter rivals, merged, he devised a new house flag incorporating features of each of the previous flags. "The emblem of the Union-Castle Line was seen at once to embody both dignity and tradition."[29]

Murray says of JC: "In bygone days, when ships were much smaller than they are today and passengers did not travel in their several hundreds, captains and their officers were able to play the social part to a far greater extent than is now possible. No commander, perhaps, was better known among travellers to and from South Africa than J. C. Robinson, a favourite of Donald Currie and a favourite, too, with most passengers by Union-Castle Line. A man of deep religious conviction, Captain Robinson would present to every new officer who joined his ship a copy of the Bible, saying: 'Here is the Book of Rules'. He was known as 'Holy Joe', and his lovable and breezy personality endeared him to all who sailed with him, whether they liked his religious idiosyncrasies or not. Children who travelled with him adored him, and many children, too, who never made an ocean voyage, for Captain Robinson was famous for the 'parties' which he gave for children when his vessel was in port."[30]

The Union-Castle line was heavily involved in carrying British troops to South Africa and casualties back. But featured at length in Murray's book,[31] and also recounted by Laurens van der Post, whose mother's cousin was involved, is an incident involving JC and 2,500 Boer PoWs.[32] This episode is described by JC in 15 and 16.

In December 1900, following rumours of a planned massed breakout of Boer prisoners, the *Kildonan Castle* under JC was sent to Simonstown and ordered to receive these prisoners – they were to be kept on board, under cover of the guns of another ship. JC "mustered all hands and reminded them that while the prisoners were on board they were not be regarded as 'anything but honourable foes who had fought for freedom', and that the ship's company, by considerate kindness and courtesy, might in no small way contribute to a better understanding in mutual relations when the war was over. ... Captain Robinson's resolution was enthusiastically adopted by the crew of the Union-Castle liner and was loyally observed by all.

"Next day some 2.500 prisoners from boys to old men, struggled up the gangway of the *Kildonan Castle*, which, 'as clean as a drawing room', was a revelation to them after the discomforts of the camp on shore. Within a few hours a metamorphosis had taken place, and a deputation waited on Captain Robinson asking for leave to hold daily services on deck, a request which, of course, was granted. So, every day at 9 a.m. and 4 p.m. there would be three services going on simultaneously: on the forecastle, amidships, and on the after well deck, and from the decks of the *Kildonan Castle* the sonorous strains of *Psalmen en Gezangen* would be carried across the waters of Simons Bay. Not satisfied with this the prisoners asked to be allowed to attend the English services which were held for the crew and which were a special feature of any ship that Captain Robinson commanded.

Kildonan Castle

"Diversion and amusement in various forms were provided for the prisoners. All on board the *Kildonan Castle* became one great family. About this time Queen Victoria died. 'The whole ship's company broke down', wrote Captain Robinson in his *Memoirs*. 'It was remarkable. A cynic might have thought that everyone had lost his own mother. "Our

Friends the Enemy" read the symptoms aright and sent their two leading men to me to express the sympathy of all their ranks with our crew and nation generally.'

"After six weeks the *Kildonan Castle* had to return to Cape Town, and the prisoners, having been transferred to two other transports allotted to them, 'climbed up into the rigging and to every available point of vantage and cheered the *Kildonan Castle* to the echo, breaking into one of their grand old Dutch psalms that was taken up by both ships with one accord, until their voices faded into the glorious sunset of a calm summer evening as they steamed out of Table Bay.'"

JC received a medal from the King, along with many other officers from the ship, on 4th November 1903.[33]

On 26 June 1904, the *Armadale Castle*, the company's new flagship under JC, steamed into Durban Harbour. This was an event because she was the first large ship to be able to enter the harbour, after much dredging and engineering work. "The day was declared a holiday and people flocked to the docks to view the ship. Special guests had even been brought down from Johannesburg by train for the event."[34] "The docking caused considerable interest with 20,000 people visiting the harbour to see the vessel over the next few days. Her master, Captain J. C. Robinson, even gave a party for school-children in the town."[35] And at a luncheon paying tribute to the engineers, "With characteristic enthusiasm Captain Robinson sprang to his feet and led the assembled company with the singing of the Doxology."[36]

In 14th January 1905, *South Africa* journal reported that the *Armadale Castle* "left Cape Town on Wednesday evening having on board bar gold of the value of £682,862 for London. This is a record shipment for London."

On February 11th 1905, the *Illustrated London News* published a drawing based on a sketch by Capt. J. C. Robinson of the *Armadale Castle*. "During a recent voyage of the Armadale Castle when the vessel was in latitude 3 deg. South, the stem's perpendicular struck a large fish close to the head, and held it prisoner for about fifteen minutes. The monster was not less than fifty-seven feet in length, and must have been eight feet in diameter. It was beautifully marked, and Captain Robinson was sorry he could not lasso and preserve it. There was keen controversy among the passengers as to its species, some arguing for a whale, some for a shark. As Mr Rudyard Kipling was on board and saw the sight, it has been suggested that the creature should be called 'Piscis Rudyardensis."[37] This event was given one-and-a-quarter pages of jocular comment in *South Africa*.[38] The paper also published JC's original sketch, and quoted him as saying "It was not a whale because it had no blowhole."

"'It is a pity you let him escape,' said the *South Africa* man to Captain Robinson when he met the Commander the other day.

"'Had I suspected in the least degree,' said the Captain in reply, 'that we had run into anything uncommon or out of the way, I would have had him lassoed by the head. That could easily have been done, and we could then have had him lashed to the ship's side for observation and measurement. But being a little anxious to save the life of the poor brute, and being for the moment unconscious of its exceptional nature, I backed out to give him a chance. Then, unfortunately, he sank. The fact of the matter is this: there was so much excitement on account of the poor thing's terrible struggles to free itself, that we were all carried away by our feelings, rather than any curiosity to know anything as to its fishy character.'"

In August 1905 the French fleet paid a ceremonial visit to England, and the *Armadale Castle* under JC was made available to French VIPs to enjoy the spectacle of their own and the British fleet in the Solent, while the on-board band played the *Marseillaise*.[39]

On 13th January 1906, *South Africa* journal reported on the Duke and Duchess of Connaught's arrival at Cape Town on the *Armadale Castle*. At Christmas 1905, JC had read out a telegram of good wishes from Sir Donald Currie to the Royals, officers and crew. JC was delighted that the Duke of Connaught (Edward VII's brother) toasted captain, officers and crew in return, as he relates in No. 23.

The last voyage shown for JC is 1906, still on the *Armadale Castle*. After that he worked onshore as Marine Superintendent for the company in Southampton. The 1901 census shows his family living in Shirley, Southampton and in 1911 he is living at Armadale, The Avenue, Surbiton with his wife, Maribel and Annalice, and two servants. By 1913 JC and his wife had moved to Balmoral Road, Parkstone, Poole, where his house was also called Armadale.[40]

When he officially retired in 1913, aged 70, *South Africa* journal published a full-page photograph of him[41] ("Our Gallery of South African Celebrities" [sic]). See pp. 223-4.

Terrible losses soon followed – JC's beloved wife Mary Ann died suddenly of a stroke at their new home in Poole on 31st October 1913.[42] The notice in *South Africa* said sympathetically: "It was only quite recently that Captain Robinson retired from his position as Marine Superintendent of the Union Castle Company, and he and Mrs Robinson had just settled down to enjoy the evening of their days at Parkstone. Now this bewildering blow has fallen on one whose married life has been one long loving romance."

The following year JC's youngest daughter Kathleen Elise, who had been working as a nurse in a TB hospital and had travelled to South Africa for her health, died in Cape Town on 14 November 1914,[43] aged about 26, and shortly afterwards his youngest son Launcelot (Lannie) (28) died when *HMS Bulwark* blew up at Sheerness on 26 November the same year, killing all on board.[44] Something of his feelings at these events can be gleaned from the "Christmas story" in No. 22.

A descendant of JC's great-uncle Matthew, Olga Wells, recalled visiting JC at Armadale: she "went to his house in Poole, which is where he is buried, and his bedroom was apparently done out like a cabin on board ship. …. She also remembered that the Captain who took over Capt. JC's ship was adamant that JC's biblical text in his cabin remained, as it had protected JC and so it would be bad luck to remove it!!" [45] (See No. 36.)

J. C. Robinson died on 25th October 1925 in Parkstone, Poole, aged 83, and was buried at St. Luke's Church there.

His daughter Annaliese/Annalice Mary went on to write religious fables for children as A.M. Robinson,[46] and to look after her sister Maribel who was crippled with arthritis.

Of JC's second son Harold Percy, *South Africa* said in 1903 that he "follows the sea, and hopes one day to be a skipper like his dad." He himself reported on his Statement of Service, 9th September 1901, that he had sailed in the *Pyrenees* from Glasgow, September 1st 1898.

"The *Pyrenees* was burnt in the Pacific and stranded at Manga Reva in the Gambia Group. We left her December 22nd of last year in a French schooner for Tahiti and from there we sailed for San Francisco in the US steamer *Australia* and remained there until the *Hougoumont* arrived." The *Hougoumont* sailed on Feb. 26th 1901, arriving at Glasgow at the end of August. From 1901 Harold was on the Royal Navy Reserve list as a midshipman; he got his 2nd Mate's certificate (036527) on 11th November 1901 and his 1st Mate's certificate 13th February 1906. He was 6'1", with a dark complexion, brown hair and brown eyes.[47] I have not found out what happened to him, but his daughter married in Kuala Lumpur in 1936.

JC's eldest son Charles Douglas had two daughters, divorced in 1910 but later remarried, was wounded in WWI, and in 1920 went back to South Africa (see No. 27) where he farmed. His twin daughters, Martha and Mary, born 1906, came to England and married. Martha became a successful children's author and Mary a clinical psychologist.[48]

Martha worked in films for a while and had a hit in 1935 with her book *Continuity Girl*. She worked as an editor, and married a fellow editor, H E Alexander. Her children's books – the first of which was shortlisted for the 1946 Carnegie Prize – dealt realistically with contemporary problems, such as the postwar housing shortage, race relations, pesticides and children in care. In her 70s she recalled "I was one of those 'rootless' children, always longing for a settled home." She died in 1987.

[1] Under the auspices of the Society for the Propagation of the Gospel. His letters to them are held in Rhodes House Library, Oxford, now part of the Bodleian.

[2] Stated on his certificate applications.

[3] Now The Pines Nursing Home.

[4] John Robinson's will.

[5] *Strand Magazine*, 1896

[6] *Bury & Norwich Post*, 12 March 1856.

[7] Discussed in his letters to Matthew kindly made available by Nicolle Ansell.

[8] Robert's younger sister Marianne and youngest brother John had followed him to Jamaica, where they married, but they too died in 1856 and 1857; their partners survived them. Joseph, the milling brother, died in 1861, a few months after his wife, leaving nine orphans.

[9] The two little girls were sent to a religious institution where their names were changed, says the family story.

[10] Stated on his certificate applications. All the voyages and ranks are taken from his applications and certificates.

[11] Stated on his certificate application.

[12] He refers to this in his first piece.

[13] See page 250.

[14] Stated on his Master's Ordinary Certificate application, 4 Nov. 1870. There were a number of ships called *Excelsior* at the time. Shaw Savill's passenger ship to Auckland under Captain Lees would be an obvious one but the sailing dates don't match.

[15] freepages.genealogy.rootsweb.ancestry.com/~blanchec/ship2.htm

[16] JC seems to have maintained close relations with his youngest brother, Arthur Sextus. Their houses in Middlesex and Southampton were within visiting distance of each other, and Arthur's daughter Annalice recalled coming home to 17 The Grove, Southampton and being warned by the maid that "the Captain" was in the living room with a gathering of other masters.

[17] 1891 census.

[18] 1901 census.

[19] *South Africa* journal, 5th December 1903.

[20] http://www.theshipslist.com/ships/lines/castle.shtml

[21] Marischal Murray, *Union-Castle Chronicle 1853-1853*, 1953, p. 57.

[22]

http://www.archive.org/stream/madeirameteorolo00smytrich/madeira meteorolo00smytrich_djvu.txt

23

http://cluster.biodiversitylibrary.org/n/naturejournal36londuoft/naturej
ournal36londuoft_djvu.txt and similar

[24] *Western Daily Press,* 8 September 1890.

[25] e.g. *The Western Times,* 26 August 1893.

[26] Murray, p. 133.

[27] Laurens van der Post, *Yet Being Someone Other,* Hogarth, 1982, p. 270.

[28] Inscription noticed by Bryan Clark, email January 2006.

[29] Murray, p. 138.

[30] Murray, p. 332

[31] Murray, p. 144.

[32] van der Post, p. 273.

33

http://boards.ancestry.co.uk/localities.africa.southafrica.general/9870.2/
mb.ashx and http://www.angloboerwar.com (search under "Kildonan")

[34] http://natal-fever.blogspot.com/2004/06/ah.html

[35] http://www.fad.co.za/Diary/diary012/diary012.htm

[36] Murray, p. 275.

[37] http://www.encyclopedia-titanica.org/captain-rostrons-monster.html

[38] *South Africa,* 4th Feb. 1905: "A Monster of the Deep: Shark, Whale or
Serpent?"

[39] Enthusiastic report in *The Times,* 8th and 9th Aug. 1905. Also *South
Africa,* 12 Aug. 1905.

[40] Stated on Mary Ann Robinson's death certificate 31st October 1913.

[41] 21st June 1913: "Captain J. C. Robinson who retires at the end of the
month after long and honourable service in the Castle Packets Company
and the Union-Castle Company."

[42] Death certificate.

43

http://boards.ancestry.co.uk/localities.africa.southafrica.general/9870.2/
mb.ashx

[44] www.naval-history.net/xDKCas1914-11Nov.htm,
www.eggsa.org/newspapers/index.php/south-african-magazine/340-
south-africa-1914-4-october-december.html,
www.unioncastlestaffregister.co.uk/shipmates_Robinson_LA_01.html
and other sites.

[45] Thanks to Angela Gibson for this information, email 7th October 2006
and Reid Robinson, November 2012.

[46] *The Prince and the Road, Prickly Pears.* Also *Birds of a Feather* about a
residential home for missionaries' children.

[47] 1st Mate's certificate, 1906.

[48] Dustjacket of *A Little Loving* by Martha Robinson, 1973.

George Lipscomb Robinson, 1862, aged 17

III: George Lipscomb Robinson, 1844-1862

The Rev. Robert's second son, George, left Jamaica to live with JC and his grandfather at Bongate Terrace as a child.[1] He was 11 when his father died, and was sent to the Clergy Orphan School in Canterbury, where he won a Warneford Scholarship and was allowed to stay on past the usual leaving age of 15.[2]

In 1862, aged 17, George was offered a post in Jamaica,[3] left school and embarked with his friend David Kerr, the son of a Scottish planter, on the brig *Columbus*.

The boys were the only passengers on the *Columbus* which sailed from Leith on 19 January 1862. On 23rd January the ship broke up in bad weather on the Skerries in the Pentland Firth and both boys drowned, along with nearly all the crew. The *Orkney Herald* carried distressing reports of the splitting of the ship in heavy seas on the Lother Rock[4] and the attempts of men from South Ronaldsay to rescue the crew seen clinging to the foremast. Only one man survived, clutching a piece of wreckage, and being picked up by boat when the tide finally turned and brought him back within reach.

The *Dundee Courier and Daily Argus* reported in its Deaths column on 1st Feb. 1862:

"Lost at sea, in the brig Columbus, of Leith, bound for Jamaica, in the Pentland Firth, on the 23rd ult., David Kerr, aged 16, eldest son of David Kerr, Esq. of 21 Warriston Crescent, Edinburgh, and island of Jamaica; and at the same time and place, George Robinson aged 17, his fellow passenger and friend."

The minutes of the Clergy Orphan School, February 1862, said: "We have all been shocked and grieved lately by the death of G L Robinson, a Warneford Scholar, who left us at Xmas. He had sailed only a day or two for Jamaica, where by the kindness of a friend, a good prospect was before him, when the Vessel was wrecked in the Pentland Firth and all on board except one Seaman perished. We can think with comfort (D.G.)[5] of the poor boy's conduct and good principles, but his untimely end will long be painfully felt by all here."

---

[1] John Robinson's will.
[2] *Foundation on a Hill: the history of St Edmund's School, Canterbury* – Jock Asbury-Bailey, 2.e., 2011
[3] Clergy Orphan School's minutes, Feb. 1862
[4] Quoted in *The Times*, 31 Jan. 1862.
[5] Dei gratia – "Thanks to God."

"High Seas: tea-clipper Leander" by marine artist Derek G. M. Gardner
Reproduced with kind permission of Mrs Mary Gardner

"Parramatta" by marine artist Jack Spurling

Joseph Trutch Robinson, 1847-1928: "Damnation Joe"

It was JC's younger brother, Joseph Trutch Robinson, our great-grandfather, who we admired as children, rather than JC of whom we knew little. There was a family story about how in a storm at sea, Joseph (as second officer) had found JC, the first officer, on his knees praying, when he should have been in charge: I concluded he was probably a bit silly.

We heard about Joseph Trutch from my mother and her sister: he had a quick temper and was known as "Damnation Joe". His wife would often go to sea with him leaving their eldest daughter to look after the children. He used to let out his cabin on the Cape route. He brought back a parrot and crocodile. His grey parrot Polly was fondly remembered as able to sing and swear (to the delight of the doctor and the Rev. Peabody).

His discharge certificates and his 1862 indenture to Devitt & Moore had been kept by his youngest son, Geoffrey, and much of the following information comes from them, along with Captains' Register listings (included in the back).

Joseph Trutch Robinson was born on 6th July 1847, at Clarendon, Vere, Jamaica.[1] (Two of his brothers were named after respected bishops, but the name Trutch is a puzzle.)[2] Joseph returned to England with his family in 1849 aged about two.

When his father died in Newmarket, he was eight. In later life he said that the Rev. Robert's death from pneumonia in February 1856 had followed from the refusal of his brothers and himself to stop skating on the ice when called: the Rev. Robert then sat down under a tree to write his sermon, and caught the chill from which he died.[3]

Joseph was sent later that year to the Clergy Orphan School in Canterbury, following his older brother George.

At 15 he was apprenticed to Devitt and Moore of 9 Billiter Street, London, on 22 July 1862 for three years.[4] Devitt and Moore were ship-owners who built up a strong connection with Australia. They owned amongst many other ships the *Vimeira* and *La Hogue*, bought from Duncan Dunbar in 1863. Joseph was described on his indenture certificate as "a native of the Island of Jamaica", and his maternal aunt Maria Wright of Holland Place, Kensington, stood surety for £50 on his behalf. Joseph was covenanted to faithfully serve his said Masters, obey their lawful commands and keep their secrets; he was not to absent himself without leave nor frequent taverns and alehouses, nor play unlawful games. In return they would "teach him the business of a Seaman" and provide him with "sufficient Meat, Drink, Lodging,

Washing, and Medical and Surgical Assistance". He was to provide for himself "all sea-bedding, wearing apparel and necessaries".

Like his older brother JC, Joseph made his first voyage on the *La Hogue*,[5] sailing to Sydney and back from July 1865 to April 1866 at the lower status of Ordinary Seaman (JC had been a midshipman). His captain was William Goddard who appears memorably as the "tutting" 2nd Mate in JC's "ghost story", No. 17. Joseph's next voyage out on the *La Hogue* from July 1866 to April 1867 was again under Goddard, to Sydney. He was now an Able Seaman (AB).

From August 1867 to May 1868 he sailed as AB on the *Parramatta* to Sydney under captain John Williams, under whom JC had sailed as a midshipman on *La Hogue* (No. 18).

The next year, July 1868 to April 1869, Joseph was back on *La Hogue* as 4th Mate under William Goddard, sailing to Sydney and returning with passengers and wool. (At the end of *La Hogue*'s subsequent voyage to Sydney, November 1869, a group of passengers wrote an appreciative letter to Goddard after "this long and arduous journey" thanking him for his "uniform courtesy and kind attention", and his "ever wakeful attention to all our wants, even in the midst of the zealous and energetic performance of your onerous and important duties.")[6]

Joseph's first four discharge certificates (which rate his ability and conduct as "VG"), show some confusion over his date of birth and especially over his birthplace. His first and second certificates, 1866 and 1867, say that he was born in "Dumferran" in 1848. The third one, from the *Parramatta*, has him born in 1849 in "Dumfirmline" and the 1869 sign-off from *La Hogue* gets his age right (21) and decides he was born in "Dumfermline". Thereafter the certificates correctly show him as born in Jamaica. A possible explanation is that, with no older family members to consult, he was misremembering "Clarendon" or perhaps one of the Scottish place names on Jamaica, such as Dumfries or Dunblane.

From November 1869 to January 1871 Joseph, aged 22, was 3rd Mate on the tea clipper *Leander*, built only two years previously. The heyday of the tea clippers lasted from about 1850-1875; the ships, built for speed, would race back to England from China with their profitable tea cargoes. Sometimes described as an "extreme" clipper, the *Leander* was rated one of the six fastest China clippers, and could carry 45 sails. This was her third voyage, and her last under Captain Petherick; she was carrying 1.137.000 lbs of tea on her return journey, which took 98 days.[7] The knowledgeable marine artist Derek Gardner, whose painting of her appears on page 238, said that small "fine" ships like the *Leander* required very careful handling in the kind of weather shown there, to ensure she held her course. "In such conditions, the captain would seldom leave the poop, snatching such sleep as was possible in a deck-chair lashed to the mizzen rigging with a canvas weather cloth to give some protection."[8]

In March 1871 Joseph joined the *Star of India* to Melbourne as 3rd Mate, serving under his brother JC (Mate) and Captain Charles Holloway. JC described the ship as "one of Soames's crack East Indiamen" (No. 1); she had been built in Dundee in 1861.[9] The ship, with 394 passengers, arrived in Melbourne in June 1871, and the *Melbourne Argus* noted with satisfaction that the immigrants "appear to be of a superior class, and have come into port in excellent health"; Captain Holloway and the design of the ship with her "spacious 'tweendecks" were praised.[10] The *Star of India* and the Robinson brothers were back in London in April 1872.

The following year Joseph was 2nd Mate on the same ship under JC and Captain Holloway, leaving in May 1872 for Colombo and Madras, and returning August 1873. His certificate number is given as 90.934.

He continued as 2nd Mate (20934) to New Zealand (Canterbury) from September 1873-March 1874, still under Holloway and Mate JC – who then went to work for Currie on the *Carnarvon Castle,* as he relates in his first piece.

From July 1874 to December 1875, Joseph was 2nd Mate (90934) on the *Star of India* under Holloway to "Foreign - Rangoon", returning to Liverpool. In February 1876 he sailed under Holloway on the same ship as 2nd Mate (0544) to San Francisco, returning to Liverpool in March 1877. He was 29.

In June 1877 he achieved his certificate as Chief Mate on square-rigged ships,[11] and from 3rd July 1877 to 4th July 1878 he served as Chief Mate (90934) on the *Leander* again, under Captain Knight, from London to China, leaving Shanghai for New York 11th January 1879 and arriving back at Falmouth 4th July and Gravesend 5th July. This was his last official voyage under sail.

There was then a pause while he married Sara(h) Frances Down Mayne (known as Fanny) in Ottery St Mary, Devon, in July 1878. He was 31. (Sarah Frances's grandfather Charles Down Mayne, a land agent and bookseller, also lived in the town.) Like Joseph, Sarah Frances was an orphan, one of eight; both her parents had died of TB. On 12th April 1879, their first child Frances Maud was born in Ottery St Mary.

Joseph's next voyage was as 3rd Mate on his first steam ship, Donald Currie's *Lapland* to Cape Town, carrying "private mails" from April to June 1879 and then as 2nd Mate from August 1879 till January 1880. The captain was James Lott.

His discharge certificates for the next three years were washed overboard, he says on his next application form, where he states he was working as Mate on the *Lapland* till April 1883.

The 1881 census shows Sarah Frances in Ottery St Mary with the baby and two aunts from Joseph's mother's family – Maria Wright and Sarah Crampton. The census taker wrote: "Husband at sea – merchant service".

In April 1883, in Liverpool, he applied for a replacement 1st Mate's certificate, his original one having been lost at sea: "about 10 miles east of Terschilling lightship in the North Sea, my berth being washed overboard with all contents." The new certificate (012714) was issued.

His next discharge certificates show Joseph working as 2nd Mate on the Cape Town mail route for the Castle line from 1883-1889 as 2nd Mate, on the *Warwick Castle* (May-July 1883, Captain J. C. Robinson), *Hawarden Castle* (July 1883-July 1885, Captain M. P. Webster – JC calls him "bluff" in No. 19) and *Grantully Castle* (August 1885-April 1886, Captain Young). He then worked on the *Hawarden Castle* again from July 1886 to May 1889 under Webster, and then under Captain Harrison. These were all mail steamers and the return voyages took about two and a half months. At 3.30am on 8th April 1889 the *Hawarden Castle* ran into the inadequately-lit British ship *Sierra Nevada* off Port Elizabeth and an inquiry was held which exonerated the captain and officers of the *Hawarden Castle*.

On 27 July 1889 at the age of 42 Joseph applied for a certificate of competence as Master of a Square-rigged Vessel. He was described as 5'8", dark complexion and hair, brown eyes. He failed in navigation, tried again and passed on 2nd August 1889.

Meanwhile his family had been growing and they moved from Ottery St Mary, to Upton Park in Essex, and then to Ilford. This was the height of the family's prosperity: at one point they had a live-in maid, a cook and a gardener. Eight of the nine children survived.

From September to December 1889 Joseph worked on the *Pembroke Castle* as 1st Mate under Captain W. Hay; he continued working on this ship as 1st Officer under Captain Harry Rigby (who competes with JC for the East London buoy anchorage in No. 6) until July 1891, and then under Captain W. Warden until 1893, always on the Cape Town mail route. His discharge certificates continued to be stamped "Very Good" for conduct and ability.

In 1894 he was 1st Mate on the *Garth Castle* (captain unreadable) and thereafter worked as 1st Mate on the *Dunottar Castle* until September 1900. In 1894 he was serving on this ship under Captain Harry Rigby, until the latter ran her into the Eddystone Rocks off the southwest coast in fog on 24th August, sustaining serious damage. She had 215 passengers on board, a crew of 156 hands, 500 tons of cargo and the South African Mails but luckily the sea was calm. At the enquiry held at the Town Hall, Westminster in September, Captain Rigby had his certificate suspended for three months only, taking into consideration "his excellent character and great length of service." The court noted that: "Masters of vessels are not justified in approaching danger in a thick fog when they are uncertain of their exact position." A slight conflict of evidence between Rigby and Joseph is reported, and the court seems to have believed the latter: "The master stated that at 4.54 another cast of lead was taken in 35 fathoms, sand and shell, but according to the chief officer [JT] who took the sounding, this cast had been taken and reported to the master by 4.50. The Court thinks that this cast must have been taken at some time between 4.40 and 4.50."[12]

Captain Webster now took over the *Dunottar Castle* until early 1895, and Captain Hay from February 1895 until April 1897. From September 1897 until September 1899 the captain signing the discharge certificates is J. B. Harrison, who also signs in September 1900.

In October 1899 at the outbreak of the 2nd Boer War, it was the *Dunottar Castle* (with Rigby as Captain, rather surprisingly, and Joseph as Mate) which carried Sir Redvers Buller and his HQ Staff to take command of the British Forces in South Africa, cheered off by a huge crowd at Southampton singing "God Save the Queen" and "Rule Britannia" and waving pocket Union Jacks.[13] [14] The young Winston Churchill was also on board and he recalled the journey in his autobiography.

At 53, Joseph Trutch Robinson must have been wondering when his captaincy would come, but in May 1901 he was Master on the newly-built *York Castle*, carrying cargo to New York for Donald Currie; a battered photo (p. 245) shows him standing on the deck, looking very weather-beaten.

From 1902-1904 Joseph captained the *Raglan Castle* on the mail run to Cape Province. In December 1903 the ship ran into "terrific seas" in the Bay of Biscay when returning to Plymouth from the Cape: "A portion of the bridge was swept away, and the commander, Capt. J. T. Robinson, was hurled to the deck, whence he was picked up unconscious and bleeding, with his head lacerated and his leg broken. For 48 hours the weather was of the wildest description."[15]

In 1905 the *Raglan Castle* was sold to the Russians for the Russo-Japanese War, and Joseph became captain of the *Berwick Castle*[16] to Cape Province. On 19th March 1907, on a voyage commencing 16th Jan. 1907,[17] the ship "in charge of a pilot" was run onto a mudbank off Mozambique[18] but successfully refloated.[19] The voyage ended on 15th May.[20]

Joseph is shown as captaining the ship after this for one more voyage, from 27 May 1907. The information supplied from the Captains' Registers gives no destination, but various English papers reported her calling at Cape Town, East African ports and Mauritius through July and

August, and Australian newspapers announced that *Berwick Castle* (Union-Castle SS Co. Ltd.) under Captain J. T. Robinson would be sailing from Brisbane on 18th September 1907 ("Steam to London via Suez"), taking on "cargo for Continental ports" including wool "for the November wool sales." She arrived in Sydney on 20th September[21] and Adelaide on 3rd October, leaving again on 8th October. She had apparently been docked and painted in Sydney. She was back in England on 18th November 1907.[22] This was an unusual voyage for a Union-Castle ship, and it was perhaps an experiment to see if it was a worthwhile venture.

In July 1908 because of the depression in shipping, the Union Castle Line decided to lay up the sister ships *Berwick Castle* and *Alnwick Castle*.[23] Joseph's employment by the Union-Castle Line ended there, at the age of 60, and unlike JC, he didn't have a pension – a family story said he had offended some important personage, though perhaps captains didn't necessarily get pensions.

Short of money, the family moved to Exmouth in Devon around 1912. Of the older children, Charles had gone to sea, and married in Australia in 1907; Maud married in 1905, having worked at an Oxford Street jeweller's; Marie worked as a nurse all her life. Ken and Theo joined the Merchant Navy: Ken[24] became a Merchant Navy Captain and an adviser to the Royal Navy in WWII. Geoffrey enlisted in the Royal Army Medical Corps on the outbreak of war in 1914. Aubrey joined the 1st Canadian forces. Leila worked as a companion in Italy when young.

Joseph died 22nd January 1928, aged 81. He and Sarah Frances are buried in Littleham churchyard near Exmouth.

There's a clear contrast between the two brothers, "Holy Joe" and "Damnation Joe": both sea captains, one was overtly benevolent, publicly recognised and applauded, the other relatively unrewarded professionally but a colourful character whose large family continues to this day.

The fact that we knew nothing but the "praying at the wheel" story suggests that Joseph resented his more successful older brother, but there were also signs he was actually devoted to him, as we were told. It was probably a complex relationship, with Joseph's last words reportedly to his brother who had died three years previously: "I'm coming, JC."

Joseph Trutch Robinson, 1864, aged 16

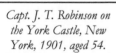

Capt. J. T. Robinson on the York Castle, New York, 1901, aged 54.

Captain Joseph Trutch Robinson and family, 1894
L-R from back: Marie, Maud
Charlie, Sarah Frances with baby Geoffrey, Aubrey, Joseph Trutch
Ken, Theo, Leila

1 Jamaica Archives, Spanish Town.

2 Charles Trutch, a doctor, magistrate and landowner in Vere is a possibility. (jamaicanfamilysearch)

3 Letter from JT's youngest son Arthur Geoffrey, 20 Dec. 1975.

4 Indenture certificate held by JT's grandson Geoffrey K. Robinson, son of the above.

5 All the information on Joseph Trutch's voyages is thanks to Geoffrey K. Robinson who compiled it from his discharge certificates.

6 http://trove.nla.gov.au/ndp/del/page/1460867

7 www.bruzelius.info/Nautica/Ships/Clippers/Leander(1867).html

8 *The Tall Ship in Art*, Blandford, 1988.

9 She is not the museum ship of that name in San Diego, California; that was originally the *Euterpe*.

10 http://trove.nla.gov.au/ndp/del/article/5849634,

11 Taken from his application for competency as Master, July 1889.

12

www.unioncastlestaffregister.co.uk/SHIP_DUNOTTAR_CASTLE_01.html

13 Marischal Murray, *Union-Castle Chronicle 1853-1953*, Longmans, 1953, p.141

14 *The Times*, 16 October 1899.

15 "Liner In The Gale" - *Shields Daily Gazette*, 15 Dec. 1903

16 She was an unlucky ship – she had already rammed a British submarine in 1904, with the loss of all the submarine's hands. This wasn't under JT.

17 List from Captains' Registers, supplied by Guildhall Library to Geoffrey K. Robinson in 1993.

18 *Times*, 21 March 1907.

19 The Lloyds record (Captains' Registers) says "Ashore Mar. 21/25, got off Mar. 30/25". Perhaps he went ashore for a few days, and the ship was refloated on the 30th.

20 Info. from Southampton City Archives.

21 http://mariners.records.nsw.gov.au/1907/09/190709.htm
http://trove.nla.gov.au/ndp/del/article/14885942

22 Ibid.

23 *Manchester Courier*, 23 July 1908.

24 George Edmund Kenneth Robinson, 1886-1958

VOYAGES OF J. C. ROBINSON

The following are taken from JC's certificate applications. Destinations from his memoirs.

Out of London

Year	Ship	Rank	Destination	Dates
1858	La Hogue 26531	Midshipman	Australia	July 29 - May 10 1859
1859		Midshipman	Australia	July 21 – April 27 1860
1860	Lady McDonald 30928			
		Midshipman OS	Australia	Aug. 15 – June 21 1861
1861		3rd Mate	Australia	Nov. 22 – Feb. 24 1863
1863	Vimeira 806	3rd Mate	Australia	June 27 – July 28 1864
1864		2nd Mate	Australia	Sept. 24 - July 28 1865
1865	Duncan Dunbar 18724			
		2nd Mate	Wrecked	Aug. 25 1865 - Nov. 4

Out of Liverpool: at least one of these voyages was to Calcutta, probably both

Year	Ship	Rank		Dates
1866	Orient	2nd Mate		Jan. 20 – Feb. 5 1867
1867		2nd Mate		Mar. 7 – May 16 1868

Out of London

Year	Ship	Rank	Destination	Dates
1868	Poonah (P&O)	4th Mate	Mediterranean	Nov. 3 – Dec. 26
1869		4th Mate	Mediterranean	Jan. 28. – Mar. 29
		4th Mate	Mediterranean	April 1 – May 28
		4th Mate	Mediterranean	June 17 – July 21
	Excelsior	1st Mate	India?	Aug. 31 – Oct. 8 1870

The following are taken from Ms 18567 in Guildhall Library. Copied by hand so accuracy not guaranteed. Where ship or rank not listed, same as previous. Italics = discharge.

Year	Ship	Rank	Destination	Dates
1871	Star of India 43925	Mate	Australia	March 4
1872		Mate	E I	April 27 May 29
1873		Mate	Australia	Aug. 31 Sept. 20
1874		Mate	Australia	*June 25*
	Carnarvon Castle 56826	Capt.	Cape, E I,US	July 30 *July 13*
1875			Cape	Aug 16 *Sept 24*
1876		.		Nov 21 Nov 23
1877	Balmoral Castle 67935	Mate		Mar 2 *June 8*
				Aug 22 *Sept 11*
				Nov 30
1878	Conway Castle 77049	Mate		Jan 18 *April 3*
	Taymouth Castle 76947	Captain		May 11 Sept 21 *Dec. 25*
1879			Cape	Jan 18 *April 5*
				Apr 16 July 26 Oct 22
1880			Cape	Jan 13 14 B.S. (in red)
	Warwick Castle 77027			Jan 30 May 7
				Aug 13, Nov 9
1881	Dunrobin Castle 73612			Feb 1
	Warwick Castle			May 20, Sept 13, ??
			Cape	Dec 16
1882			Cape	May 27, July 5, Sept 26
1883				Jan 26, May 9
	Roslin Castle 87126		Cape	Nov 20
1884				Feb 26
	Norham Castle 87101		?F	July 9
	Pembroke Castle 87157		Cape	Nov. 26

1885	Roslin Castle	Cape	April 1, July 7, Sept 29
1886		Cape	Feb 3, April 28,
			Aug 17, Nov 24
1887	/s/	Cape	Mar 16, June 7
All marked /s/ = steam from now on)			Sept 13, Dec 7
1888	Roslin Castle		Feb 14,
	Pembroke Castle	Cape	May 9
	Norham Castle	Cape	Aug 15 Oct 23
1889		Cape	Jan 30 April 24
			July 16 Oct 18
1890	18/1 Roslin Castle	Cape	Jan 14 April 8 July 1
			Sept 19 Dec 30
1891		Cape	Mar 20 Aug 13
	Dunottar Castle 98152	Cape	Nov 19
1892		Cape	Feb 11 April 21
			July 14 Oct 6
1893		Cape	Jan 12 April 6
			June 29 Oct 5
1894	Tantallon Castle 102855	Cape	Jan 23 April 5
		B[altic?]	June 12
		Cape	July 10 Sept 18 Nov 27
1895		Cape	23 Jan, 5 April
		Baltic	12 June
		Cape	10 July 18 Sept, 27 Nov
1896		Cape	Feb 21
	Dunvegan Castle 105854	Cape	Sept 3 Nov 25
1897	Dunvegan Castle	Cape	Feb 17 Apr 28 July 7
1898	Carisbrook Castle 108351	Cape	June 8 Aug 16 Oct 29
1899		Cape	Feb 16, Apr 26, July 19
	Kildonan Castle 112615	Cape	Nov 1
1900		Cape	March 3 May 29 Oct 12
1901		Cape	March 13 May 29 Dec 5
1902	Walmer Castle 114839	Cape	Mar. 13 May 23 July 24
			Sept 25, Nov 28
1903		Cape	Jan 30 April 3 June 6
			Aug 5
	Armadale Castle 118350	Cape	Dec 3
1904		Cape	June 2, Aug 3
			Oct 6 Dec 7
1905		Cape	Feb 8 April 14 Aug 17
			Oct 22 Dec 22
1906		Cape	Feb 22 April 26 June 28

No more entries.

Some more of JC's ships

P&O's Poonah 1862

Icelana

Tony Haslett Collection

Taymouth Castle

Tony Haslett Collection

Dunvegan Castle

Tony Haslett Collection

Walmer Castle

Tony Haslett Collection

Armadale Castle

VOYAGES OF JOSEPH TRUTCH ROBINSON

Taken from his discharge certificates by Geoffrey K. Robinson. (S) = sail.

SHIP	No./Ton	Rate	From	To	Port
La Hogue (S)	26531/1331	O.S.	25/07/65 - 18/04/66		Sydney
La Hogue (S)		A.B.	26/07/66 - 09/04/67		"
Parramatta (S)	54740/1521	A.B.	24/08/67 - 13/05/68		"
La Hogue (S)		4th Mate	25/07/68 - 18/04/69		"
Leander (S)	56878/882	3rd Mate	01/11/69 - 18/01/71		China
Star of India (S)	43925/1040	3rd Mate	04/03/71 - 27/04/72		Melbourne
Star of India (S)		2nd Mate	29/05/72 - 31/08/73		Colombo & Madras
Star of India (S)		2nd Mate	23/09/73 - 25/06/74		Canterbury Bight NZ
Star of India (S)		2nd Mate	28/07/74 - 12/12/75		Rangoon
Star of India (S)		2nd Mate	28/02/76 - 17/03/77		San Frisco
Leander (S)	56878/848	Chief Mate	03/07/77 - 04/07/78		China, NY

Steam from here on

Lapland	65778/822	3rd Mate	22/04/79 -15/06/79	Cape
Lapland		2nd Mate	13/08/79 - 04/01/80	Cape

Missing certificate(s): application form shows Lapland 22/04/79-14/04/8.

The following voyages are all to Cape Town; later "Cape Mail Service"

SHIP	No./Ton	Rate	Dates
Warwick Castle	77027/1892	2nd Mate	04/05/83 - 18/07/83
Hawarden Castle	87076/2721	2nd Mate	27/07/83 - 08/10/83
Hawarden Castle		2nd Mate	19/10/83 - 29/12/83
Hawarden Castle		2nd Mate	25/01/84 - 04/04/84
Hawarden Castle		2nd Mate	18/04/84 - 27/06/84
Hawarden Castle		2nd Mate	01/08/84 - 09/10/84
Hawarden Castle		2nd Mate	24/10/84 - 01/01/85
Hawarden Castle		2nd Mate	13/02/85 - 23/04/85
Hawarden Castle		2nd Mate	08/05/85 - 15/07/85
Grantully Castle	81601/2233	2nd Mate	14/08/85 - 21/10/85
Grantully Castle		2nd Mate	06/11/85 - 15/01/86
Grantully Castle		2nd Mate	12/02/86 - 21/04/86
Hawarden Castle		2nd Mate	16/07/86 - 22/09/86
Hawarden Castle		2nd Mate	08/10/86 - 15/12/86
Hawarden Castle		2nd Mate	14/01/87 - 23/03/87
Hawarden Castle		2nd Mate	09/04/87 - 15/06/87
Hawarden Castle		2nd Mate	01/07/87 - 08/09/88
Hawarden Castle		2nd Mate	23/03/88 - 29/05/88
Hawarden Castle		2nd Mate	15/06/88- 21/08/88
Hawarden Castle		2nd Mate	07/09/88 - 13/11/88
Hawarden Castle		2nd Mate	14/12/88 - 20/02/89
Hawarden Castle		2nd Mate	08/03/89 - 16/05/89
Pembroke Castle	87157/2520	1st Mate	27/09/89 - 13/12/89
Pembroke Castle		1st Mate	07/01/90 - 21/04/90
Pembroke Castle		1st Mate	27/05/90 - 07/08/90
Pembroke Castle		1st Mate	02/09/90 - 15/12/90

Pembroke Castle		1st Mate	06/01/91 - 19/04/91	
Pembroke Castle		1st Officer	12/05/91 - 20/07/91	
Pembroke Castle		1st Mate	20/08/91 - 28/11/91	
Pembroke Castle		1st Mate	08/01/92 - 16/04/92	
Pembroke Castle		1st Mate	26/05/92 - 02/09/92	
Pembroke Castle		Mate	29/09/92 - 12/12/92	
Pembroke Castle		Mate	05/01/93 - 15/04/93	
Garth Castle	82849/2350	1st Mate	26/10/93 - 01/01/94	
Garth Castle		1st Mate	10/01/94 - 26/03/94	
Dunottar Castle	98152/3069	Mate	05/04/94 - 03/06/94	
Dunottar Castle		1st Mate	28/06/94 - 25/08/94	
Dunottar Castle		1st Mate	20/09/94 - 17/11/94	
Dunottar Castle		Mate	29/11/94 - 28/01/95	
Dunottar Castle		1st Mate	21/02/95 - 20/04/95	
Dunottar Castle		Mate	17/10/95 - 14/12/95	
Dunottar Castle		1st Mate	09/01/96 - 07/03/96	
Dunottar Castle		1st Mate	19/03/96 - 16/05/96	
Dunottar Castle		1st Mate	11/06/96 - 08/08/96	
Dunottar Castle		1st Mate	20/08/96 - 18/10/96	
Dunottar Castle	98152/3070	1st Mate	10/11/96 - 09/01/97	
Dunottar Castle	98152/3069	1st Mate	04/02/97 - 03/04/97	
Dunottar Castle	98152/3139	1st Mate	16/09/97 - 12/11/97	
Dunottar Castle		1st Mate	17/02/98 - 18/04/98	
Dunottar Castle		1st Mate	21/07/98 - 17/09/98	
Dunottar Castle		1st Mate	13/10/98 - 12/12/98	
Dunottar Castle		1st Mate	02/02/99 - 01/04/99	
Dunottar Castle		1st Mate	13/04/99 - 11/06/99	
Dunottar Castle		1st Mate	06/07/99 - 04/09/99	
Dunottar Castle		1st Mate	12/10/99 - 09/12/99	
Dunottar Castle		1st Mate	21/12/99 - 17/02/00	
Dunottar Castle		1st Mate	15/03/00 - 13/05/00	
Dunottar Castle		1st Mate	24/05/00 - 27/07/00	
Dunottar Castle		Mate O.C.	03/08/00 - 29/09/00	

Information from Captains' Registers at Guildhall Library. All steam.

York Castle	112489	Master	23/05/1901	New York
Raglan Castle	108187	Master	29/10/1902	Cape
Raglan Castle		Master	29/01/1903	CP
Raglan Castle		Master	03/06/1903	
Raglan Castle		Master	07/09/1903	
Raglan Castle		Master	25/04/1904	CP
Raglan Castle		Master	17/08/1904	
Berwick Castle	114822	Master	29/08/1905	CP
Berwick Castle		Master	13/03/1906	CP
Berwick Castle		Master	27/08/1906	
Berwick Castle		Master	16/01/1907	CP

"Ashore 21/15, got off Mar 30/25"

Berwick Castle		Master	27/05/1907	(Australia)

Some of JTR's Ships

Lapland –Tony Haslett Collection

Hawarden Castle – Tony Haslett Collection

Grantully Castle – Tony Haslett Collection

Pembroke Castle – Tony Haslett Collection

Garth Castle – Tony Haslett Collection

York Castle – Tony Haslett Collection

Raglan Castle – Tony Haslett Collection

Berwick Castle– Tony Haslett Collection

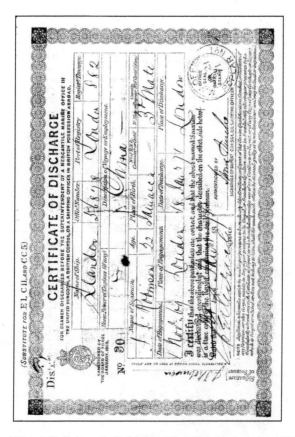

*3rd Mate J. T. Robinson's discharge certificate from the Leander, 1871,
signed by Captain Petherick*

CAPTAINS' SIGNATURES

mostly from JTR's discharge certificates

	William Goddard
	J. B. Harrison
	W. Hay
	Charles Holloway
	Capt. Knight
	Capt. Petherick
	Harry Rigby
	J. C. Robinson
	J. T. Robinson
	W. Warden
	M. P. Webster
	John Williams
	Capt. Young

Bongate Mill, Appleby

The Rev. Robert Robinson, 1814-1856
Father of J. C., George Lipscombe and Joseph Trutch Robinson

Direct Descendants of John Robinson

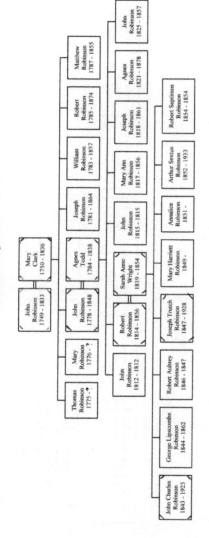

Descendants of John Charles Robinson

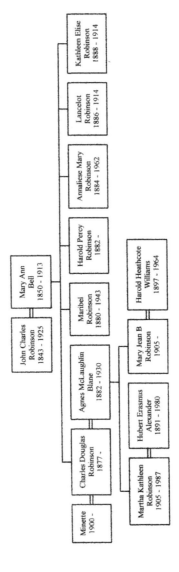

Direct Descendants of Joseph Trutch Robinson

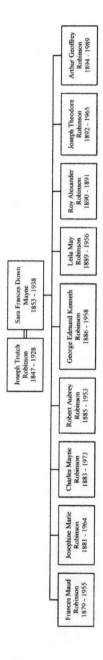

Lightning Source UK Ltd.
Milton Keynes UK
UKHW03f1646170418
321216UK00001B/16/P